BURNING TANKS AND AN EMPTY DESERT

This book is dedicated to past and present members of the Royal Army Medical Corps, who in war are often in the forefront of the battle. The supreme British decoration for valour is the Victoria Cross. Only three soldiers have received this decoration *twice*. Two of these were regimental doctors, Captain Arthur Martin-Leake and Captain Noel Chavasse.

BURNING TANKS AND AN EMPTY DESERT

Based on the unpublished journal of
Major John Sylvanus MacGill, MB, ChB, MD,
Royal Army Medical Corps

JOHN PHILIP JONES

authorHOUSE®

AuthorHouse™
1663 Liberty Drive
Bloomington, IN 47403
www.authorhouse.com
Phone: 1 (800) 839-8640

Published by AuthorHouse 10/19/2015

ISBN: 978-1-5049-5028-2 (sc)
ISBN: 978-1-5049-5029-9 (hc)
ISBN: 978-1-5049-5027-5 (e)

Library of Congress Control Number: 2015915265

Print information available on the last page.

This book is printed on acid-free paper.

CONTENTS

LIST OF MAPS

LIST OF PLATES – FIRST SECTION

1. JSM in 1939

2. British Light tank, 1940

3. British Cruiser tank, 1940

4. British Infantry tank (Matilda), 1940

5. German 88mm anti-tank gun, 1942

6. German Panzer IV tank, 1942

7. Somme, 1940: destroyed Queen's Bays Cruiser tank

8. Surrender of 51st Highland division, St. Valery

9. British Stuart tank, 1942

10. British Cruiser tank (Crusader), 1942

11. British Grant tank, 1942

12. British Sherman tank, 1942

13. JSM's tactical map of Cyrenaica

14. JSM's sketch of sun compass

LIST OF PLATES – SECOND SECTION

LIST OF FIGURES

FOREWORD

by Brigadier J.R. Smales

John Smales is a British soldier who had a long and distinguished career as a Regular army officer. He served in the 14th / 20th King's Hussars, which he commanded between 1984 and 1986. He was on the Directing Staff of the British Army Staff College, Camberley, from 1981 to 1984, which is a job for a military intellectual. He ended his Regular career in command of 107th (Ulster)Brigade from 1993 to 1996.

Of all the aspects of history war must be the most written about. Studies of the theory of warfare proliferate and reach back through the ages, and are respected and consulted to this day, such as Sun Tzu and Clausewitz. The descriptions of the Peloponnesian Wars by Thucydides remain fascinating and authoritative. Studies of campaigns by scholarly men and women abound. Commanders by sea, land or air publish their experiences, to justify their actions, to establish and record the truth (or their perception of it) before those involved have died, and to give credit to those who fought with them. Politicians write of war from the point of view of their own backgrounds. And of course there are the innumerable memoirs of individuals who took part, always popular with readers, as they can understand and relate to the actions and experiences of individuals nearer the lower end of military hierarchy, and are thrilled by tales of individual derring-do, often written by men with that permanent grin that comes from carrying a dagger between your teeth.

In this book John Philip Jones has achieved something exceptional. He tells the story of two campaigns, giving factual detail about the overall background while cleverly bringing events to life through the eyes of an individual who was present at the time and, though deeply involved in combat, was not so near the sharp end as to lose the broader perspective of the battle. Through the eyes of Dr. John Sylvanus MacGill, the atmosphere of the fighting and the responses of the people in it are brought to life and bring colour and human interest to the narrative of the campaigns and battles.

The first campaign is the German conquest of France 1940. Most people remember only the desperate retreat of the British Expeditionary Force to the coast, the dramatic counter-attack at Arras, and the miraculous evacuation from Dunkirk. Professor Jones deals in more detail with the campaign on the Somme and the Seine where the lately-arrived British Armoured Division, inadequately trained, with an inferior organization, encountered the Germans as they advanced southward through France. The enemy were by now tired, but were battle-hardened, and had thought out their tactics and trained to apply them. The French, who had the BEF under command here, were by now disorganized and demoralized. After a flurry of unrealistic plans and orders – and without informing the British – they asked the Germans for an Armistice, which was agreed. It was only the energy and moral courage of General Sir Alan Brooke which allowed the second British evacuation of France to be so successful. This aspect of the 1940 campaign is all too often neglected, and Professor Jones gives it some much needed illumination. It was also the first time in the Second World War that British tanks were used as Divisions, and it is interesting to see later in the book what lessons were learned in France and whether they were applied in North Africa.

Dr. MacGill was Medical Officer of the Queen's Bays, and kept a journal while he was with them. At 39 he was the oldest and thus the most experienced and mature officer in the regiment, with greater experience of life than most. Through his eyes we see the unruffled calm and old-fashioned attitudes of a famous and distinguished cavalry regiment, recently equipped with tanks after giving up their horses, finding themselves outmatched by what was at the time the finest army in Europe. Their stoical acceptance of casualties, their maintenance of personal standards, morale and discipline in conditions of chaos, their uncomplaining attempts to carry out orders which they must swiftly have realized were futile, are moving, and make one realize the value of the British Regimental System, which the author explains so clearly. As a system it is not economic, nor, in the eyes of the outsider, particularly efficient to run. But the cohesion it achieves and the sense of family it engenders produce pride, enduring loyalty and high morale, proof like nothing else against defeat and disaster. The spirit is long-lasting. As one whose own regiment has just celebrated its 300th Anniversary I know the value of that 'golden thread' which links us with the past and each other. Regiments are reluctant sometimes to give up traditions and change attitudes; but this produces a certain staunchness which is invaluable in war.

The campaign in North Africa up to Alamein is a complex story, with frequent changes of Generals, vast areas in which to maneuver, changing and developing doctrine and tactics, and a demanding and complicated re-supply system. It is a period of history in which we should take pride. We were the only nation which was fighting the Axis powers until Hitler attacked Russia in June 1941, and until the Americans arrived in North Africa in November 1942 we were on our own there. Professor Jones not only outlines simply and clearly the to-and-fro of the battles, but with the help of the Medical Officer's journal brings to life the real feeling of living in and from your vehicle in the Libyan Desert for month after month. Having served there for three years in the early '60s in Armoured Cars, reading the MO's experiences took me back. I once more felt the contrast of chilly night and blazing day, and was reminded how we used to keep our greatcoats on until mid-morning, as the thickness of the material retained the cool of night for hours, despite the bright sunshine. His descriptions of long drives seeing nothing, navigating by sun-compass across the waste are real, as is the feeling of relief when you find yourself at the right place, and the feeling of dismay when you reach what you think is your destination and there nothing to be seen. Such descriptions are masterly.

Dr. MacGill does not dwell on the horrors of war, and Professor Jones, rightly, does not do so either. Indeed the displays of emotion at casualties that we see nowadays would have seemed out of place and a sign of weakness at that time. But reading the book you can see that all were at the highest hazard. Dr. MacGill lists the officers, with comments, and you read that a high proportion of them were killed. His own successor in the regiment was killed at Alamein. His experience of burns injuries, commonplace in armoured vehicles, was such that he was sent to the USA to lecture American doctors on the subject. Both the men of the Queen's Bays and their doctor regarded death and injury as normal events in war, to be dealt with as quickly and efficiently as possible, and not allowed to interfere with the main business of defeating the enemy. Compassion existed, of course it did, but both the victims and their comrades would have been embarrassed and uncomfortable if it were shown over-dramatically.

It is interesting and pitiful to read of the consistent superiority of German tank design. It was only in late 1942 that the Grant and the Sherman appeared in the desert to give us and the Americans little more than parity, and as the war progressed the Allies consistently failed to match German developments in Armour. It is surprising, even disgraceful, that the two most technologically and industrially advanced nations in the world should not have designed tanks superior to the enemy's, particularly as Russia – invaded and with much of her territory occupied – could design and produce in large numbers the excellent T34 tank.

These considerations did not affect the Queen's Bays. Like every other cavalry regiment they were only a few years from that wonderful but superseded weapon, The Horse. Their thinking, their attitudes, their sense of superiority, their very identity had been dependent on it for hundreds of years, and their ethos and their professional mastery were bound up in it. The Cavalry Spirit, which means appreciating the value of maneuver, the ability to make quick decisions under stress, the development of an 'eye for the ground', which is the ability to appreciate rapidly and while on the move the effect that your surroundings will have on your tactics, were all invaluable. But to expect recently converted units to appreciate the strengths and weaknesses of their equipment, and to work out how best to use it, all in the stress of combat, was too much to ask. Britain led the world in armoured warfare and in tank development after the First World War. But this lead had been abandoned for economic reasons ten years before the Second World War, and had to be caught up at great cost of blood and kit during the fighting.

In this book we get the feel of a typical and good cavalry regiment of the period: brave, intelligent, quick thinking, cheerful. But as Dr. MacGill records, still spiritually mounted on horses which remained, he notes, of more interest to many of them – men as well as officers – than women. This feeling prevailed throughout the war. They were not alone. The poet Keith Douglas served in North Africa with The Sherwood Rangers, a historic Yeomanry regiment that had changed its horses for tanks.

Douglas was – with terrible inevitability – killed in Normandy in June 1944. He was twenty-four, but during his short lifetime he made a notable contribution to the literature of the Second World War. He lamented the horse's disappearance from the British Army, and in his poem *Aristocrats*, he detected the influence the horse still had, even after the massive changes brought about by armoured warfare, on the thinking and attitudes of these well-bred sportsmen from the Shires. In Douglas's words:

> *Here then*
> *under the stones and earth they dispose themselves,*
> *I think with their famous unconcern.*
> *It is not gunfire I hear, but a hunting horn.*

John Philip Jones has produced a fascinating book which combines the facts of history with the experiences of an individual doctor and the story of a brief but dramatic period in a regiment's life. I have been both gripped and educated, much helped by the excellent illustrations and maps.

PREFACE

This book is the fruit of an old friendship. The hero of the work, Dr. John Sylvanus MacGill (JSM), a family doctor and senior partner of a practice in Denton, near Manchester in the north of England, had two sons. The older son, John, and I have been continuous friends since our early twenties. The MacGill family knew another Scottish medical family, called Lees. who lived a few miles away. (They first met briefly in 1941 when Dr. MacGill was entertained by British families in Cape Town when *en route* to Egypt. The Lees family had been evacuated there.) Shortly after the time when I first knew John, I met Dr. Lees's daughter Eileen and she became a serious girl friend. A few years later she introduced me to Wendy, who became my wife. We have been married for fifty-seven years! I only remember meeting JSM once or twice. The last occasion was shortly before we went to live in Holland. This was a time when many people embraced with enthusiasm the birth of the European Economic Community (now the European Union), and major firms often sent young executives to Europe to get experience. Some time later, John and his family went to live in Belgium. We all eventually were posted back to Britain. I only knew John's younger brother Neil slightly. He became a professor of philosophy in a Canadian university and died prematurely and unmarried.

In about 2010, we were staying with John MacGill and his wife Vivien at their home in Ascot, and he mentioned casually that his father had left a drawer full of relics of his war service: his medals (including the Africa Star with the 8th Army clasp), a journal mainly hand-written, a few sketches, and some albums of photographs. He was a good photographer, and before the war he had devoted time and interest to taking artistic black and white photographs, using a top-quality camera.

He did not take his expensive equipment on active service, and in any case photography was forbidden by military regulations. However, he bent the rules and used a snapshot camera to take a host of sometimes striking photographs, a number of which are to be found in this book. Note particularly **Plates 6, 18, 23, 30, 32, 33, 35, 36, 43, 45, 47, 52, 55.**

After I had spent a couple of hours with the journal and other exhibits, I said that this had the making of a book. I took all the material back to America and started working through the papers with the closest interest. I had shortly before published a book based on a contemporary journal kept by a fighting soldier. (*Battles of a Gunner Officer. Tunisia, Sicily, Normandy and the Long Road to Germany,* by John Philip Jones, based on the unpublished diary of Major Peter Pettit, DSO, TD, HAC.) By trial and error I had learned that a book of this type cannot be made to work unless the diary is fitted into a broader framework. This means that the work has to be a compact book of general history, but using the diary to illustrate many of the high points.

This led me to 'read around' the two most important scenes of Dr. MacGill's active service. The first was Northern France, south of the Somme. After the Dunkirk evacuation in early June 1940, the British armour was concentrated and deployed south of that river. JSM was the Regimental Medical Officer of the Queen's Bays, a historic cavalry regiment that fought in tanks. It operated alongside two other long-established cavalry regiments, the 9th Lancers and the 10th Hussars, in the 2nd Armoured Brigade, which was a major element of the 1st Armoured Division. This division fought unsuccessfully because of overwhelming enemy strength, but it got back to Britain more or less intact. JSM returned to England from Brest in northern France, five weeks after the Dunkirk evacuation. He traveled standing on the crowded deck of a steamer sailing at full speed to evade U-boats. His wife had believed that he must be dead until she got his telegram from Plymouth.

The second scene was the North African desert, where there was a prolonged ding-dong series of battles. (Much fighting had taken place during 1941, and Rommel had constantly made his presence felt.) The 1st Armoured Division arrived in December 1941. During 1942, it participated in the Battle of Gazala, which was followed by the loss of Tobruk and the withdrawal of the 8th Army to the El Alamein position, where three battles were fought: the first two defensive but the third the turning point of the Second World War. JSM was originally still with the Bays, but in June 1942 he was promoted to be Second-in-Command of the 1st Light Field Ambulance, an exclusively medical unit that received patients transferred from Regimental Aid Posts in its vicinity, most of the casualties coming from the Bays, the 9th Lancers and the 10th Hussars. The 1st Armoured Division fought in the successful Battle of Mareth in March 1943. This was an old but strong French defensive line that opened the way to Tunis, where the division arrived in May 1943.

These episodes from the Second World War have generated a large and rich literature containing hundreds of titles. My own library contains 112 works, listed in the Bibliography at the end of this book. I believe that these are the cream of the crop. Within these 112 volumes, I have isolated twenty-seven.. These are the most important primary works, i.e. those written by people who were there during the events they described. The best-known of these authors were the highest-ranking soldiers: Brooke, Alexander, Montgomery, Horrocks, de Guingand, and – from the other side of the hill – Britain's formidable antagonist Rommel. In his extraordinary combination of tactical flair and frenetic energy, he outperformed the British generals. However, by the time of the major assault at El Alamein in October 1942, the British were deploying massive weight which helped clinch the victory. In the field of military memoirs, some more junior soldiers left unforgettable accounts, and I mention particularly Major Armstrong, Lance Corporal Merewood, and Major (later Brigadier) Daniell. JSM's journal is of course in this category. I have also included the regimental histories of the Queen's Bays, the 9th Lancers, the 10th Hussars, and the 11th Regiment, Royal Horse Artillery (Honourable Artillery Company). These works are substantially based on individual accounts by members of all ranks who fought in these regiments. They therefore all count as important primary works.

Because of my plan to write a compact work of history with the journal providing highlights, it is important to set the scene in some detail. In doing this, I have introduced each chapter with a separate *italicized* paragraph summarizing the content. I used this technique in *Battles of a Gunner Officer,* and readers found it a useful way of understanding the relevance of the journal in the overall history. The first four chapters of this book are more history than journal. But the balance shifts in Chapter 5, and the last five chapters are substantially based on the journal although they also include a historical narrative.

The journal reads well and needed only light editing. This is not surprising since its author had a rigorous Scottish education at school and university. He tells a fascinating story, especially about his active service in the desert when he was with the Bays, a first-class Regular regiment that maintained the highest standards. The junior officers were often regarded as gilded youth because they were elegant and rich, but they were also well trained and were excellent leaders who were popular with their men. The officers suffered many casualties, a higher proportion than in the other ranks. Dr. MacGill was older than most (he was born in 1900) and he constantly played Bridge and took a regular dram of whisky with his Commanding Officer, who was the same age. The younger officers presumably preferred champagne when they could get it!

During their time in the desert the Bays lost many men as well as officers, although the regiment was mercifully spared the number of casualties that were common in all branches of the service during the First World War. The journal does not devote too much attention to heroic medical procedures. In any event sickness generally caused more casualties than wounds. The Medical Officer's jobs in the Regimental Aid Post were first aid and triage, which meant passing as many men as possible down the line to a Field Ambulance (where JSM was himself to serve from June 1942).

The only beneficial effect of modern war is that it increases medical knowledge. The most important medical advance during the Second World War was the introduction of antibiotics, a British invention but one that the American pharmaceutical industry was able to put into mass production. Providentially fairly large supplies became available just before the invasion of France in June 1944. They were not there during the North African campaign.

This book contains an outline of the chain of medical services that were set up, with considerable efficiency, to move patients along the link to receive increasingly complex attention from medical and surgical specialists. (**Figure 2**). The treatment of wounds was carried out more effectively in the dry climate of the desert than it was in the jungles of the Far East. Motor ambulances were plentiful, and for longer distances there were air ambulances and, during the latter part of the campaign, hospital ships that took patients to Alexandria. (JSM travelled in such a ship on one occasion.) Dr. MacGill had taken a postgraduate MD degree in Tropical Medicine, especially Sleeping Sickness, and this was of considerable value to so many of his comrades who were stricken with tropical diseases during their service.

Many people have given me help in writing this book. As always, my first thanks go to my wife Wendy. Despite the confusion of my dictation and written drafts, not to speak of my constant amendments, she always produces an immaculate computer-generated manuscript. She is also my best critic, and I always listen to and act upon her frequent criticisms of the clarity and style of my prose. What she says always leads to improvements.

John MacGill, who had unknowingly initiated the whole enterprise, has played a continuous and most helpful part in its development. He, Vivien and I have been discussion partners, and he has read the whole manuscript during its various stages. His comments have always been valuable and I have amended the text accordingly, despite a few small disagreements about American and English spelling! In fact, I eventually decided to write the book in British English. JSM's journal was of course written with British spelling, and it seemed sensible to be consistent throughout the book.

Brigadier John Smales has played a special role. A Regular army officer, he served in a distinguished cavalry regiment, the 14th / 20th Hussars, which he rose to command. The original 14th were known as 'the Emperor's Chambermaids.' On guest nights the officers drank champagne out of a loving cup, which is a large silver chamber pot that had been owned by King Joseph of Spain, Napoleon's brother. It was booty seized during the Peninsular War in 1813. The 14th Hussars have been amalgamated twice, and are now the King's Royal Hussars.

The loving cups of champagne continue to be drunk by officers in the combined regiment. John Smales entered the Staff College, an important rite of passage, and he graduated high on the list and became a Staff College instructor, to help educate the next generation of the most promising officers. He ended his career commanding a brigade. During his service he served for three years in Libya, which gave him a first-hand understanding of the North African desert. In his retirement, he is now a well-known battlefield lecturer and guide. He has read the manuscript of this book and made a number of helpful suggestions that I have incorporated. He is the author of the lucid and perceptive Foreword that distills the essence of my book, and I am most grateful to him.

I thank a number of friends for their advice on aspects of this work. They include members of the medical profession, particularly Dr. Robert Daly, Dr. Gregory Eastwood and Dr. William Stewart, whose poem on the subject of triage appears at the end of Chapter 1. I am also grateful to three friends who have considerable knowledge of military history: David Bennett, Professor at the Maxwell School of Syracuse University; Charles Pettit, former Major in the Honourable Artillery Company; and Anthony Simpson, former Major in the 21st SAS Regiment – Artists. I was puzzled about JSM's three medical degrees, and Wendy's Scottish cousin, Michael Dickson, very kindly set me straight.

Justine Taylor, Archivist of the Honourable Artillery Company, is ever-helpful and made available six impressive photographs of the desert war. She also provided me with the war diary of the 11th Regiment, Royal Horse Artillery (HAC). My friend Dymphna Byrne very helpfully steered me through the British regimental records at the National Archives in Kew.

Finally, my thanks go to professional consultants in Syracuse, New York: Scott Bunting of Fresher Graphics, who designed the cover which has been much admired, and the ten computer-generated maps that are notable for their simplicity and clarity; and Sharon Pickard and Collin Becker of Industrial Color Labs, who carried out a good deal of photographic work with their customary skill.

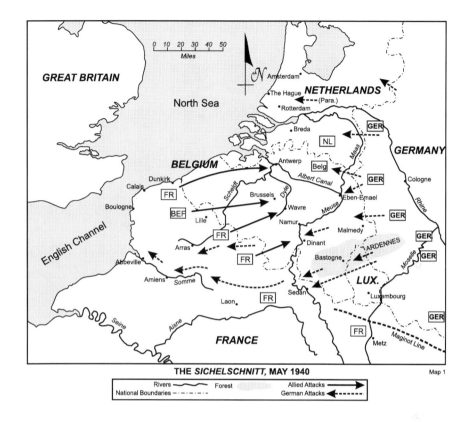

THE *SICHELSCHNITT*, MAY 1940   Map 1

| Rivers ———— | Forest | Allied Attacks ———▶ |
| National Boundaries —··—··— | | German Attacks ◀------- |

THE *SICHELSCHNITT*, 1940

On 10 May 1940, the German army began its assault in the west, with parachute landings in the Netherlands and assaults in south-eastern Belgium. Following an agreed plan, the British Expeditionary Force and the 1st and 7th French armies moved north-east into Belgium, where they were soon engaged. A powerful German armoured force now moved out of the Ardennes Forest and swept, north of the Somme, to reach the Channel coast. This was the *Sichelschnitt*, the Sickel Cut that isolated the British and French and forced their evacuation from Dunkirk between 27 May and 4 June.

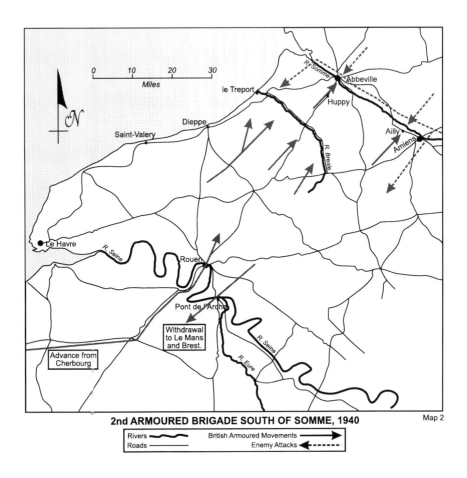

2nd ARMOURED BRIGADE SOUTH OF SOMME, 1940

Map 2

Rivers	British Armoured Movements ➤
Roads	Enemy Attacks ◄-------

2ⁿᵈ ARMOURED BRIGADE SOUTH OF THE SOMME

The under-strength 1ˢᵗ Armoured Division, containing the 2ⁿᵈ Armoured Brigade, was only deployed in France after most of the British army had been evacuated from Dunkirk. The tanks landed in Cherbourg and moved to the area south of the Somme, while strong German armoured columns were advancing to the river. The 2ⁿᵈ Armoured Brigade attempted unsuccessfully to stop them. A number of engagements followed, and most of the 51ˢᵗ Highland Division was captured at Saint-Valery on 11 June. There was now no future for the 1ˢᵗ Armoured Division because of superior enemy strength. It therefore moved south and west to Brittany, and sailed from Brest to Britain, having destroyed its tanks to prevent their capture.

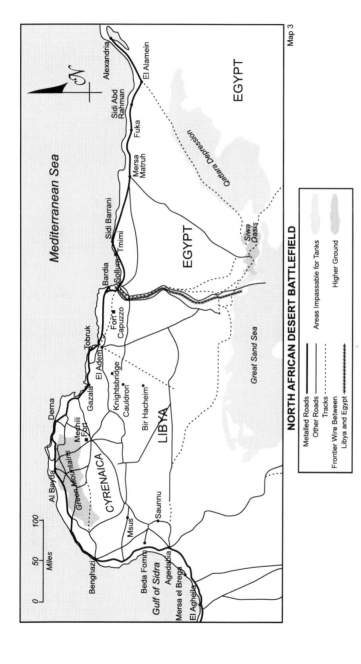

NORTH AFRICAN DESERT BATTLEFIELD

The battlefield was barren and large: 300 miles as the crow flies from Alexandria west to the frontier 'Wire' between Egypt and Libya, and then another 300 miles from the 'Wire' to the port of Benghazi. The only metalled road followed the coastline, going through the important port of Tobruk before getting to Benghazi, in the large bulge of Cyrenaica, where much fighting was to take place. The actual distances travelled were longer than the direct distances, although the fighting was mostly concentrated in the desert regions south of the escarpment which rose up from the coast. The southern desert contained a number of tracks, although most of the area was difficult 'going' for tanks.

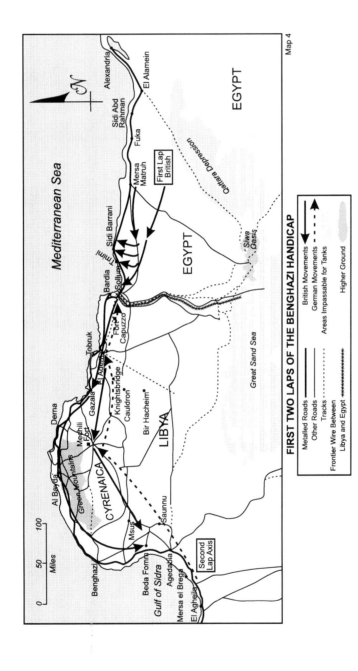

FIRST TWO LAPS OF THE BENGHAZI HANDICAP

Metalled Roads ——————	British Movements
Other Roads ————	German Movements - - - - →
Tracks · · · · · · ·	
Frontier Wire Between	
Libya and Egypt ✻✻✻✻✻✻✻✻✻✻	Areas Impassable for Tanks
	Higher Ground

Map 4

THE FIRST TWO LAPS OF THE BENGHAZI HANDICAP

The entry of Italy into the war in June 1940 saw 150,000 men of the Italian 10th Army garrisoning Libya but not demonstrating any aggressiveness. Their British opponents, commanded by General Wavell with Lieutenant General O'Connor reporting to him, moved in total secrecy to carry out a large-scale raid in December 1940. This grew into a major operation and netted tens of thousands of Italian prisoners. Unfortunately, Wavell now had to weaken his force. At the same time the German Afrika Korps, under General Rommel, landed and without delay mounted an attack on the British force. By 15 May 1941, Rommel had reached the 'Wire' separating Libya from Egypt. However, he did not capture Tobruk, which remained isolated and became a source of trouble for him.

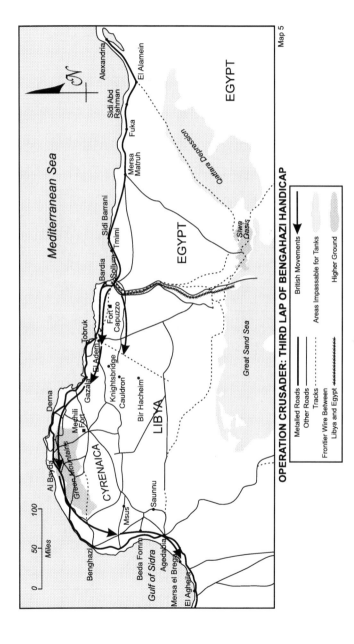

OPERATION *CRUSADER*: THIRD LAP OF BENGAHAZI HANDICAP

Map 5

OPERATION *CRUSADER* – THIRD LAP OF THE BENGHAZI HANDICAP

Under pressure from Churchill, Wavell made a riposte, codenamed *Battleaxe*, which was too weak to succeed. Partially as a result of this failure, there was now a change of command, and General Auchinleck took over as Commander-in-Chief of the Middle East. He refused to move precipitately in the desert, but made a well-planned attack named Operation *Crusader* which was launched on 18 August 1941. It was commanded by Lieutenant General Alan Cunningham, whom Auchinleck had appointed. He had a large number of tanks but they were inferior to the substantial numbers of Panzer III and Panzer IV that opposed him. The attack proceeded with difficulty in view of Rommel's defensive skill, but Tobruk was relieved. After six weeks of hard going the 8th Army completed successfully the third lap of the Benghazi Handicap.

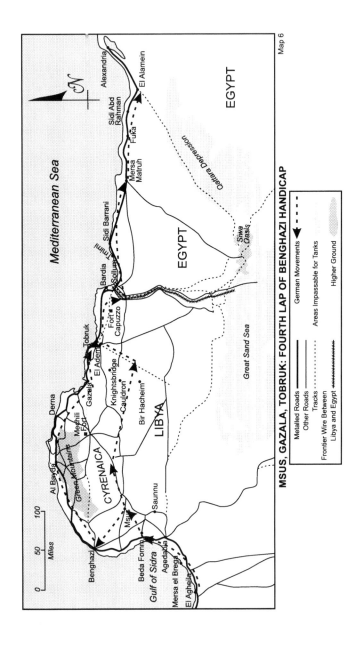

MSUS, GAZALA, TOBRUK: FOURTH LAP OF THE BENGHAZI HANDICAP

Map 6

Legend	
Metalled Roads	German Movements
Other Roads	Areas Impassable for Tanks
Tracks	
Frontier Wire Between	
Libya and Egypt	Higher Ground

MSUS, GAZALA, TOBRUK: FOURTH LAP OF THE BENGHAZI HANDICAP

In early 1942, Rommel had received tank reinforcements and was able to attack the 8th Army with his customary ferocity. On 20 January, the 1st Armoured Division encountered the enemy, but Rommel maintained the initiative. The British fought a series of piecemeal engagements until the pace of the fighting slowed. Rommel had meanwhile received a restraining order from his superiors. The two sides were not in battle for two months, and spent the time reinforcing a defensive line running south from the small port of Gazala. When Rommel resumed the offensive at the end of May, there was confusion in the British command, and Auchinleck was eventually compelled to take personal command of the 8th Army. He decided to take a blocking position, sixty miles west of Alexandria, based on the small railway station of El Alamein.

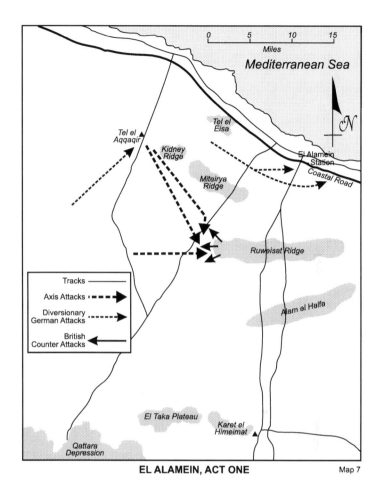

EL ALAMEIN, ACT ONE   Map 7

El ALAMEIN, ACT I

The El Alamein line, running south for forty miles from the railway station on the coast to the totally impassable Qattara Depression, was a reasonably good defensive position. The desert was flat, but there were three small ridges that offered a tactical advantage for the defenders by providing observation; these were Miteirya, Ruweisat and Alam el Halfa. More than two weeks were to pass before Rommel returned to the offensive. Auchinleck judged correctly that Rommel would attack the Ruweisat ridge, but this was preceded by diversionary moves in the north. The result of the assault on Ruweisat was a soldiers' battle, with small gains and losses, local counter-attacks, and heavy artillery fire (the particular strength of the 8th Army). The German soldiers kept their fighting spirit, but this was less true of the Italians. El Alamein Act I, successfully blocked any further advance by Axis troops, and after the position had been fully secured, the British began to receive greater-than-ever reinforcements of men, tanks and supplies.

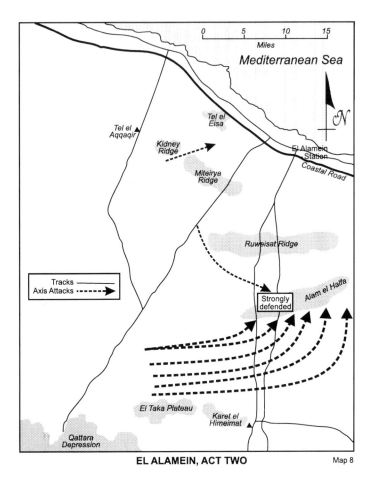

EL ALAMEIN, ACT TWO   Map 8

EL ALAMEIN, ACT II

Montgomery now commanded the 8th Army. He received reliable *Sigint* reports that Rommel would be resuming his assault, and the German *Schwerpunkt* was likely to be the Alam el Halfa ridge. Montgomery's plan was to hold a static position in overwhelming strength and allow Rommel's attacks to wash against an impregnable British position. On 30 August 1942, the expected attack by the Panzerarmee Afrika began, in great strength from the south of the ridge and with a less powerful thrust from the north. Rommel's forces were greeted by the fire of 400 tanks (dug in hull-down), 300 anti-tank guns, and 240 field guns, all protected by a dense minefield. By 3 September, Rommel's troops had retreated to their start line, with the loss of fifty guns, fifty tanks, and 400 other vehicles.

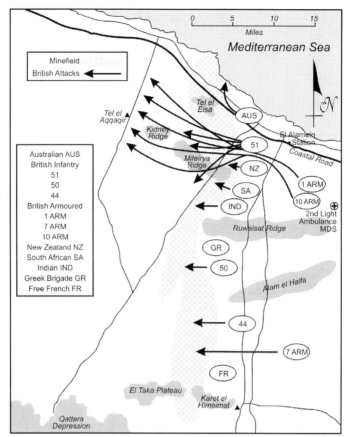

EL ALAMEIN, ACT THREE   Map 9

EL ALAMEIN, ACT III

By October 1942, the 8th Army had been substantially reinforced and Montgomery prepared to take the initiative. A vast minefield now separated the two armies, and this had to be tackled before any breakthrough. Montgomery deployed eight infantry and three armored divisions, fully manned and equipped, while Rommel had a similar number of divisions, but all under-strength. The battle opened with a night assault. The date had been determined by the longest possible period of darkness, which was 23 October 1942. A spectacular artillery bombardment opened the battle, then in the northern (XXX Corps) sector, the infantry advanced, accompanied by sappers to clear the minefields. Progress was slow and the cost was heavy. Meanwhile, XIII Corps further south made diversionary attacks that did their job. By 27 October, Montgomery paused to regroup and adjusted the angle of his attack. Then on 30 October, he made his plan for the long-awaited armored breakthrough in the northern sector, and the two armoured divisions of X Corps at last surged through the enemy defensive lines. Montgomery had forecast accurately that the battle would take twelve days.

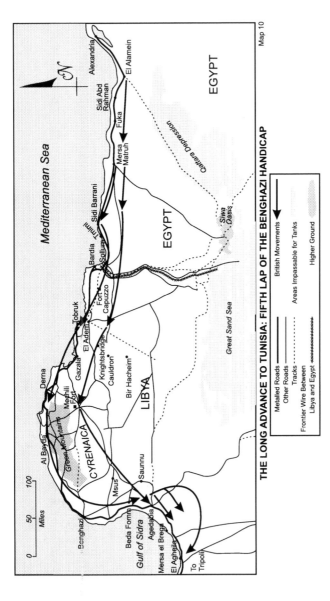

THE LONG ADVANCE TO TUNISIA: FIFTH LAP OF THE BENGHAZI HANDICAP

Map 10

THE LONG ADVANCE TO TUNISIA – FIFTH LAP OF THE BENGHAZI HANDICAP

After the battle of El Alamein, both sides were exhausted, having suffered major casualties. The 8ᵗʰ Army's pursuit of the enemy to the west was made difficult by the limited capacity of the single metalled coast road, particularly since seasonal rains turned the desert into mud, which slowed the progress of all vehicles. And it was not an uninterrupted progress for the 8ᵗʰ Army because Rommel maintained effective control of the Panzerarmee Afrika, which also later received reinforcements. The 1ˢᵗ Armoured Division, including the 1ˢᵗ Light Field Ambulance in which Dr. MacGill was serving, advanced to Tmimi, on the coast 250 miles beyond El Alamein. They were to remain there for a number of months. With the British advance to Benghazi on 20 November, the fifth lap of the Benghazi Handicap had been a decisive triumph for the 8ᵗʰ Army. It reached Tripoli on 23 January 1943.

CHAPTER 1

AN ARMY UNPREPARED

When Britain began to rearm belatedly during the late 1930s, she had the best and largest navy in the world; a small air force that was very soon swallowing a disproportionate share of the defence budget; and an army that still fulfilled its traditional rôle of garrisoning the British Empire and had almost half its men overseas. In 1939 Britain confronted Germany – a first-class military power – and when battle was joined in 1940 the British Army was shown to be deficient in numbers, in equipment and in doctrine, and this was especially true of the armoured regiments: those that fought in tanks. Britain had invented the tank – a potentially war-winning weapon – and first used it tentatively in September 1916. But it took almost two years for an effective tactical method to be developed: the All-Arms Offensive that broke the trench deadlock in August 1918. Unfortunately, during the 1930s, it was the German Army that studied intensively and formulated effective All-Arms tactics, and these led to the victory of the Panzers in France in 1940. In contrast, British Army doctrine governing the use of armour remained an anachronism. This book describes the active service of a cavalry regiment converted to tanks, viewed through the eyes of its medical officer. Because of the conservatism of the British Army, a problem exacerbated by the shortage of tanks, it took three years or more before the generals learned how armour should be used effectively.

Tradition, with its Strengths and Weaknesses

The British Army is a collection of regiments, and in this respect there is no other army in the world like it. The infantry regiments are recruited on a regional basis, a system that encourages regional

1

loyalty to underpin the soldiers' loyalty to their regiments. The British Army has had a long history, dating from 1537 when the Honourable Artillery Company came into existence. This was and still is a non-Regular regiment. As far as the Regular infantry is concerned, there has always been a chronological ranking beginning with the Royal Scots, raised in 1633. An infantry regiment's position on the list – its order of precedence – is always jealously guarded (although the amalgamations of regiments since the Second World War have caused a good deal of confusion.) The cavalry regiments have a similar ranking, beginning with the Life Guards, raised in 1660. The Army is merely one example of how Britain, as a result of its long history, resists homogeneity: a point plentifully illustrated by the following totally unconnected examples of how the British refuse to accept uniformity and simplicity when there is any way of finding differences.

There are wide variations in British regional speech: more than in the United States with its population five times as large. The British Parliament, despite the small size of the country, has more constituencies than the United States House of Representatives. A movement exists in Britain to split the United Kingdom by making Wales and Scotland (and even the Shetland Isles!) independent. The ranks of the British titled classes are wondrously complex, and so is the awards system by which members of the public can received a strange array of decorations and medals for services to the country. Britain has always been fond of obsolete units of measurement: tons and hundredweights; miles and furlongs; unusual descriptions of guns e.g. 6-pounders and not 57mm; and the pounds, shillings and pence that only disappeared in the 1970s, long after all other major countries had gone metric. The British police have always been based on independent county constabularies, with no central body like the FBI or the gendarmeries of continental Europe. The oldest British universities, Oxford and Cambridge, have a fragmented structure. In contrast to monolithic institutions like universities in America and other countries, they are composed of individual and quite independent colleges – a number that has grown since the Second World War – which represent a greater source of loyalty to their members than the university itself. Perhaps most strikingly, the British population is composed of a number of social groups with clear distinctions, even in today's supposedly classless society. George Orwell described himself as being in the lowest stratum of the upper middle class!

The British Army, with its jigsaw puzzle of regiments, is made up of six broad groups. With a delightfully mixed metaphor, these are called 'teeth arms' – those involved directly in combat – infantry, armour, artillery, air, engineers and signals. There is also a range of supporting arms: transport, ordnance, medical, chaplains, pay, military police and others. This book is concerned mainly with a unit and an individual from these groups: a cavalry regiment and its Regimental Medical Officer (RMO), who was a member of a larger organization, the Royal Army Medical Corps (RAMC). The RMO was Dr. John Sylvanus MacGill, a family doctor who had been in practice in Denton, near Manchester. The regiment was armoured but formerly cavalry, the Queen's Bays (2nd Dragoon Guards). Often referred to simply as the Bays, it was named after the regiment's horses, which were different shades of brown, with black points (mane and tail). It had a curious nickname, 'Rusty Buckles.' During the 18th Century the regiment had returned to England from Ireland, with steel buckles still on their uniforms, because they had not received the army order to change them to brass. 'Rusty Buckles' also became the name of the Bays' march, played on parade.

At the beginning of war in 1939, the British Regular Army numbered 374,000 men, including the substantial number of Regular reservists who were experienced men who could be instantly mobilized although these needed training to bring them up to speed. (There were no women yet.) In addition, there were 457,000 members of the Territorial Army (TA), enthusiastic part-time soldiers who were mobilized just before war was declared, although the war was to demonstrate that Territorial troops needed at least a year of training and military discipline before they were ready for battle. Conscription, introduced in 1939, increased the size of the Regular Army, initially by 34,000 men; but the conscripts needed even more training than the Territorials. It was therefore the end of 1940 before Britain became a nation at arms. By then conscription was providing a large flow of recruits and many women were joining the armed services in non-combatant jobs. Conscription soon put a great strain on the Regular Army, whose officers and NCOs had to train the recruits. And equipment, which was always in short supply, had to be shared with the units and sub-units containing large numbers of conscripts.

Training was a matter of the first importance, and the reason why the partially trained Territorials and the untrained conscripts needed at least a year before they were ready for action was because three separate disciplines had to be rigorously imposed. The first was living and working under military regulations. The second was personal skills: for the infantry, skill at arms and minor tactics; for the armour, driving, maintenance, gunnery and signals. The third discipline was training in progressively large units, which in armour meant troop then squadron then regiment, followed by joint training with artillery and infantry. Before the invasion of France in June 1944, many British troops had been training hard in Britain for three or even four years.

In 1939, the infantry and armoured force was made up of ninety-two regiments: sixty-nine in the infantry recruited from different parts of the country, and twenty-three in the armour. Just before the war, the armoured units were put together into one large group called the Royal Armoured Corps (RAC). This comprised the Royal Tank Regiment which had emerged from the First World War, together with twenty-two ancient cavalry regiments which had exchanged their horses for tanks during the inter-war period. In 1939 some of these regiments were still learning their new skills, a difficult process because of the shortage of tanks. Each infantry regiment had at least two battalions and the Royal Tank Regiment had more than two. (The name 'battalions' was later changed to numbered Royal Tank regiments). But in the cavalry each regiment remained a unique entity, with no multiple battalions. As conscripts swelled the size of the army, the newcomers boosted the numbers of battalions in the infantry and Royal Tank Regiment. The cavalry however expanded much less; only six new cavalry regiments were raised, and these were to be disbanded at the end of the war.

An infantry battalion (generally described as a unit) had about 850 men: a number that was quickly eroded by casualties when battle was joined, with reinforcements often not large enough to replace the losses. An armoured regiment (also described as a unit) had only three-quarters the strength of an infantry battalion. The infantry had more regiments than the armour; many more multi-battalion regiments, which multiplied the number of units; and more men per unit. The infantry therefore had *seven times* as many men as the armoured force. But despite its small total size, the armour had an extremely important rôle in battle. It also had by far the greatest deficiencies in equipment and doctrine: for a start, there was an obvious need for a big increase in its total size. The problems were not easily solved and were to persist for many months of fighting in the North African desert. A major improvement followed the arrival of large numbers of American tanks in 1942, and by this time the army was making progress in improving its armoured tactics.

The long and honourable tradition of the British Army inevitably led the officers and men to become conservative in their attitudes. This led to pride in the regiment, which was highly beneficial because it stiffened the sinews of individual members in the face of the enemy, and helped units survive losses in battle and still remain militarily effective. But tradition also often meant problems of parochialism. Love of regiment was often so strong that officers and men were unhappy to be posted elsewhere, despite the frequent need of their services in other regiments, on the staff, or in training positions. Regimental pride also led to rivalry between regiments. Although this was generally healthy, very occasionally it was counter-productive because it hindered cooperation.

In the background there was also a matter of social class. There was always a rigid division between officers and the rank and file. Officers rarely came from the ranks with the exception of quartermasters, one per unit, who were former warrant officers and did not usually rise above the rank of captain. But within the commissioned ranks there were also more subtle gradations. Although there were no differences between the jobs that different regiments performed, and they all had equally long and bloody histories, there was a well understood but unwritten hierarchy of regiments.

Officers were recruited from a limited number of sources: members of the small group that made up the aristocracy and landed gentry, and the larger number of established families in the educated *bourgeoisie*: serving and retired officers in the armed services; members of the learned professions (the Church, medicine and the law); elected politicians, especially parliamentarians; senior permanent officials in various branches of government (the Home Civil Service and Diplomatic Service, the Indian Civil Service and the Colonial Service); and prosperous members of the financial and business communities. Very few officers entered the army with a university degree, but they had nearly all attended the Royal Military College, Sandhurst, where candidates for the infantry and cavalry were trained for eighteen months, or the Royal Military Academy, Woolwich, where candidates for the artillery, engineers and signals spent two years. Fees were charged at Sandhurst and Woolwich although there were a few scholarships. Cadets at these establishments usually, although not always, had come from public schools (English terminology for fee-paying private schools). When they joined their regiments, the vast majority of young officers were required to have at least a small private income because their pay was meagre and hardly enough to cover their messing and other expenses.

Things only became different after the end of the Second World War when the newly-unified Royal Military Academy, Sandhurst no longer demanded fees, and life in an officers' mess became simpler. Some officers had larger private incomes than others, and this factor contributed to the pecking order of the different regiments. Hubert Gough, one of the many cavalry officers who became generals in the First World War, as a subaltern in the 16th Lancers received from his father a private income three times the size of his army pay. Looking back at his time in this very stylish regiment he wrote: 'I do not remember ever seeing a whisky and soda, still less beer or plain water, at any of our meals.' But Gough and his brother-officers consumed large quantities of champagne, claret and port. Many cavalry regiments have royal connections. The Queen's uncle the Duke of Gloucester served in the 10th Hussars; her cousin the Duke of Kent was in the Royal Scots Greys; another cousin Prince Michael of Kent served in the 11th Hussars; and her grandson Prince Harry recently left the army after ten years as an officer in the Blues and Royals.

Of the ninety-two regiments of the infantry and cavalry, twenty-nine were considered more exclusive than the others and accounted for about ten percent of the strength of the army as a whole, including the other 'teeth arms' and the services. The twenty-nine attracted more aristocratic and richer officers, and in particular those who already had family connections with the regiment. The group was made up of the five regiments of Foot Guards; the Green Jackets (two of the small number of infantry regiments known as Rifles); and the twenty-two regiments of cavalry (two regiments of Household Cavalry and twenty others). The Royal Horse Artillery (the members of which are selected from the greater numbers in the Royal Artillery), should be added to the twenty-nine, to make thirty in all. Twenty-eight of the thirty were exclusively Regular (the Green Jackets being the exceptions). However, during the course of the war they all received and made good use of conscripts.

Cavalry in all countries tends to be associated with aristocracy, with its historical connections with chivalry, knighthood and *noblesse oblige*. However, as mentioned, all these regiments carried out jobs which were the same as those done by other regiments. And although these exclusive regiments had impressive historical records, these were no different from most other regiments in the army. Incidentally there was another curious idiosyncrasy about the cavalry. A number of the regiments, including the Bays, had the word 'Guards' in their titles, but this did not imply the same direct connection with the Sovereign that was enjoyed by the Foot Guards and Household Cavalry. Six of the most senior Cavalry units, including the Bays, were at one time known as Horse regiments, which denoted that they were heavy cavalry, and had a superior status and received more pay than other regiments. In 1788, higher authorities decided to bring all regiments into line, which meant that the Bays lost their title of Horse regiment, and also their extra pay. As compensation, all the regiments of Horse, including the Bays, were given the honorific title of Dragoon Guards.

This is a reminder of the rich history and traditions of British regiments: history symbolized by the Colours, Standards and Guidons, and the guns – the Colours – of the Royal Artillery. Regiments all have silver cups and table decorations, much of it historically important. They all proudly bore nicknames that had emerged from the shadows of regimental history: 'the Donkey Wallopers' (the Life Guards); 'the Old Farmers' (the 5th Dragoon Guards); 'the Straw Boots' (the 7th Dragoon Guards); 'the Bird Catchers' (the 1st Dragoons); 'the Lily-White Seventh' (the 7th Hussars); "the Dirty Dozen' (the 12th Lancers); and many more.

Although the Bays were mechanized in 1936, the style of the officers' mess did not change. The officers were still 'horsey', although they no longer had to follow the practice of all mounted regiments by which young officers work with the men they command in 'mucking out' the stables every morning. Both at home and on active service, the officers brought some comfort to their lives by dining formally on many evenings and purchasing luxuries, even in the desert. Before joining the regiment, young officers had to be accepted by the higher ranks. The newcomers were all relatively rich, had good manners and impeccable accents, were well-tailored and led stylish lives. They took their profession seriously, and if they had not become tank experts before 1939, this was because there was a crippling shortage of machines on which to train.

What has been said so far has been confined to the commissioned ranks, and officers accounted for only five percent of the strength of every infantry or cavalry regiment. However, regimental pride and exclusivity has always permeated all the ranks. The troopers in every cavalry regiment regarded it with the same pride as their officers did, and inevitably tended to be patronizing towards the members of other regiments. The men in the ranks of the cavalry regiments had great affection for their horses. Nevertheless, the conversion to tanks was not totally unwelcome, for two reasons. First, the time taken on care and maintenance was much less than was demanded by the horses; and second, the mechanical skills the men were taught would be of great value when they eventually returned to civilian life.

Every regiment in the army had its own badge, which was always worn on the cap and often also on the collar, lapels and epaulettes of the tunic. Some of these badges were also rich with historical symbolism. Before the First World War, when the infantry wore scarlet and the cavalry wore blue full dress, all regiments had visible differences in their uniforms. During the inter-war period full dress became obsolete and the khaki uniform introduced during Queen Victoria's reign became the plain and undecorated kit that was now universally worn. But differences were built in, as if to deny the word uniform in its original meaning. The khaki tunics were fastened with a row of buttons and every regiment had its own design: the majority had brass buttons, but the Rifle regiments had black ones. The officers in each regiment of Foot Guards – always idiosyncratic – had their tunic buttons clustered in a different way from those in the others. The buttons of the Royal Horse Artillery are in the shape of miniature cannon balls. The Scottish regiments had specially-tailored tunics that were cut away at an angle below the belt, to display the kilts of the Highland regiments, each with its own tartan, and the trews of the Lowlanders, again with their own tartans. (The Highlanders wore their kilts in battle until 1918.) The Royal Welch Fusiliers (note the spelling) had their unique Flash: a bunch of black ribbons hanging from the back of the tunic collar. Officers in the Inniskilling Dragoon Guards wore dark green 'overall' trousers below their khaki tunics, and officers of the 11th Hussars wore distinctive red ones that gave the regiment its nickname 'Cherry Pickers.' Many regiments had distinctive headgear: the Royal Tanks, all the Scottish regiments, some of the Irish ones, and a couple of regiments of cavalry.

Even with the introduction of khaki battledress just before the Second World War – a uniform designed to be worn in the field by both officers and men – differences started popping up, such as coloured lanyards worn around the shoulder, small differences in badges of rank between regiments, and coloured cloth patches at the top of the arms of the tunic. (The 1st Armoured Division had a cloth patch with a symbol of a white rhinoceros on a green background.) There was also a fascinating array of coloured side caps that were not issued free but which soldiers were happy to buy with their own money. The war gave birth to some new regiments, and the Commandos were very proud of their green berets, and the airborne troops equally proud of their maroon ones. When in action, both regiments were reluctant to use steel helmets and continued to wear their berets.

Tanks: How They Were Used, and How They *Should* Have Been Used

The efficiency of an army's armoured force depends on three factors. The first is the overall strategic doctrine of the army as a whole, which determines the number of armoured divisions in comparison with infantry divisions. The second factor is tactical: the internal composition of an armoured division. This is a formation that should be sufficiently large – and with the right balance of armour, infantry and artillery – to carry out independent tasks on the battlefield. The third factor is the quality of the tanks themselves. In all three aspects, the British Army in 1939 had serious deficiencies.

The original type of division was infantry and was well established before the First World War and had not changed much by 1939. Three battalions made up an infantry brigade. Three brigades made up a division, which also included a substantial amount of artillery. However, before the Second World War there was no agreement about how an armoured division should be organized. At one extreme, it could be three armoured brigades plus supporting forces from infantry and artillery. At the other extreme, an armoured division could be a three-part balance of one armoured brigade, one infantry brigade and one artillery brigade. Typically, the British Army eventually compromised and chose two armoured brigades plus a small amount of infantry and artillery.

However, the German Army went for the All-Arms concept, with an equal balance between armour, infantry and artillery. They also added powerful anti-tank guns, and dive-bombers to increase dramatically the power of the artillery. In May 1940, the Panzer divisions were the *Schwerpunkt* – the spearhead – of the German Army that cut across France. Infantry divisions followed and consolidated, forming defences against any counter-attacks. After the dramatic success of the 1940 campaign against France and the German invasion of Russia in 1941 which was conducted on similar lines, the Panzer-led offensive became more difficult to repeat. This was because of the growing power of anti-tank weapons. In the North African desert in 1941-1942, the lesson that the British Army took from its battles with the Afrika Korps was that unprotected British armour was all too often knocked out by German 88mm guns, and unprotected German armour by British 6-pounders. When Montgomery, now a Lieutenant General, arrived on the scene, he used his infantry divisions to crack the crust of the German defences at the Battle of El Alamein. The three British armoured divisions penetrated the gaps and pushed forward. However, the armour was much less aggressive than Montgomery had hoped, and this pointed to continuing problems with the organization of the typical armoured division. It is necessary to look back to understand why things were still not right.

An Inchoate Tactical Doctrine

Although Britain had invented the tank during the First World War, it was two years before the army learned how to handle this powerful new weapon effectively. As a result of hard experience that tanks could capture ground but not hold it, the British Army at last appreciated the lessons that tanks had to be employed *en masse*, and work in close cooperation with other 'teeth arms'. This led logically to the All-Arms Offensive. This was pioneered by the British Army and put into effect in August 1918 by General Rawlinson's 4th Army, when infantry, armour, artillery and air attacked in accordance with a tightly-coordinated plan. It proved to be a war-winning innovation.

The British Army during the inter-war period continued to pay lip-service to the value of the All-Arms Offensive. But it did not form part of routine peacetime training, mainly because the individual arms of the service continued to pursue their own training programs. This was particularly true of the Royal Air Force.

Defence budgets were also always very restricted. However, the German Army operated differently, and the All-Arms Offensive became an article of faith. One reason is that influential German officers studied the works of the British military analysts J.F.C. Fuller and Basil Liddell Hart. Paradoxically, the British military doctrine that had been derived from notable British successes in the battlefield was studied more seriously in Potsdam than in Aldershot. The result was the formation of many well-armed and well-balanced Panzer divisions, with a considerable emphasis on tactical air power. This was partially integrated into the division and partially organized independently to provide close support.

The problem with the British armored force in 1939 was not entirely the outcome of years of financial stringency. There had also been doctrinal disputes. One faction in the army saw armour as essentially a support for the infantry, while another visualized it as a new incarnation of cavalry, whose job was to lead the charge. This was a reflection of a sharp cultural difference between the Royal Tank Regiment and the Cavalry. What was at the time known as the Tank Corps was established during the First World War. Its experience, at the Battle of Cambrai in November 1917 and in the All-Arms offensive in August 1918, produced two doctrines that penetrated the psyche of the regiment. These were the need to fight tanks *en masse*, and the demand for strong support from infantry and artillery. As the cavalry regiments became mechanized after the war, the Royal Tank Regiment remained suspicious that the Cavalry was still imbued with its traditional belief in shock action and cold steel.

The notion of the All-Arms offensive, with the armour integrated into a formation that included all the 'teeth arms,' with all of them operating to a single tactical plan and one set of orders, did not receive much support, although it had demonstrated its effectiveness in August 1918. J.F.C. Fuller, a senior staff officer in the War Office, pushed the idea of All-Arms and described it in strong and persuasive English. However, Fuller's writings were (as mentioned) studied more seriously by German than by British officers.

Fuller was ordered in 1927 to set up an Experimental Mechanized Force, comprising two armoured regiments, an infantry battalion, a field artillery regiment and an engineer field company: a force of All Arms in miniature. This experiment had a very short life, partly because of the wide variations of equipment within each of the five units. But Fuller was also responsible. This became known as the Tidworth Scandal, and put back the development of British armoured doctrine for a number of years. Meanwhile, a handful of intelligent and forceful officers became interested in the future of armour, and were stimulated by the second of the British military gurus of the inter-war period, Basil Liddell Hart. In 1937 Liddell Hart became an adviser to Leslie Hore-Belisha, the reforming Minister of War. The most aggressive and imaginative of the officers influenced by Liddell Hart was Percy Hobart (who coincidentally became Major General Montgomery's brother-in-law).

Britain led the world in tank design during the 1920s, but further progress slowed down because of the economic depression. However, this period saw a development that reflected the views of different army factions and which muddied the waters. Work was slowly started on three separate types of tank, and each was eventually manufactured in a number of different versions. They were all tracked; had inadequate offensive armament that was not powerful enough to fight tank-on-tank;

and a modest amount of armour plating to protect against enemy fire. The three were called Light: 12-feet in length and intended for battlefield reconnaissance; Cruiser: 18-feet and intended for offensive action; and Infantry, also 18-feet, strong, heavy and slow, and built to support advancing infantry.

In 1933 Hobart was appointed to command the 1st Tank Brigade. It was composed of three regiments of tanks and little else and gave some indication that armour was going to operate as an independent force on the battlefield, like a cavalry brigade of old. In 1934, this brigade was expanded into a Mobile Division, but there was still no clear idea about whether it would be the equivalent of a cavalry division, or a support for the infantry, or a more balanced force. Its composition – a compromise based on too many tanks and too little infantry and artillery support – reflected this dilemma. Command of this division was given in 1937 to Major General Brooke, an officer with a future who would eventually become Chief of the Imperial General Staff (CIGS). Eight months later, Brooke handed over to Major General Evans, who was to take it to France in May 1940. It was then named the 1st Armoured Division and equipped with relatively ineffective tanks and weak support from the other 'teeth arms'. It was a plan ripe for disaster.

Of all the deficiencies in the Royal Armoured Corps in 1939, the greatest was the shortage of tanks – a direct result of financial stringency – with only 375 on the books in 1936. Of these, 209 were Light models, two-thirds of them obsolete. Improvements brought about by Hore-Belisha in 1937 meant that more tanks were soon in the pipeline, but the bulk of them had not reached the armoured units when war was declared. The astonishing result was that it was not until May 1940 that the 1st Armoured Division landed in France, by which time the campaign had been virtually lost. Nine individual armoured units had been in France since the beginning and had been distributed among the infantry divisions, which is not a good way of employing armour. Except for the remarkable exploits of an armoured car regiment, the 12th Lancers, and a partially successful counter-attack near Arras, the armour made little contribution to the operations of the British Expeditionary Force (BEF).

The Armoured Division: British Weakness and German Strength

The 1ˢᵗ Armoured Division that went to France was organized on the compromise pattern. It had two armoured brigades and a weak support group of infantry and artillery. The 2ⁿᵈ Armoured Brigade was made up of three historic cavalry regiments: the Bays (raised in 1685), and the 9ᵗʰ Lancers and 10ᵗʰ Hussars (both raised in 1715). They had all begun converting to armour three years before war was declared, but tanks were in short supply and the regiments were still learning on the job. They were equipped with Cruisers and Light tanks. The 3ʳᵈ Armoured Brigade (of Infantry tanks) comprised only two regiments, 2ⁿᵈ and 5ᵗʰ Royal Tanks. The division fielded a total of 357 tanks, but 143 were Cruisers, 114 Light machines, and 100 of the slow Infantry tanks, mostly early models with a machine gun but no artillery. In summary, the 1ˢᵗ Armoured Division was weak and lop-sided.

In addition, British anti-tank weapons were feeble. The infantry had .55 inch anti-tank rifles, with a range of 250 yards, which had an alarming recoil and probably did more damage to the shoulder of the soldier firing it than to the tank he was shooting at. The basic Royal Artillery anti-tank gun was the 2-pounder (40mm), a complicated weapon that made little impression on German armour. The Germans however had increasing numbers of effective anti-tank guns. The 88mm which was being introduced – an anti-aircraft weapon also engineered to fire horizontally – was particularly formidable, and even as late as 1945 there was no anti-tank gun in the world that was as good. (**Plate 5.**)

When the BEF eventually received the 1ˢᵗ Armoured Division in May 1940, the Germans fielded ten Panzer divisions opposing the French and British Armies. For the British, this was the beginning of a long learning process. By the end of the war, the British Army had raised eleven armoured divisions, all stronger and better balanced than the 1ˢᵗ Armoured Division of 1940. But in 1944 the German Panzer force had been made even more powerful to match the large numbers of Russian, American and British divisions the German Army was now facing. Most British armour went to France in 1939-1940: nine separate units, followed in May 1940 by the 1ˢᵗ Armoured Division. But another armoured division existed at the time. This now took the name of the

Mobile Division (the same name as the experimental 1934 formation) and was stationed in Egypt; it was even less strong than the 1ˢᵗ Armoured Division. But it was eventually strengthened and re-named the 7ᵗʰ Armoured Division and with its memorable name of Desert Rats it was to fight its way across North Africa, and then from Normandy to the Baltic.

The first commander of the Mobile Division was Major General Hobart, who had great ability but an intolerant personality that made him unpopular and led to him being sacked by the Commander-in-Chief of the Middle East in 1940. He returned home and in his retirement he became a corporal in the Home Guard, the part-time local defence volunteers. However, Churchill plucked him away for higher things. He was re-appointed as an armoured divisional commander, and was eventually given the job of creating a new and specialist armoured division for the invasion of France in 1944. It was a case of a round peg at last finding a round hole. This formation, the 79ᵗʰ Armoured Division, developed a range of machines called 'Funnies': swimming tanks, bridge-laying machines, flame-throwers, flails that used chains to beat the ground to destroy mines, and a number of other remarkable contraptions. They landed in Normandy on D-Day, 6 June 1944, and fought their way in a glorious path towards Germany until the end of the war.

The way in which British armour evolved between 1940 and 1944 makes an instructive story. Chapters 4 to 8 describe the to-and-fro of battles between the British 8ᵗʰ Army and the German Afrika Korps. British armoured tactics gradually changed, better tanks arrived, and the structure of a typical British armoured division was adapted to match. But the British Army had still not got it quite right.

Finally, before the invasion of France in 1944 a typical armoured division had become much better organized and was at least twice as powerful – in part because it had better weapons – than the 1ˢᵗ Armoured Division of 1940. The 1944 Armoured Division had four armoured regiments, four battalions and a company of infantry, four artillery regiments, and three squadrons and a troop of engineers. By that time, the fighting in North Africa had proven the worth of the British 6-pounder (57mm) anti-tank gun. The better 17-pounder (76mm) was to arrive later in

1944. These were more effective than anything that had gone before, but they were still outclassed by the German 88mm gun.

The Deficiencies of British Tanks

In one respect – and only one – the British Army in 1939 was superior to the Germans. The British Army had a mechanized 'tail': the rear echelons used heavy and reliable trucks. In contrast, much of the German Army transport was horse-drawn. This was to cause a real problem when a German division had to cover long distances, as in Russia; and the need for large supplies of fodder every day was a logistical nightmare. The German Afrika Korps had no horses because of the desert climate, but it was often immobilized for lack of gasoline, which had to be shipped across the Mediterranean. In Western Europe at the end of the war, even elite German divisions had to rely on a rag-bag of vehicles of different types, some mechanical and some still horse-drawn. The British Army had to abandon a vast number of trucks on the beaches of Dunkirk, and these became a generous gift to the German Army, although many were to be abandoned for a second time in the snows of the Eastern Front.

Another small but positive advantage of the British Army was that it was equipped with two types of vehicle that were tactically very useful. The first was the universal carrier, also known as the Bren gun carrier, a low-slung tracked vehicle weighing three tons. It had armoured sides and an open top so that the soldiers on board had to wear steel helmets. With a crew of three, carriers could manage to transport a dozen men for short distances in great discomfort. They were sturdily built, with robust engines, and were used in infantry battalions as transport to move reinforcements and supplies under fire.

The second vehicle was the armoured car. This had a long history with the British Army, and armoured cars were widely used in the Middle East during the First World War and the inter-war period. They were also used by the Royal Air Force, which had a special ground force that used them. There were a number of models of armoured car, but they all ran on wheels not tracks, which meant that they did not perform well when they moved across rough country. (Both the German and American armies had half-tracks, which were better than armoured cars in this respect.) The Humber armoured car, used in 1940, weighed seven tons and had protective armour that was proof against small-arms fire. At the beginning of the Second World War, British cars had two machine guns of different calibres, but the cars' purpose was not to engage in a shooting war. Their job was reconnaissance, which meant exploring suspicious but not obviously occupied places on the battlefield until they bumped into the enemy, at which time they radioed reports to headquarters and then got away at their top speed of 45mph or more. In 1940, the 12th Lancers made a name for themselves as an armoured car regiment in the BEF; and the 11th Hussars built an astonishing reputation in 1940-1941 against the Italians and later the Germans in the North African desert.

British tanks were a different matter, and in 1940 were inferior to the German armour. In particular, the German models had a far superior balance of armour, mobility and fire power. The main models are summarized in **Figure 1**.

	BRITAIN			FRANCE	GERMANY	
	Light	Cruiser	Infantry			
	VI	III	II		III	IV
	(Matilda)					
Weight (tons)	5.5	14.75	26.5	33	15	17.5
Maximum/minimum armour (mm)	14/4	14/6	78/20	80/40	30/10	30/8
Gun (mm)	-	40 (2 pounder)	40 (2 pounder)	75/47 **2**	37 or 50 **2**	75 1
Rifle-calibre machine gun	**2**	1	1			
Maximum road speed	35mph	30mph	15mph	25mph	30mph	26mph

FIGURE 1
MOST MODERN MODELS OF TANKS IN 1940

The three qualities that mattered most were a tank's offensive capability (the number and calibre of its weapons), mobility, and the protection to the vehicle and its crew. This was mainly a matter of the thickness of the armour. (The two figures for armour in Figure 1 refer to the heavier protection on the front of the tank and the lighter protection on its side and rear.) The number of men in the crew was also relevant. The Light tanks (**Plate 2**) had 3-men crews (commander, gunner, driver), which meant that they could bail out quickly if the tank were hit, especially if it caught fire, when the vehicle became a death trap. The problem became greater with Cruisers (with five men) and Infantry tanks (with four men).

All the British, French and German tanks had machine guns, mostly rifle-calibre (.303 inch in the British army), but a few with the heavier .5 inch. The bullets fired from these could neutralize unprotected infantry, but they were of little use if the enemy built protected defensive positions. They were also not much use against tanks and dug-in anti-tank guns. To be effective, a tank had to have artillery pieces that could fire high explosive or solid shot (for use against enemy tanks). The absence of artillery made the British Light models almost valueless, and after the 1940 campaign they were phased out and replaced by armoured cars, many of which now had light artillery.

The British Cruisers (**Plate 3**), built for the old cavalry rôle of rapid offensive action, had less armour than the German machines, and the 2-pounder gun was soon outclassed as more Panzer IV tanks were brought to the battlefield. (**Plate 6.**) The British Infantry tanks (now called Matildas) had impressive armour, but they were desperately slow. (**Plate 4.**) This is because they were built for a traditional type of infantry assault, the pace of which was determined by men slowly advancing in the open. The superior models were in short supply in 1940, and most of the Infantry tanks with the BEF in France were armed only with a single machine gun, and were therefore as valueless as the Light tanks. The French Char B was by far the best allied machine, but it was not effectively used because it was dispersed in 'penny packets.'

What is strikingly obvious about this description of the British Army's tanks was the urgent need for better models. New designs were already under way, but most were soon shown to have problems. The proving ground for the British tanks was going to be the North African desert.

A Scottish Doctor Joins the Bays

John Sylvanus MacGill (JSM) was born in 1900 in British Guiana (now Guyana), which is near the Equator. He was a son of the manse, his father being a minister in the Presbyterian Church of Scotland. JSM moved to the healthier climate of Scotland at the age of seven after a dose of malaria. At the age of thirteen, he entered Merchiston Castle School in Edinburgh, and at eighteen became a medical student at Edinburgh University, which has always possessed one of the most prestigious medical schools in the world. He received his joint baccalaureate in medicine and surgery (MB, ChB), the medical qualification that permitted him to practise. He later completed a study of tropical diseases, especially sleeping sickness caused by the tsetse fly: a common ailment in British Guiana. His knowledge of these was valuable when he was with the Queen's Bays in the North African desert. This specialist study led to an MD degree, not an everyday qualification in Britain even now. During his time at Edinburgh he spent some months during the last year of the First World War as a cadet in the Edinburgh University Officers Training Corps. A photograph exists of him looking immaculate in tunic, breeches and puttees. Until 1938 this was to be his sole experience of military life.

After he had graduated, he decided to go into general practice and joined his uncle, Dr. Wakefield MacGill, in a flourishing partnership in Denton, a working-class town on the eastern edge of Manchester. He became known as Dr. John, to distinguish him from his uncle. When his uncle retired, he was replaced by a new partner, Dr. Robertson, who was eventually conscripted into the army. This made it necessary for Dr. John to return to the practice in 1943.

The list of 7,000 patients cared for by the practice included a number of private patients who paid their own fees, and a larger number who were members of what was known as the Panel, a system by which families with low incomes could pay a small sum of money every week and in return receive routine medical attention. (The Panel system disappeared in 1948 when the British National Health Service was introduced.) JSM was a dedicated doctor. Every day he held an open surgery in three separate locations at which patients arrived without appointments, and he also made up to twenty house calls every day. (House calls were

universal in Britain until well after the end of the Second World War.)
His personal transport improved with his professional progress. As a
newly qualified physician, he visited his patients on a bicycle with his
doctor's bag in a satchel behind the back wheel. He then progressed to a
motorcycle, and when he had a comfortable income he travelled by car.
With a typically Scottish respect for education, he gave his two sons a
first-class private education at school and university. He later also helped
to cover the cost of his grandchildren's school fees.

In 1938, when it was clear that war was approaching, the British
Government doubled the size of the Territorial Army. JSM joined it
and was immediately commissioned in the RAMC. (**Plate 1.**) The
RAMC is an independent corps founded in 1898. Medical Officers in
the RAMC are attached to a regiment and not actually members of it.
JSM's wife did not like the idea of his joining the TA; she destroyed his
first application but his second effort was successful. He was embodied
just before war was declared and remained in uniform until 1943, when
he returned to Manchester (as already mentioned). Wartime conditions
were difficult for his wife, who took the responsibility of running the
practice with the support of locums, doctors temporarily employed
to serve JSM's patients. Most were Irishmen; as citizens of the Irish
Republic they were not required to join the British armed services.

In 1939 JSM was posted to the Queen's Bays and served in Britain
until the regiment was shipped to France in May 1940. At the age
of thirty-nine he was one of the three oldest officers in the regiment,
the others being the Colonel and the Quartermaster. To the young
officers, the three were thought to be of a different generation. The
Colonel and JSM played Bridge together (co-opting young officers as
partners). The job of the Regimental Medical Officer when the unit
was away from the battle area was to maintain the health of more than
600 men. He had orderlies to help him with dressings and other routine
procedures, but they were not qualified nurses. He held sick parades,
medical inspections, and he immunized the men against a variety of
diseases. He had to be pro-active and always on the watch for signs
of infection. The most important of these were symptoms of diseases
associated with 'horizontal refreshment'. (This euphemism came from
Major General Montgomery, who came close to being sacked in 1940
because he had established properly-supervised brothels for his troops.)

In battle, the RMO had to set up a Regimental Aid Post (RAP) not far from Regimental Headquarters, in a place that was as well protected as possible to prevent men from being wounded a second time. Stretcher bearers, who were mostly members of the regimental band, brought in the patients and the RMO had to work unrelentingly and speedily at first aid. His function was also triage, to evaluate the degree of urgency demanded by different wounds. This meant deciding between three alternatives: first, the wounded soldier could be saved but needed immediate treatment and then sent down the line; or second, he would live but could be treated with less urgency and then probably also sent down the line; or third, he could not be saved, in which case he would not be moved but given all comfort possible. Wounded enemy troops arriving in the RAP were given the same attention as JSM's comrades. The Endnote that concludes this chapter is devoted to the important topic of triage.

The Bays, with JSM as part of the regimental family, were shipped around Africa to Egypt towards the end of 1941. During his whole time in the army he more than earned his pay. Much of his work in Africa was devoted to patients who had been burned when their tanks caught fire, and he developed special expertise in this field. After the end of the North African campaign he was flown to the United States, to share this knowledge by giving lectures to large numbers of medical officers in the American Army. The desert was a tough learning experience for everybody in the British Army. But unlike so many campaigns in 20th Century wars, it ended in clear victory.

Endnote

The only person who is qualified to make a triage decision is the doctor treating the patient. Although the doctor often has to make up his mind hurriedly, the medical profession is fully conscious of the vital importance of the decision that is made.

Dr. William Stewart, a distinguished neurosurgeon who was in practice in Syracuse, New York, and is now retired, was a United States Navy Surgeon who served in the Vietnam War. He was chief of neurosurgery on a hospital ship that covered I Corps off the coast of Vietnam.

Wounded soldiers were moved rapidly by helicopter directly from the Regimental Aid Posts to the deck of the hospital ship. They were then put in line for triage.

Many years after the war, Dr. Stewart wrote a number of poems, in free verse, about his experience on active service. These came straight from his heart. Here is the beginning of a poem entitled, quite simply, *Triage.*

'Medical history, duty stations, graduation date.'
The record tells all.
My brother's Academy classmate.
Were they acquainted? This one can't tell me now;
There's a spent bullet through his brain.

Both front and back; dicey manipulation between.
Four to five hours to make it clean.
Certain residual if all goes well.
Time to get started with this day's Hell.

No, this one must wait;
Three more heroes just came through the gate.
Still, chances are good; I'll do them all in three hours or so.
Triage: best for the unit, not for the one
Who marched with my brother a few short years ago.

Wounded pour in.
Easy pushes difficult to the end of the line.
Brain swells, pupils dilate, time runs out for the last in line.

CHAPTER 2

A PHONEY WAR AND A TERRIFYING JOLT

On 3 September 1939 Britain confronted Germany, a strong, politically united and militaristic country well-prepared for modern war. Britain would be fighting alongside France. Despite the major contributions of her navy and air force, Britain was also going to send a second British Expeditionary Force (BEF) to fight on the left of the French armies. (The first BEF had gone to France in 1914.) But Britain would be very much the junior partner on land, and the British Commander-in-Chief, General Gort, was to come under the orders of the French Commander-in-Chief. In this broad fashion, the pattern of 1914 was being repeated, and it is not surprising that even informed observers saw the Second World War as a continuation of the First, as if there had just been a twenty-one year hiatus between the Armistice of 1918 and the outbreak of hostilities in 1939. But those people who drew the inference that the Second World War would follow the pattern of the First were soon shown to be wrong. Compared with 1914, the French Army was much weaker because its morale had been eroded by its fixation on defence. In contrast, the German Army was stronger than in 1914 because of its highly developed tactical doctrine and weapons, and its superbly trained soldiers. After an astonishing seven months of military inactivity, the German lightning bolt struck.

The Second BEF Goes To War

This book is mainly about one small element of the second BEF, a Regular cavalry regiment converted to armour, the Queen's Bays (2nd

Dragoon Guards). It came to the battle area late because of delays in supplying its equipment, and arrived in May 1940 as part of its parent formation, 1ˢᵗ Armoured Division. For the first months of inaction over the winter of 1939-1940, a period known as the Phoney War, nine armoured units (unconnected with 1ˢᵗ Armoured Division) had formed part of the BEF's Order of Battle. But they had been distributed in 'penny packets' (to use British military jargon) to individual infantry divisions. The sole exception was two tank units, 4ᵗʰ and 7ᵗʰ Royal Tank Regiment, which together formed an under-strength armoured brigade. The German Army quickly demonstrated that the British policy of dispersing tank units and using them on a small scale was not an effective way of conducting modern warfare. As discussed in Chapter 1, the effectiveness of an armoured division depends on three factors: first, the army's overall policy governing the use of armour; second, the internal organization of the division, in particular the balance between armour and infantry; and third, the effectiveness of the tanks compared with those they would meet in battle. In 1939 the 1ˢᵗ Armoured Division was defective in all three respects.

There was no such controversy about infantry divisions. An infantry division was, as the name suggests, composed mainly of marching soldiers. It had a total of at least 15,000 men, infantry plus other arms of the service, making it a complete 'orchestra of war'. For many years the infantry division was seen as the main piece on the military chess board, a useful way of measuring the strength of competing armies, although the internal organization of a division varied to some extent country by country.

France, with its long tradition of peacetime conscription, mustered the equivalent of more than seventy divisions garrisoning the eastern and northern frontiers. (Some troops were in fortress regiments and not organized in divisions.) The French also had a number of divisions on the Italian frontier and overseas. The French divisions varied a good deal in quality. Many were manned by elderly reservists and were ineffective fighting formations: something startlingly obvious to interested independent observers like Winston Churchill and senior British officers.

The French had begun the First World War imbued with the spirit of the offensive, a response to her humiliating defeat at the hands of the Prussian Army in 1871. An impassioned zeal to attack was not a doctrine that could withstand the weight of modern defensive firepower, and it produced a horrendous rate of loss: 250,000 French soldiers killed, wounded and missing during the first *three weeks* of fighting in the First World War. Since the Germans were occupying French soil during the whole course of the war, there was no let-up in the French Army's continuous but futile assaults on the German lines, and these relentless attacks were to lead to widespread mutinies in 1917. The losses in the French Army bit deeply into the national psyche and led the French to rely, from the early 1930s, on the Maginot Line. This was a chain of forts along France's eastern frontier, magnificently-engineered and mainly sunk underground. However, before 1939 the French General Staff realized – quite correctly – that the German Army would attack from the north, through Belgium. This meant that the Maginot Line would be easily by-passed and would remain a quaint anachronism and symbol of an outdated strategy.

All ranks in the BEF were conscious of low morale in much of the French Army. In addition to its defence-mindedness, the rigid, 'top-down' method of command practised by the French did not encourage good morale and self-respect for the simple reason that it squashed local initiative. The British General Staff's awareness of the French lack of energy and fighting spirit contributed to General Gort's eventual decision to evacuate the BEF from France. He was certain that if he continued to fight on French soil the armies on the British flanks would not hold, and this would lead to immediate defeat. Gort was ultimately responsible to the British Government despite the fact that he had a place in the French chain of command. It is never easy to serve two masters, but Gort had a good grounding in common sense.

The French Army possessed about 2,000 tanks, and had relatively recently formed them into armoured divisions, four heavy and three light. These had not had time to carry out exercises to test their military effectiveness. Each of the four heavy divisions had 150 *Char B1* tanks, which by the standards of the time had heavy firepower and were well protected with armour. There were also three light mechanized divisions, each of which had 220 less powerful but still relatively effective vehicles.

All these tank formations were farmed out to infantry divisions, and were therefore unable to provide any real armoured 'punch'.

The German Army was similar in size to the French. Facing Belgium, Luxembourg and the Ardennes Forest, where the Germans would be attacking in May1940, there were two Army Groups made up of seventy-three divisions, all well-trained and relatively uniform in quality. Surprisingly, the infantry divisions used horse-drawn transport, which caused many problems including the need for large amounts of fodder. Most importantly, ten of the divisions were Panzer. The Panzer division was the most powerful engine of modern warfare, and comprised armour, infantry, artillery and airpower (in particular the terrifying Stuka dive bomber), all operating together with well-honed skill. The Germans boosted the offensive power of their Panzer Divisions by concentrating them into Panzer Corps. The Commander of the largest of these was soon to be legendary, Lieutenant General Guderian (an officer whose unusual name reveals his Armenian origin). The overall commander of the Army Group planning to make the main attack was Colonel General von Rundstedt, whose Chief-of-Staff was Lieutenant General von Manstein. Like all other leaders of the German Army, von Rundstedt, von Manstein and Guderian had been selected early for their intellectual power and sent for two years of intensive education at the War Academy in Potsdam to prepare them to join the German Great General Staff, a very small body but one widely considered to be the most impressive concentration of military brain-power in the world.

The German General Staff had studied armoured warfare more carefully than the British, and had drawn firm and positive conclusions from the British 'All-Arms' offensive of August 1918. This was the direct progenitor of the Panzer Division. The German Army also had another comparative advantage. Unlike the practice in other armies, the Germans always laid great emphasis on self-reliance and individual initiative among the lower ranks. While a British infantry battalion often contained thirty officers, a German battalion had fifteen. Sergeants commanded platoons, and were prepared to command companies if the officers became casualties. This traditional policy encouraged small groups of German soldiers to exploit local opportunities and maintain continuously the momentum of the attack. The Germans also had more aircraft, 3,700 compared with 2,600 in the French and British squadrons. German airpower was also directly under the command of the army (unlike the substantially independent RAF).

The German Army was therefore well-prepared in fighting spirit and doctrine for an offensive war. But surprisingly its 2,500 tanks on the Western Front were by no means superior to their antagonists. Almost 1,500 German tanks were obsolete, and the remaining vehicles were barely a match for the best French armour. The German superiority on the field of battle was therefore in morale and organization rather than in military hardware. The Germans however took pains to develop effective anti-tank guns, and this was to pay great dividends later in the war.

In contrast to the substantial forces mobilized by the French and Germans, the BEF in early May 1940 had been built up to only ten divisions. These, plus two that arrived later, would advance into Belgium to meet the advancing Germans. Then, after this British force had been cut off by the Germans who had advanced to the Channel coast, four extra British divisions came on the scene. The total size of the BEF therefore became sixteen divisions, six Regular and ten Territorial. Many of the Territorials were put to work at the beginning, digging and building defences and guarding and strengthening the lines of communications. The troops also had to train intensively, although this was not one of Gort's priorities. However, some of his senior subordinates trained their troops ferociously. In particular, Major General Montgomery's 3rd Division fought extremely well for this reason.

The divisions in the second BEF were all infantry, except 1st Armoured Division which only began to arrive on 20 May. (As mentioned, nine armoured regiments had already been distributed in a single small brigade and individual units over the army as a whole.) In 1940, the British infantry division at full establishment had ten battalions, in three brigades each of three battalions, plus a machine-gun battalion armed with forty-eight Vickers medium machine guns. There were also three Royal Artillery field regiments and one anti-tank regiment; four field companies of Royal Engineers; a full array of services: signals, transport, ordnance, medical, police etc; and an armoured regiment attached *ad hoc*. The Regular divisions were organized in this way, but some of the Territorial divisions did not have their full complement of guns, mortars or light machine guns (platoon weapons).

For comparison, the first BEF, having suffered terrible casualties during 1914, mustered eleven divisions in April 1915, when it was eight months into the war. But the composition of these divisions was very different from those in the second BEF. In the first BEF, the divisions were virtually all Regular troops (with a small number of Territorial units slotted in alongside the Regulars). But the sixteen divisions in the second BEF were made up of six Regular and ten Territorial, with a small number of Territorial units in the Regular divisions and a stiffening of Regular units in the Territorial divisions. In the First World War, Territorials had been sent to foreign garrisons to replace Regulars who were sent to France to join the first BEF. After 1915, large numbers of these Territorials also came back to join the BEF. By this time they had become reasonably well trained, unlike the Territorials in the second BEF. The uniformly high standard of training of the first BEF contributed to its formidable fighting reputation.

Limited conscription had been introduced in April 1939 and it was extended with the coming of war in September. The Regular army could not immediately train a large influx of recruits at the same time as forming the strongest element of the BEF. This meant that very few conscripts joined the BEF and some of those had not even passed their recruits' course in musketry. The large numbers of Territorials in the BEF had undergone varying amounts of part-time training in peacetime, but the experience of the period after 1941 reinforced the lessons of the French campaign that non-Regular troops needed a year or more of full-time service and military discipline to make them fully fit for war.

The BEF in 1940 had clear problems: first, a much smaller size than the French and German armies; second, too little armour: a number of independent regiments and only a single armoured division arriving at the end of May; and third – most serious of all – the incomplete training of two-thirds of the force. The Regular divisions were well led and fully trained, but the Territorials – all volunteers – relied on enthusiasm, comradeship and regimental pride rather than the practised military skills of the Regulars. These factors meant an unusually heavy strain on the commanders of all ranks, especially the generals, and in particular General Gort, the Commander-in-Chief.

When Gort was a regimental officer in the Grenadier Guards in the First World War, he was celebrated for his bravery and personal leadership and won a record number of awards for gallantry, including the Victoria Cross. During the Second World War he was forced within months to make brutally hard decisions, and in these he demonstrated moral courage as robust as the physical courage he had shown when he was in his early thirties. But Gort had a negative side. He did not have outstanding brain-power and had a reputation for being fixated on military minutiae, with no focus on the 'big picture'. He was also associated with the unsavoury episode in early 1940 which led to the dismissal of Gort's political chief, the Secretary-of-State for War, Leslie Hore-Belisha.

In 1937 Hore-Belisha became the Secretary-of-State for War, the Cabinet Minister who was responsible for the Army and who had to represent it in the House of Commons. He was an able and energetic politician with a business background, but he was also ambitious, vain and publicity-conscious. Gort, aged fifty-one, was one of the relatively young senior officers whom Hore-Belisha selected for promotion, in order to bring new life into the British Army, whose senior officers were often lampooned and shown in popular cartoons as white-moustached figures called Colonel Blimp. Gort shot ahead to become the professional head of the Army, the Chief of the Imperial General Staff (CIGS), and he immediately cooperated with Hore-Belisha to bring about changes. At this time the Defence Budget was at last being increased, after years of funds inadequate to keep the army up-to-date. But with the increases, the Royal Air Force began to swallow a disproportionate share, to prepare the country for assault from the air and to build a powerful bomber force to take war to the enemy. However, Hore-Belisha and Gort made the best use of the funds available, and army equipment was improved, large numbers of junior officers were promoted after they had been stuck in their present rank for decades or more, and the Territorial Army was doubled in size.

Nevertheless, the generals distanced themselves from Hore-Belisha because of his public persona and the publicity that surrounded him, and also because he was a Jew. (Anti-Semitism sometimes showed its ugly face even in Britain.) They also thought that Hore-Belisha was being unduly influenced by Liddell Hart, the military analyst whose writing was (as mentioned in Chapter 1) being followed carefully by senior officers of the German Army. The generals' dislike of the Secretary-of-State was reciprocated, and immediately before the war Gort was given command of the second BEF: it was thought because Hore-Belisha wanted to get him away from Whitehall. But the antipathy between Hore-Belisha and the generals continued, and when he visited France at the beginning of 1940 he did not hide his opinion that a stronger defensive line of concrete pillboxes needed to be built. As the result of this, Gort went behind Hore-Belisha's back and prevailed on the Prime Minister, Chamberlain, to sack him. Gort and the generals saw Hore-Belisha's words as interference by a civilian in strictly military matters: despite the fact that Hore-Belisha was Gort's superior and an elected member of the House of Commons. This conspiracy reflected particularly badly on Gort and on many other senior officers in France. It might have done lasting damage if events had not soon precipitated a military crisis, a time when everybody – soldiers and civilians alike – had to buckle down and fight a war.

In the BEF as a whole there was no shortage of military talent. Six of the senior officers managed to climb the greasy pole to become Field Marshals: Gort, Dill, Brooke, Alexander, Montgomery and Templer. Eight others built successful and in some cases outstanding careers as army or corps commanders: Leese, Anderson, Crocker, Dempsey, Horrocks, Lumsden, McCreery and Ritchie. Lumsden is a fascinating case. In 1940 he made his name as a Lieutenant Colonel, commanding the 12th Lancers, the BEF's sole armoured car regiment. When British General Headquarters was shrouded in the fog of war, the 12th Lancers provided eyes and ears, moving over the battlefield to locate and report from trouble spots. After the evacuation of the BEF, Lumsden was given command of a brigade in Britain and in October 1941 posted to North Africa, where he commanded a division then a corps. (He will reappear in later chapters in this book.) He was sacked by Montgomery after the battle of El Alamein because Montgomery did not judge him to be aggressive enough. Lumsden's men had for a year faced the often superior German tanks and the deadly 88mm anti-tank guns, and he was reluctant to demand even more sacrifices. He was subsequently given a most unusual appointment and sent to the Pacific as the British liaison officer with the American forces. He developed a strong rapport with the anglophobic General Stilwell and the autocratic General MacArthur. But he was killed in 1945 in a Kamikaze strike, one of the few senior British officers to fall in battle in the Second World War.

The 'Impassable Ardennes Forest'

As soon as the BEF arrived in France, most of the troops were put to work building a strong defensive line in the north (hence the importance of the concrete pillboxes that were the cause of Hore-Belisha's downfall). The French Commander-in-Chief was General Gamelin, who was also responsible for French forces overseas, although the Western Front was his first concern. Gort came under Gamelin, and General Doumenc, Commander of French land forces; but more directly under General Georges, who commanded all the army groups in the north west. Later, Gort was also put under General Billotte, the commander of the 1ˢᵗ Army Group, earmarked for operations in Belgium, where the enemy assault was expected. In this way the BEF sank down the chain of command, a chain now connecting Gamelin to Doumenc to Georges to Billotte and finally to Gort. The result was confusion, caused by the length of the chain, made worse by the uniform lack of 'grip' by all the senior French commanders, and made even worse by inadequate communications. A chain so complicated led to impossible difficulties in reacting quickly to changing battlefield conditions. And it was soon to be a problem even to Gamelin. He did not get on with Georges and got into the habit of giving orders directly to Gort. Gamelin himself was totally isolated in his gloomy headquarters at Vincennes, north-east of Paris. With no direct telephone or radio connections, contact with his command was made by using motorcycle dispatch riders!

The whole organization had been assembled *ad hoc* and the senior officers had no experience of working with one another. Gort was forced increasingly to operate independently. The BEF was compact and, in contrast to the French, was to show itself to be a relatively efficient fighting force. The long-service Regulars who comprised one-third of the strength had good, sometimes outstanding, leaders and the men had had years of training; the Territorials who comprised the remaining two-thirds had received at least a modest amount of training and possessed the enthusiasm that came from their being volunteers.

The French Army was from the beginning totally oriented towards defence. But this was not true of their antagonists. The German state was highly centralized and the decision to attack and the broad lines of strategy were determined by Hitler himself, who was nothing if not aggressive. As early as October 1939 he had issued orders to attack France as soon as the German Army had been properly prepared. Hitler assumed – correctly – that France would easily be defeated; and also – less correctly – that England would then sue for peace. Hitler's ambivalent attitude towards Britain led him to believe that Britain would be grateful to keep her Empire as a *quid pro quo* for German domination of the European Continent.

The Germans planned to assault France from the north, passing through the Netherlands and Belgium (in contrast to the 1914 Schlieffen Plan, under which the German Army went only through Belgium). The sweep through France itself in 1940 would be mechanized, thus obviating the fatal flaw of the Schlieffen Plan: that the increasingly footsore soldiers had to march, and cover only about twenty miles a day. (This was a process that took so long that the French were able to develop a powerful riposte, the result of which was the first battle of the Marne.) The French in 1940 assumed that the German invasion would follow broadly the Schlieffen Plan. Their guess was right as far as the initial German plan was concerned. But the plan that was eventually implemented was changed in an important way.

The time at which the German assault in 1940 was to take place depended on four things: first, favourable weather; second, how quickly the Germans could digest the dismemberment of Poland which took place in September/October1939; third, how much time was needed to deploy and prepare the massive forces that would invade France; and fourth, how soon a sophisticated General Staff plan could be developed. This plan had been partially worked out in January 1940, but it was immediately compromised. This was the result of a German aircraft landing in Belgium because the pilot had lost his way. This aeroplane carried on board an important part of the German invasion plan, and in no time the document was copied and in the hands of the Dutch,

Belgians and French. To say the least, it was surprising that a secret and very important operational plan should have travelled in an aircraft flying close to hostile territory. Following this unfortunate incident, the German strategy should have been changed immediately. And indeed a major modification was eventually made, with Hitler's direct involvement.

Von Rundstedt, whose powerful army group was to play the greatest rôle in the forthcoming invasion of France, was losing faith in the plan because it was so similar to Schlieffen that it would hold no surprises to the French. In his skepticism he was influenced by von Manstein, his Chief-of-Staff, a soldier of unquestioned brilliance. It was expected that when the Germans invaded Belgium, the BEF and a major part of the French Army would move north to meet the German attack. Von Manstein conceived a plan of great subtlety: a strategy of encirclement to lure the Anglo-French armies to Belgium, and into a trap. Then, when they were committed to battle, there would be a full-blooded assault across northern France in a western direction along the line of the River Somme, to separate the forces in Belgium from the rest of the French Army. The most powerful element in the German Army, the Panzer divisions, would spring out of the Ardennes Forest in southern Belgium and Luxembourg, crossing the formidable River Meuse, then charging across northern France to reach the English Channel coast. This sweep, which the Germans called the *Sichelschnitt* (the Sickle Cut) would isolate all the Allied armies in Belgium in an increasingly constricted pocket and this would lead to their destruction.

The central headquarters of the German Army, and in particular the Commander-in-Chief, Colonel General von Brauchitsch, were for a long time unenthusiastic about the *Sichelschnitt*. The Ardennes Forest was dense, had thick mud, and would hinder the movement of armoured forces. The French view was that the Ardennes was quite impassable. The Americans were to make the same disastrous misjudgment in December 1944 when the German Army sprang another surprise: a surprise that led to the Battle of the Bulge. Hitler during the early years of the war possessed an extraordinary strategic flair (among his many less desirable personal qualities). He had in fact thought of the Ardennes before von Manstein. The Führer unhesitatingly supported the *Sichelschnitt*, and he had the will and the authority to make it happen. It turned out to be one of the most dazzling military manoeuvres in the long and unhappy history of warfare.

The German attack from the west began with a powerful and most unusual prelude. Early in the morning of 10 May 1940 – auspiciously the day on which Winston Churchill became Prime Minister – German parachute troops landed near the Dutch cities of The Hague and Leyden, and on the crossings of the Meuse in eastern Belgium. Glider-borne infantry also attacked the important Belgian fort of Eben Emael and seized it by a *coup de main*. Meanwhile Rotterdam was being pounded from the air, and the Dutch Army showed itself to be no match for the Germans. The Netherlands was traditionally neutral and was in no position to resist a powerful opponent. The country surrendered on 15 May and Queen Wilhelmina and her Government escaped to Britain. Dutch fighting men who escaped subsequently fought as members of the British armed services, and people who joined the Dutch Underground were a constant irritant to the German occupiers of their country.

Unlike the Dutch, the Belgians had suffered war during the twentieth century, and they did everything they could to avoid a repetition. Belgium had terminated its military alliance with France in 1936, and refused to allow any staff talks between the Belgian Army and the French and British for fear of provoking the Germans. The isolation of Belgium was to be a problem when the Germans invaded the country on 10 May. The French and British put into effect their plan to march north across the Belgian frontier, but close cooperation with the Belgian Army was going to be difficult. The French and British left behind the positions in northern France with their pillboxes that the BEF had so laboriously constructed during the winter.

During the fighting that followed, the German Army seized and kept the initiative because it was better armed, generally better trained, and single-mindedly aggressive. It did not outnumber the defending forces. Because the German Army held the upper hand, the French/British/Belgian armies were forced to respond the whole time to German pressure: a situation that almost always leads to a loss of balance. The positions occupied by the defenders were based on three river lines. In the east, the River Dyle flows in a loop from south to north, fifteen miles to the east of Brussels. Fifteen miles to the west of Brussels, the

River Dendre flows from south west to north east. Finally, twenty miles further west still is the great River Escaut (Scheldt in Flemish), which also flows south west to north east.

The French and British, together with the Belgians who by now realized that they would have to cooperate, took defensive positions on the line of the Dyle. From right to left (i.e. south to north from the Franco-Belgian border), the formations deployed were the French 1st Army; then the British I Corps and II Corps; then the Belgian Army of twenty divisions, which was to fight remarkably well during the following days, although widely criticized later. The French 7th Army, having attempted to move north to support the Dutch, arrived on the left of the Belgians. The British I Corps was made up of three divisions, two Regular and one Territorial (1st, 2nd and 48th); II Corps had a similar composition (3rd, 4th and 50th Divisions). There were three senior officers in these corps who were to make formidable reputations later in the war, Lieutenant General Brooke (commanding II Corps), Major General Alexander (1st Division) and Major General Montgomery (3rd Division). The tough fighting in Belgium and France and the retreat to Dunkirk provided unmistakable evidence that they had the brains, experience, temperament and determination needed for high command. Above all, they demonstrated coolness and 'grip'.

The Dyle was a weak line of defence yet the British, who started digging energetically on 11 May, made effective preparations for the looming attack. On the whole front the defenders outnumbered the attackers, although the Allied left had been weakened by the surrender of the Dutch Army and some Germans were infiltrating the left flank. Ominously, the attackers included a Panzer corps of two divisions, with 600 tanks.

However, assaulting the Meuse was the key priority for von Rundstedt. As a result of heavy German air bombardment, artillery fire and infantry attacks, the French and Belgians were pushed back and blew the bridges over the river. Without any delay the German infantry crossed in small assault boats and the engineers got to work building pontoon bridges. On 12 May a German Panzer division, commanded by a soldier whose name would shortly be a household word, Major General Rommel, got over a weir on the river. During the next two days substantial

German forces crossed the pontoons and brushed aside feeble French counterattacks. The road to Belgium was open. By now the remaining Panzer divisions had moved into and through the Ardennes Forest and were poised to begin the *Sichelschnitt* by seizing Sedan. (**Map 1.**)

It was on 14 May that the Panzers came into their own. The defenders of Sedan, two French divisions of elderly Reservists, offered no resistance and actually ran away. The overall effect of this blow on the French commanders was psychological as well as physical, since Sedan had been the scene of the terrible French defeat at the hands of the Prussians in 1870. This second fall of Sedan unnerved the French and deadened their offensive spirit. There were no counterattacks because there were no reserves. General Georges broke down in tears. Perhaps he sensed what was to come, because the dramatic sweep of the *Sichelschnitt* was now released and it was to take the Panzer divisions to the Channel coast with extraordinary speed, and they would arrive there on 20 May.

The British and French Armies in Belgium were now in serious trouble. The troops on the Dyle had to start withdrawing without delay because of the imminent danger of their being enclosed in a pocket. However the withdrawal could not be a headlong retreat, but had to be a controlled tactical withdrawal. This is a difficult operation of war although there was an established method of carrying it out. The procedure was for a sub-unit (e.g. a battalion if a brigade was retiring) to occupy a stop line, well behind the front line. The troops in contact with the enemy would then thin out from the rear, if possible under cover of darkness. They would then fall quietly back through the stop line which would then become the front line. The process would then be repeated, with the troops in the stop line thinning out towards a new stop line in their own rear. As the soldiers retreated they of course made life as difficult as possible for the enemy, e.g. by blowing bridges.

This rather complex manoeuvre is less difficult for trained Regulars than for untrained men. Four of the BEF's Regular divisions were in the two British corps on the Dyle. The initial withdrawal was carried out without too much loss.

By 19 May the British had been forced back to the Dendre. (On 15 May the French 7th Army had been shifted to the south to join the main body of their compatriots. This left the Belgians as the sole protection of the BEF's northern flank). During the days of the BEF's retreat, two factors made a bad situation worse. First, the Germans had total command of the air and German aircraft were a constant menace to the weary, but not demoralized, British troops. The second problem was the large numbers of refugees who clogged the roads and added to the overall cloud of gloom.

The strain had been borne so far by the better-trained elements of the BEF, since I and II Corps contained four of the five Regular infantry divisions. Gort now made the difficult but essential decision to bring untrained and incomplete Territorial divisions into the battle. Between 16 May and 20 May, six divisions moved north towards the British line in Belgium, which was behind (i.e. west of) the Escaut. These divisions were the Regular 5th, and the Territorial 23rd, 12th, 42nd, 44th and 46th. The 42nd and 44th went into the line more-or-less intact. And Gort had a special rôle for the 5th, which joined the 50th to make an *ad hoc* formation called 'Frankforce'. The remaining three Territorial divisions were sent into action piecemeal, a policy that proved disastrous. They were destroyed by stronger German formations: a process described in military jargon as defeat in detail.

The *Sichelschnitt* was all the time surging forward and the leading Panzer corps was soon approaching Amiens and Abbeville. On 20 May, while the BEF was holding the line of the River Escaut/Scheldt, its southern flank was in considerable peril because the French 1st Army had pulled back to avoid the danger of being surrounded. Significantly, the British General Headquarters was thinking ahead and began to make plans for a withdrawal to Dunkirk, sixty miles from the Escaut.

While the BEF was in such a difficult position, that of the French Army was worse. It was without a plan and had no reserves. Between 10 May and 19 May, fifteen French divisions had been destroyed and many more were in danger. Gamelin was sacked on 19 May. His replacement General Weygand was, like Gamelin, in his late sixties. On 21 May, Gort and senior officers in the BEF met General Billotte and found him deeply depressed. He had a car accident later that day and died on 23 May.

During this troubled period, Gort and his senior officers were the only commanders on the Western Front to demonstrate 'grip'. But the concept of counter-attack, which was an article of faith in the German Army, did not have a high place on the British and French agenda. The initiative was always with the Germans, which inevitably meant that the French and British had to concentrate so much on defence that they could not devote the time needed to develop forceful and well-balanced plans to hit the enemy. But despite the pressure he was under, Gort organized a counter-attack that might have been an important tactical victory had it been supported by a vigorous and complementary French move.

The French had admittedly made two small and isolated counter-attacks, on 17 May and 19 May, under the command of a soldier with real fighting spirit and who would soon be internationally famous, Brigadier General de Gaulle. The light division he commanded was equipped with small tanks with thin skins and inadequate guns, and they made no impression on the Germans they attacked. Nevertheless these minor operations shook the nerve of the German commanders and as a result made them more circumspect during their further advance.

The British plan was to launch an attack from the west of Arras, assaulting in a southerly and then easterly direction to meet a thrust that the French had promised to make to the north. Gort put together 'Frankforce' of two divisions for the specific purpose of doing this job, but there were so many calls on elements of these divisions that all that could be made available for the counter-attack were two armoured regiments (the under-strength brigade of 4th and 7th Royal Tank Regiment), two infantry battalions, two field batteries, two anti-tank batteries, and four infantry platoons of miscellaneous specialist troops. This force was divided into two equal parts, making them effectively two weak brigade groups: a force far short of the two complete divisions that had been originally allocated. These two brigade groups were to make Britain's first armoured offensive of the Second World War. The force mustered seventy-four tanks, all in poor mechanical condition. Fifty-eight were three-man Light vehicles armed only with machine-guns. The remaining sixteen were the heavy but slow Infantry tanks, called Matildas. Most were the early models. Later ones were much better armed and were to give a good account of themselves and became celebrated in the North African desert.

On 21 May, the two columns moved forward. Communications were poor, some units got separated from the main force, and the advancing troops were constantly impeded by streams of refugees. The troops nevertheless made a number of successful attacks and did much damage and captured prisoners. But except for some brief support from a single French light armoured division, there was no sight of the French supporting force. The anticipated French counter-attack was never in fact launched. Despite its small scale, the British counter-attack badly shook the German generals. Rommel, commanding the 7th Panzer Division, was only able to stop the British because he used his 88mm anti-aircraft guns as deadly anti-tank weapons: the first time that they were used in this way. The Germans' respect for the British probably influenced their disastrous decision to halt their own assault on Dunkirk a few days later. Most importantly, the Arras counter-attack suggested what results might have been achieved if it had been mounted with a strong, concentrated force of heavy infantry machines. The only force of concentrated armour that was available was the 1st Armoured Division, which included the Queen's Bays in which JSM was serving. This was only just arriving in France and was not yet ready for battle.

On 21 May, the BEF was occupying a perimeter based on the line of the Escaut, stretching for thirty miles. The Escaut River line was its furthest point, and this was to be shortened slightly when the British retreated a little further back behind the river on 23 May. From this new position the front line followed a route back to the right and another to the left. Both ended on the Channel. The coast line occupied by the BEF covered almost 200 miles. Dunkirk was in the centre of it; and the most extended part of the British defensive positions was sixty miles distant from this port. These positions were relatively firm but the flanks were vulnerable, particularly after the Belgians surrendered on 28 May. And the British had few reserves. However, the senior British commanders never lost their nerve. They had firm control of their formations and units and were able to respond with professional skill to the continued German pressure.

With strong German forces now on the Channel coast, the two major ports of Boulogne and Calais were in the German Panzers' path as they advanced towards the BEF holding the Dunkirk perimeter. Boulogne is fifty miles (80km) west from Dunkirk along the coast, and Calais is half way between Boulogne and Dunkirk. General Dill (CIGS) in Whitehall provided what limited resources he had available to help Gort mount an improvised defence of Boulogne, to support the French who were already in and around the town. The operation lasted between 22 and 24 May, and was an expensive failure, except that it succeeded in delaying the 1st Panzer Division for three complete days.

Calais was a proposition that would call for larger forces. These were mainly made up of three important units that had been taken away from 1st Armoured Division before it sailed from Britain: one armoured regiment (3rd Royal Tank Regiment), plus 30th Infantry Brigade (made up of two highly-trained 'motor' battalions, 2 King's Royal Rifle Corps and 1 Rifle Brigade). The absence of these three units would be a real problem when the 1st Armoured Division was in contact with the enemy before the end of May. On 19 May, the troops already in Calais were an infantry platoon and two batteries of anti-aircraft gunners. They were joined on 22 May by the Queen Victoria's Rifles, a Territorial regiment affiliated with one of the two battalions in 30th Brigade. 3rd Royal Tank Regiment, with forty-eight tanks – Cruisers and Light models none of which was yet ready for action – landed on 23 May. It promptly received contradictory orders, and as parts of the regiment moved forward, they bumped into the 1st Panzer Division and a number of tanks were soon knocked out.

Brigadier Nicholson, commander of 30th Infantry Brigade, now arrived on the scene and took overall control. The units in his command, 3rd Royal Tanks plus his own two battalions and the Queen Victoria's Rifles, were all short of equipment and ammunition. At this time the 10th Panzer Division took over from 1st Panzer Division, which by-passed the town and made for the British forces in the Dunkirk perimeter. Calais was heavily shelled and dive-bombed and was attacked from three sides. The transports that had brought the troops to the town had sailed away, probably as a result of some misunderstanding due to contradictory orders. The only response that Nicholson could make was to order a fighting withdrawal. Finally, under French pressure, he was told by London – with Churchill's reluctant agreement – to fight to the end. With no more resources to continue the fight, the British troops on 26 May laid down their arms. The tanks were destroyed by their crews. The surviving men spent five years in German prisoner-of-war camps; very few got away.

The only redeeming feature of this débâcle was that the attacking Panzers suffered many casualties and their further advance was delayed by three days. These three days, together with the similar delay achieved by the British at Boulogne, probably contributed to the escape of the bulk of the BEF from Dunkirk.

CHAPTER 3
DISARRAY AFTER DUNKIRK

Twelve divisions of the BEF, a few having suffered heavy casualties, began to be evacuated from Dunkirk on 27 May. Despite the loss of equipment, the men – the raw material from which a new army would be built – were to arrive home in surprisingly high spirits despite their defeat. Proven leaders had by now emerged – notably Brooke, Alexander and Montgomery – plus a cohort of eight men who would before long be commanding corps and armies. Most importantly, Churchill had the unwavering support of Parliament and the country. Public opinion in Britain believed that the evacuation from Dunkirk marked the end of the campaign in France. However, it was by no means over. South of the Somme – the river followed by the German Army when it sliced across France from east to west – the 1ˢᵗ Armoured Division in which Dr. MacGill was serving, was cut off with three others. Of these four, the 1ˢᵗ Armoured Division was the weakest because three of its most important units had been directed to Calais and forced to surrender. The four divisions were not all that remained south of the Somme. A larger number of British soldiers were manning the long 'tail' that connected the BEF to the ports at which its enormous supplies had landed, most of which would fall into German hands. The soldiers got away, but the abandoned equipment included all the tanks that the British had left, and JSM's ambulance. However, large numbers of men would eventually get back to Britain.

The Fate of the 1ˢᵗ Armoured Division

During the latter part of May, Gort's focus was on the task that many considered impossible, withdrawing the BEF across the Channel from

Dunkirk. For reasons that are still unclear, the German Army halted well before it reached the BEF's shrinking perimeter; the sharp British riposte at Arras was probably remembered and caused the generals to think twice. Between 27 May and 4 June, 338,000 troops were lifted from the beaches. It was a phenomenal achievement by the Royal Navy, which not only employed its own ships and those of the Merchant Navy, but also mobilized at short notice a fleet of small boats manned by amateur yachtsmen. There were heavy casualties among the sailors and also the defending airmen, whose actions were not always visible to the troops on the ground. 110,000 of the evacuated soldiers were French and the majority of these were returned to France a few days later when it was still thought that the fighting could continue. The British losses at Dunkirk in guns, trucks, tanks and stores were gigantic. But the most important component of the BEF – the troops of all arms –survived to fight another day. The rescue of the BEF, for which there was no alternative since Britain was determined to go on fighting, was deeply resented by many French people. Even de Gaulle, who got away to Britain to rally the Free French, was widely criticized for his desertion; to the Vichy French he became a marked man.

The total size of the BEF had been sixteen divisions, but the remaining four only came to battle after the first twelve had been sealed off in the north. Of these four, the 1st Armoured Division arrived at Cherbourg on 20 May; and the celebrated 51st (Highland) Division moved to the west after having been with the French Army and inactive on the Maginot Line. A third new division, named after its commander, Major General Beauman, was put together on 31 May from troops from the line of communication. It was composed of nine (later twelve) infantry battalions, mainly Territorials, plus a small amount of artillery, a few engineers, and nothing else. Finally, the 52nd (Lowland) Division arrived in France on 7 June, because even as late as this, Churchill and the generals in London still refused to believe that the campaign was over. The rôle of these four divisions was unclear and remained so, which meant that operational plans had to be made at short notice. The initiative was still in German hands and as a result long-term planning was quite impossible.

An additional complication was the continued presence of the line of communication (L of C) troops, commanded by Major General de Fonblanque, who was in an isolated position immediately after the Dunkirk evacuation. This line stretched from Cherbourg to the Somme, although the most important sector was the 20 miles (30km) from Le Havre to the Somme: territory which was soon to see much military activity. Control of the L of C was difficult and depended on good communication with sub-units. These had been well established over the winter and worked well. The strength was 100,000 (*sic*) troops, divided into semi-independent units to protect the enormous stockpiles of supplies (many of which were eventually to fall into enemy hands). After the reorganized BEF had been landed later in June under Brooke's command, he quickly made the decision to evacuate the whole force, including the L of C. (This will be described later.)

After Dunkirk, there were five British Major Generals with independent commands south of the Somme. They were not organized into a single force, and they had to wait for the return of Brooke on 13 June for there to be an overall commander.

Major General Evans commanded the 1st Armoured Division. Its components were one complete brigade, 2nd Armoured Brigade (Queen's Bays, 9th Lancers and 10th Hussars); and one incomplete brigade, 3rd Armoured Brigade (2nd and 5th Battalions, Royal Tank Regiment. The third regiment, 3rd Royal Tanks went, as explained, to Calais and would be lost there). There was a single Light Anti-Aircraft/Anti-Tank regiment; and two field squadrons of Royal Engineers. The infantry component, 30th Brigade, would also be lost in Calais. Because of the removal of 30th Brigade before it sailed to France, the 1st Armoured Division was given a Territorial battalion, 2/6 East Surrey Regiment. The division was now a very weak force. Most of the division's tanks had only machine guns except for a few that had small artillery pieces, so that the absence of three important units was made worse by the division's lack of well-armed tanks. There was every sign that the division was going to be isolated because there was no other British armour, and all-too-vulnerable because of its endemic weaknesses.

The biggest supply port for the BEF was Le Havre. However, this was now considered too close to possible German activity. The 1st Armoured Division was therefore diverted to Cherbourg, at the top of the Normandy peninsula. The port was full of British troops from the rear echelons who were trying to get back to Britain. The division with its tanks and heavy equipment took some days to unload but was ready to move on 20 May. Its destination was Rouen: a distance from Cherbourg of 155 miles (250 km), on a road that went in a south-easterly direction. Armoured units normally travel on tank transporters to save wear on their caterpillar tracks. However, there were no transporters and the tanks had to move under their own power, which meant that they were not in the best shape when they arrived. And an awful problem was that the roads were clogged with refugees.

The Queen's Bays, the senior regiment in the 2nd Armoured Brigade, mustered fifty tanks, twenty-nine Cruisers and twenty-one Light models. There were no replacements for tanks that might be knocked out or break down. The Cruisers had only recently been allocated to the regiment, and the Light tanks had not yet had their machine guns fitted. (These were their sole armament.) The officers and men had had no time to exercise with their equipment and had to learn as they went along. The drive from Rouen is graphically described by Dr. MacGill.

JSM Journal (completed after the events)

> We landed at Cherbourg and travelled by road to Rouen. I had a staff car (a station wagon) full of medical equipment, and a driver and medical orderly. The three of us occupied the car. Our progress was very slow as the tanks could not go very fast, and the roads were blocked by an endless stream of refugees going the other way, most in cars, with a mattress tied to the roof to stop bullets from the air. Every now and then a car with refugees would stop, and the people would all scramble out crying 'Les avions boches!', and fling themselves into the ditch at the side of the road. Then a German plane would fly in low along the road, machine-gunning all the way.

> As we stopped at each village we came to and I got out of the car, there was an awful smell and I said 'Gosh, French villages do have a nasty smell,' but later I discovered that the smell was coming from the

camouflage netting on the top of the car which was made of hessian and rope that smelt of tar. If the car had to be parked in the open, the netting was let down all round so that the car was invisible by air. There were a lot of dead cows in the fields, enormously swollen.

After travelling for less than a week we arrived at the area south of Rouen on the north bank of the River Seine, and were in action against German tanks. During the journey I was not able to take off *any* of my clothes, and only took my boots off once, at the side of the road, to change my socks to the other foot and put on my boots again. This was supposed to be very comforting to the feet, but I doubt it.

He then describes the unruffled demeanor of the Bays as battle approached; they had been well prepared. To them, warfare was seen as a natural continuation of the peacetime activities of a well-trained and self-confident unit, a 'crack' regiment of Regular soldiers.

JSM Journal, continued

All the time we were in France I only slept one night in a house; it was always in woods, forests, or often orchards. I had a map of the battle area which I had to consult several times a day. We never slept more than one night anywhere but were always on the move. After three weeks the map was filthy dirty – black with dry mud – and you could hardly see the names of the towns on it.

One night we arrived at camping ground after dark and I threw down my bed roll on the ground under a tree beside my car. I could not sleep, I felt as if something was digging into my back, I was too tired to bother looking. In the morning I found I had been lying on an empty bottle.

The night I slept in a house I was with the Colonel of the Queen's Bays, and in the morning we found that the only loo was a double one in the garden with no screens, so there was me and the Colonel sitting side-by-side in full view of several houses round about. I nearly forgot to mention the house that we had slept in was unoccupied, as were all the other houses in the village so there were no people to see us anyway. They had all gone on the road south, joining the refugees. The German Army was about a mile away, and there was no stopping them as far as we know but the fifty tanks of the Queen's Bays.

I was attached to regimental headquarters and hob-nobbed with the Colonel, the Second-in-Command who was a Major, the Adjutant a Captain, and two or three young staff officers. Having joined the Territorial Army before the war, I was only a Captain though I was thirty-nine and older than the Colonel. The Queen's Bays headquarters was most extraordinary. Each evening the officers' mess truck came forward and the mess waiters laid out a long table under the trees, and we sat down to a three-course dinner with white cloth etc. We had the wireless going so that we could hear from London what was happening in France where we were. One night it poured and some drops of rain were falling in my soup, then some fool left the wireless on in the rain all night and it never worked again. Every night there was one face missing when an officer was wounded or killed, and then another would appear in his place.

Rouen is on the River Seine, which meanders in a number of large loops to reach the sea, thirty-five miles (fifty-six km) to the west. The German Army, securely on the River Somme after the *Sichelschnitt*, was occupying positions about sixty-five miles (104km) north-east of Rouen. The area between the Somme and the Seine was where the 1st Armoured Division would fight and lose many of its tanks in action. The division's first encounters with the enemy took place at the German crossings over the Somme, which were well to the north of Rouen. The Channel coast is forty-five miles (seventy-two km) north of Rouen, and the small port of Saint-Valery on the coast was where the 51st Division was later to be surrounded. To the east, there was open access into the heartland of France, but if British detachments moved in this direction, they would find it increasingly difficult to get out. The main locus of the action was at the German crossings on the Somme. (**Map 2.**)

It was not long before the Panzers were moving aggressively to get over the Somme and establish firm crossings. Major General Evans, who was now under French orders, began to receive contradictory instructions: to attack north across the Somme (an impossible assignment); to support a French attack on Amiens (also impossible); and to assault the German bridgehead north-west of Amiens. This job was given to the 2nd Armoured Brigade, including the Bays. Evans's instructions from the French involved separating his two armoured brigades. These were to receive virtually no support from various French light cavalry divisions that were equipped with thin-skinned, lightly armed tanks, and even included some relics of nineteenth century warfare, mounted cavalry units.

On 23 May, the Brigade moved up to positions seven miles (ten km) south of the Somme, with the aim of blocking the German crossings. On 24 May the Bays made a premature attempt to cross the river at Ailly, upstream from Abbeville, and the outcome was as might have been expected. The regimental history of the Bays did not mince words about this action, which had called for so much sacrifice by the Regiment and an under-strength infantry battalion that fought alongside it, the 4 Border Regiment from the Beauman Division.

A History of the Queen's Bays, 1929-1945

The Regiment in their first action had been rushed into battle against first-class German troops of all arms without adequate time for preparation and without any artillery to support them. As a result their gallant individual efforts and those of 4 Borders were dissipated in a number of minor actions, none of which had any chance of success, or was within supporting distance of another. (**Plate 7.**)

On 27 May, Evans ordered the 2ⁿᵈ Armoured Brigade to make a larger-scale attack on a prepared German defensive position at Huppy, also upstream at Abbeville. The brunt of the assault was taken by the 10ᵗʰ Hussars. There was no artillery support, and the Bays were in no position to join the main assault on the right. The British effort, although carried out with great bravery, was met by withering anti-tank fire. Even the relatively small 37mm German anti-tank guns could rip open the British tanks. The German tactics, which would later be perfected in the North African desert, were to refuse to meet tank with tank, but to lure British tanks into a nest of anti-tank guns. The result of the Huppy attack was disastrous, and the 10ᵗʰ Hussars lost twenty out of their thirty vehicles, and some of the remainder were badly damaged.

The 10ᵗʰ Royal Hussars in the Second World War

> The enemy's line appeared to be echeloned right back and to be well defended along its length with anti-tank guns . . . Our mission had failed, not through any shortcomings on the part of the regiments concerned; indeed many desperate and gallant deeds were done, even if some of the fighting was most unorthodox according to current tactical doctrine.

Brigadier McCreery (Brigade Commander) called a halt before he committed his third regiment, the 9ᵗʰ Lancers. Some distance to the north, near the coast, the 3ʳᵈ Armoured Brigade attacked and made modest progress. But its two regiments lost eighteen tanks before Brigadier Crocker (Brigade Commander) pulled back the main body of his armour. McCreery and Crocker, aged forty-two and forty-four respectively, were to make their names in the desert campaign in North Africa and eventually ended their careers as four-star generals. The assault on the German crossings of the Somme was the 1ˢᵗ Armoured Division's first battle. It lost 120 tanks: sixty-five in action and fifty-five from mechanical breakdowns, many caused by wear on the caterpillar tracks. Fortunately the losses in tanks did not mean corresponding losses in men because many of the crews managed to bail out of their tanks and survived. The remnants of the Queen's Bays and 10ᵗʰ Hussars were temporarily amalgamated into a composite Regiment and began to sort themselves out.

Medical services in the field were efficiently organized within divisions. (**Figure 2.**) Each division had three Field Ambulances, one per brigade. These were medical units whose job was to treat wounded men who were sent down from the Regimental Aid Posts (RAPs). Field Ambulances had a number of sub-units: Advanced Dressing Stations (ADSs); Main Dressing Stations (MDSs); and Casualty Clearing Posts (CCPs). (CCPs were established when there were large distances between the ADSs and MDSs, although they were soon found to be too weighed down with equipment to keep pace with a battle of movement.) Each Field Ambulance, commanded by an RAMC lieutenant colonel, was staffed by RAMC officers (qualified doctors and commissioned nurses) plus many orderlies who could turn their hands to much routine work. A Field Ambulance had reliable motor ambulances for transferring patients across the battlefield, which was a much more mobile environment than during the First World War. Badly wounded men were evacuated to permanent hospitals, and later in the war air ambulances were common. (In Normandy in 1944, the ubiquitous DC3 Dakota aircraft moved men from airstrips behind the front line straight back to England.)

Figure 2 should be read from top to bottom, i.e. stretcher bearers carried patients for a quarter-mile to the Regimental Aid Post; after this, an ambulance took them five miles to the Forward Dressing Station, etc.

The distances between the different stages depended on the battle conditions and terrain. The notional figures in the diagram are reasonably typical for Europe. In the desert in North Africa, the distances could be twice as great.

Despite obvious difficulties, the journey from the RAP to the rear was often rapid. Lance Corporal Merewood of the Queen's Bays, fighting in his Grant tank, received a nasty wound. He bailed out and was picked up in a scout car driven by a fearless sergeant. Dr. MacGill at the RAP gave Merewood a shot of morphine and he was soon in an ambulance. (pp. 142-143.)

THE ENEMY

BRITISH FORWARD DEFENDED LOCALITIES
Up to a quarter mile
Stretcher bearers

REGIMENTAL AID POST
Five miles
Motor ambulance

FIELD AMBULANCE FORWARD DRESSING STATION
Five miles
Motor ambulance

FIELD AMBULANCE MAIN DRESSING STATION
Five miles
Motor ambulance

CASUALTY CLEARING POST
One hundred miles
Motor ambulance or
air ambulance

BASE HOSPITAL

FIGURE 2
THE EVACUATION OF CASUALTIES

During JSM's service, the Base Hospital in France was in Rouen; in Egypt, it was in Tobruk, and later Alexandria; in Tunisia it was in Tripoli.

When the regiment was in contact with the enemy, JSM was constantly treating patients, always under difficult conditions. The RAP moved daily with Regimental Headquarters because the Bays were fighting a moving battle. The job of a Regimental Medical Officer on the

51

battlefield, often under fire, was first aid. But combined with this was triage: making instant decisions about the seriousness of wounds. The most seriously injured men – generally the majority – were passed back as quickly as possible down the line to an Advanced Dressing Station. Again, depending on the seriousness of the wound, the worst cases would go further back. When he could, JSM visited the British Military Hospital at Rouen where many of his patients had ended up.

JSM Journal, continued

> Some of the wounded I had to attend to had been lying out two or three days before they were found, and their wounds were covered with live maggots. It sounds terrible, but it was not as bad as it sounds, because the maggots prevented sepsis, and once the maggots had been killed with ether the wounds were clean.

> One officer I had to examine was dead, and I could not find any sign of injury at all; I do not know to this day what killed him. We buried him in a clearing at the back of a big house, and discovered afterwards that it was the tennis court. One morning I was called to see a trooper who had been taken ill in the night. He was lying under a tree in an orchard. I found that he had pneumonia and sent him off to hospital at once. One day I was asked to examine a woman who was pregnant, and a refugee on the run. They wanted to know if they could go on any further, so I examined her in the straw on the floor of the barn and she was not in labour so I said she could go on. Of course I never saw her again so I do not know how she did.

> I visited the British Military Hospital in Rouen, which was only a few miles from our area of operation, and had a chat with several of our men who had been wounded and sent there. The Colonel of the Field Ambulance, to which our wounded were sent in the first place, told me that the whole of the Main Dressing Station (MDS) of another Field Ambulance were 'in the bag'. The

Germans surrounded them and took them all prisoners before they knew what had hit them. That was about 150 men, and all because their Colonel had sat in camp and did not know what was going on.

We called the Colonel of the Field Ambulance I was visiting Dangerous Dan because his name was Daniel, and we gave him this nickname because he had some curious ideas about medicine, and was very keen on manipulation of the vertebrae for all complaints, even a cold in the head – this was osteopathy. But I will say this for him, he knew his job as Officer Commanding a Field Ambulance, which is a total of 200 men and forty-five vehicles.

He spent all his time at Brigade (that means Brigade Headquarters) where he drank numerous glasses of sherry and cracked jokes with all the Staff Officers. At the same time he heard all that was going on and was right in the picture, and got on the blower to his MDS and told his Second-in-Command when he had to move, and where to, so that his unit did not get captured. Of course he was a Regular Army soldier, but so was the Colonel who was captured, come to think of it. Later, when we were in the North African desert, Dangerous Dan was promoted and was our Assistant Director of Medical Services (ADMS).

Brooke's Forlorn Hope

In the Peninsular War early in the 19th century, the commanding officer of an infantry battalion would call for a small number of volunteers – called a 'Forlorn Hope' – whose task was to make a suicidal attack against a French fortified position. The phrase is resonant, but it is a mistranslation of Dutch words meaning 'lost troop.' The inaccurate and the real meanings of this term describe equally well what was now going to befall the British Army in France.

On 2 June, Lieutenant General Brooke had returned to London, having left the evacuation of II Corps in the hands of Major General Montgomery. Brooke was now given the news that he was to return to France to command a new BEF. The deplorable condition of the French Army was fresh in his mind, so that the prospect of a return to France filled him with pessimism. His command was going to include three formations already in France, the 51st (Highland) Division, the hastily assembled Beauman Division, and the much-reduced 1st Armoured Division. He was also taking over the 52nd (Lowland) Division, which already had a brigade in France and would be complete on the ground on 7 June. It was planned that further divisions would later be added: the 3rd Division after it had been re-equipped, and the 1st Canadian Division, at the time in England. Brooke would report directly to General Weygand, but ominously and despite recent experience, Weygand still believed that the German crossings of the Somme were vulnerable to attack. He intended to throw good money after bad.

The 51st (Highland) Division had more men and more supporting arms than other British infantry divisions. It was also tied to its recruiting area with stronger bonds of sentiment than was the case with any other Territorial division in the British Army. It had spent the winter on the eastern frontier of France and had not taken part in the disastrous incursion into Belgium. It was now ordered from the east to join the 1st Armoured Division, which had on 27 May fought its brief and abortive battle near Abbeville.

Because of Weygand's continued intention to attack the German crossings on the Somme, he put the available British troops into the French IX Corps on the extreme left of the French line. He then ordered Major General Fortune, Commander of the 51st Division, to cobble together a group comprising the 51st Division, and most of what remained of the 1st Armoured Division (the combined regiment formed from the Bays and 10th Hussars, and the divisional artillery. The other tank units in the 1st Armoured Division were fully occupied in recovering and repairing their knocked-out vehicles.) He was also allocated two French divisions. This was a clumsy ad hoc arrangement, with communication problems and language difficulties. Fortune's new command had little chance of operating effectively, but he was rushed into taking the offensive on 4 June. His hurried and badly-prepared attack, again on the Abbeville sector, was an expensive failure.

This unsuccessful foray meant that the 51st Division had lost its balance when the German Army struck. The French Army was already unbalanced, but unfortunately this was now a permanent condition. After the evacuation of the BEF from Dunkirk, which was completed on 4 June, the triumphant Germans picked over the detritus of the BEF perimeter, and large numbers of abandoned trucks were later used by the German Army during the invasion of Russia in 1941. While the evacuation was going on, the German General Staff was methodically developing a plan for a massive sweep south from the line of the River Somme. This plan envisaged an encirclement like the one that had been executed with such spectacular success by the *Sichelschnitt*.

The new attack, launched on 5 June, was a double thrust: partly a direct attack and partly a swinging hook from the left. The advancing German soldiers had high spirits because of their uninterrupted successes in the campaign. The French IX Corps, which included the 51st Division, was hit hard by the direct attack, and some Highland battalions suffered devastating casualties. The 51st Division then moved back, reinforced by a weak brigade of the Beauman Division. Attacks on the German left flank by the 1st Armoured Division and other parts of the Beauman Division were too weak to have an effect. Meanwhile the German left hook was pushing forward. When the direct German thrust arrived in Rouen on 9 June, IX Corps became encircled in a large pocket south of the Channel coast. The left hook would also have caught the remnants of the 1st Armoured Division and the Beauman Division if they had not pulled back to the Seine and then south of it just before the arrival of the Germans in Rouen. (**Map 2.**)

One simple fact illustrates both the difficulty of this move and the extent of the medical care provided to the fighting troops. When the British military hospitals in the sector of operations north of the Seine were moved back to Brittany, *450 trucks* were needed to transport the medical stores.

Meanwhile, parts of the French IX Corps and the 51st Division, with the battalions attached to it, were holding a river line fifteen miles (twenty-four km) from the Somme. Seventy miles (112km) to the south-west behind the Highlanders' positions, the major port of Le Havre was capable of evacuating the troops. But they had to get there first. The day after the 1st Armoured Division had pulled back to Rouen, the retirement of the 51st Division was blocked by a German thrust that reached the Channel coast. Before this happened, Major General Fortune managed to send ahead a force of four battalions to secure the port of Le Havre and arrange transportation to take the main body away later. (These four battalions, which included one of the Regular battalions in the otherwise all-Territorial division, eventually escaped after the main body had been encircled.)

The fate of the 51st Division was now sealed. It reached the small port of Saint- Valery, a place too small to handle anything larger than a few small vessels, and these could not get into the port because of thick fog. Nevertheless, more than 2,000 soldiers, half British and half French, managed to slip away and were evacuated from another small port not far away. The Germans – by now numbering five strong divisions, including Major General Rommel's 7th Panzer – soon surrounded the British positions and attacked with strong artillery support. The French commander was the first to raise the white flag, on 11 June. Fortune, with great reluctance, soon did the same since he realized that further resistance would be futile. A photograph exists of Fortune, a justifiably disheartened commander, standing next to Rommel. As befitted an officer of the German General Staff, Rommel was well groomed, calm and professional. (**Plate 8.**)

The loss of the 51st Highland Division was a bitter blow to Scotland. The War Office wisely decided to re-form the division without delay, embodying the small numbers of troops who had got away from France. The new division trained hard in Britain for two years and was then sent to North Africa, where it fought heroically at the Battle of El Alamein in October 1942. After this successful clash of arms, it battled across the desert and led the triumphant victory parade in Tripoli. The wild, tribal music of the pipes and the bronzed battalions that followed brought tears to Churchill's eyes. The division then went to Sicily and after the victory there returned to Britain. It landed in Normandy shortly after D-Day and, after some initial problems, fought its way through north-west Europe to reach the north German plain, where in May 1945 the German Army surrendered.

After the evacuation at Dunkirk and while the original 51ˢᵗ Highland Division was retreating to Saint-Valery, the Bays were preparing to retire south of the Seine.

> *JSM Journal, continued. (Dr. MacGill later added a description of his activities in 1941/1942 in the North African desert. These were quite different from his experiences in France.)*

So when Dunkirk was being evacuated, we were in the area of Rouen, north of the River Seine and 125 miles (200km) south of Dunkirk, and still in contact and operating against German armour. Of course, we knew nothing of what was happening at Dunkirk and only heard about it afterwards. Next we had orders to retire across the River Seine, and blow up the bridge after we had crossed. So we crossed by the Pont de l'Arche and the bridge was blown up as soon as we were all across, so that the Germans could not follow us, and we had a bit of peace from them for a while. It was like a lull after the storm. Instead of continuous gun fire, night and day, all was quiet. Several times when I was sleeping in the grass under a tree I was woken up in the morning about 05:00 by the dawn chorus of birds singing. They made a lot of noise around 5 o'clock. Ever since then, if I am up now at home and open the window and hear the birds singing, it makes me think of France in the war.

Likewise, if I am sitting out in the garden on a warm summer day and the sky is blue, I think of the desert and the war: where we lived, worked, ate and slept in the open with the sky as our roof, night and day, all the time I was there, for eighteen months. We were only in tents in static periods, otherwise it was the panoply of heaven that we looked up to all the time. So when I sit out on our garden seat and I look up at the sky it brings it all back to me, and if a plane goes over, it seems all the time like the desert. Of course this only applied when we were out of earshot of the guns and all was silent around: as when, after the Battle of Msus, the Bays were LOB (left out of battle), having lost about thirty-five tanks and retired to Divisional Headquarters to await replacements. I recollect at one stage in that battle I had three tank crews – about twelve men – clinging to the outside of my scout car, as their only means of transport after their tanks had been knocked out. There were only seventeen tanks left and these were formed into a Composite Squadron and I went as Medical Officer to them with an ambulance. Incidentally, when you wakened in the early morning in the desert, away from the battle area, there were no birds at all. So there was complete silence.

Lieutenant General Brooke, who recently had been knighted as a reward for his command of II Corps, arrived in Cherbourg on the early morning of 13 June. The new BEF was a very slim force. Most of the 51st (Highland) Division had already been forced to capitulate. The 1st Armoured Division and the Beauman Division had both been much reduced by casualties. Only the 52nd (Lowland) Division was complete. (One brigade had arrived earlier, and the remainder came to France on 7 June.)

Brooke's headquarters were to be at Le Mans. After ordering that the lines of communication should be evacuated since they were no longer needed, his job was to visit the French commanders to whom he would be reporting. He drove to Orléans to visit General Weygand, and then accompanied by Weygand he visited General Georges. Brooke had been brought up in France and was bilingual, so that there was no difficulty of mutual understanding. Even after Brooke's early disenchantment with the French Army, he was appalled by the negative attitude of the two French generals. The situation map that Georges produced demonstrated clearly that the French Army was no longer a cohesive fighting force.

The only constructive proposal that Weygand put up for consideration was to build a redoubt – a strong defensive line – with a length of 93 miles (148km) across the base of the Brittany peninsula. This would initially hold the Germans and might be a place from which a future offensive could be launched. The strength of the German Army was undiminished, and it continued to make rapid progress: Paris had fallen on 14 June. It was a ludicrous idea that a defensive line – constructed by a thoroughly demoralized French Army aided by tiny numbers of British troops – could effectively block the German columns.

It was only 15 June, and Brooke now made up his mind. His views were no different from what they had been before he had left France at the time of the Dunkirk evacuation. Back in his headquarters, he managed to get a telephone call through to the newly-appointed Chief of the Imperial General Staff (CIGS), General Dill, and instructed him to stop any further reinforcements going to France. Later that day, Brooke made another call to Dill and recommended evacuation. Dill was with the Prime Minister. Perhaps as a foretaste of their future relationship, Brooke and Churchill now had a vigorous verbal duel, since the Prime Minister found it impossible to believe that all was lost. However – again as was to happen on many occasions when Brooke himself was CIGS – after fighting to the end, Churchill accepted the wisdom of his professional advisers.

The Slow Journey Home

With great care, Brooke supervised the embarkation of the remains of the British Army from France. On 15 June, he heard the broadcast of Marshal Pétain announcing that the French Army must cease firing while he negotiated with the Germans. Brooke himself left France on 18 June and had an adventurous journey across the Channel. Between 16 and 23 June, 144,000 British troops, including those from the line of communications, were transported to Britain from Cherbourg and the Brittany ports. There were also numbers of French, Polish, Czech and Belgian soldiers. The Queen's Bays and the rest of the 1st Armoured Division, having withdrawn from the Seine, moved south and west and eventually reached Brest. They navigated with the help of Michelin maps, since no British Army maps of the area had been provided.

JSM Journal, continued

We had orders to retire and did so gradually over the next two weeks. Once we were camped near a school and in the morning the children came and I spoke to some of them. I could understand them much better than the adults because they spoke very slowly. The boys looked funny in their grey smocks and black stockings. To one little boy I said 'Vous parlez Français très bien', and he laughed and laughed. My conversation with adults usually occurred when we arrived at a strange village, and asked the first person we came across 'Quel est le nom de ce village?', hoping to find out where we were, but if they told us the name of the village it was usually pronounced to us so peculiarly that we did not know what it was. We came across quite a lot of railway lines, but never saw a train – there just were not any running at all. We always parked vehicles under trees so that they could not be seen from the air, and we were camped in a wood once and found a large pond. It was a round pond about twenty yards across and six feet deep. The water was clean – an ideal swimming pool. We bathed in it, in the nude of course, and it was great. It was June, and very hot so the swim was very enjoyable. Next day when we went there the pond had gone. It was made by a dam with a sluice gate at one end of a depression in the ground; some fool had taken away the sluice gate and all the water had flowed away.

We retired south in easy stages, and when France surrendered we were at Le Mans, about 150 miles (240km) from Paris. Word came through that France had surrendered at 03:00 on Saturday 15 June, and the whole division made a bee-line to Brest. My driver could not be found so we had to go without him. I never heard what happened to him, but I expect he got a lift home from someone. Brest is 225 miles (360km) from Le Mans, we arrived there on the same Saturday night, 15 June, and went straight to the docks, where we destroyed all the vehicles and abandoned all our kit, and embarked on the ships with only what we stood up in. It was not like Dunkirk at all. The ships were tied up to the wharf and all we had to do was to walk up the gangway to the deck. The only similarity was that we were being bombed by the Jerries all the time.

There were two ships, about the size of Isle of Man steamers, and each took about 8,000 to 10,000 men who were packed like sardines – standing room only! They sailed on Sunday evening, and as I was standing on the deck by the rail, it was a bright moonlight night, and I could see the other ship sailing alongside about a quarter of a mile away. It was all in darkness, no lights of course, just a black shape tearing through the water. What struck us most about it was that it was sailing *very fast*. It was going flat out, I have never seen a steamer before or since going so fast, with smoke pouring from the funnel and its white bow wave was almost up on its deck. Those ships were going as fast as they could to beat the U-boats. They just looked as if they were racing each other. Luckily there were no U-boats about or we would have had it.

We landed at Plymouth on Monday morning, and with all the fuss and bother of disembarking and marching to camp about ten miles away, it was not until Tuesday that I could send a telegram. There must have been a lot of telegrams sent that day – about 20,000 of them in fact. One of the officers of another regiment took a French girl on the ship to England with him. She must have been the only woman on the boat with about 10,000 men. When we got to England he took her to his home, and I heard later he married her. Then in a few days I got forty-eight hours leave and was on the train to Manchester.

The previous five weeks had been particularly hard for JSM's wife, Dorothy, who had heard nothing of her husband since the time of

Dunkirk. She had two small boys at a day school, and she had to transport them without a car, since there was no petrol for private motoring. She also had to run a busy two-man medical practice. She had given JSM up for dead when she received his unexpected and wonderfully welcome telegram from Plymouth, followed soon afterwards by his arrival home on short leave.

The Queen's Bays had learned a great deal in France. The first lesson was that their tactics were wrong: the way in which British armour had been employed was totally ineffective against a sophisticated enemy. Second, the British tanks the Regiment had been given were too feeble to stand up to the German Panzers and anti-tank guns: even the obsolescent 37mm, let alone the later generations of 75mm and 88mm guns that were to be encountered in North Africa. The third lesson was more positive. Although the Regiment lost all its tanks, most of the men survived. One reason was that, with a tank holding a 3-man crew, bailing out after the vehicle had been hit was not too difficult. Fourteen soldiers in the Regiment had fallen in action, and the total number of casualties – killed, wounded and missing – was no more than fifty. This is a serious enough number, but it did not eviscerate the Regiment. The number of patients treated by Dr. MacGill during the campaign was smaller than the number of men he was to treat in the North African desert. But by then the Regiment was fighting many battles, and some of them would be won. The Regiment had better tanks than it had in France, and at last the British Army was learning how to use them.

1. JSM in 1939

Studio photograph of Dr. John Sylvanus MacGill on being first commissioned in the Royal Army Medical Corps, Territorial Army,

August 1939.

Copyright MacGill Family.

2. British Light tank, 1940

Photographed in England. This 5.5 ton vehicle had light armour and two rifle-caliber machine guns. It was totally outclassed by German tanks.

Copyright Imperial War Museum (IWM), negative MH 9293.

3. British Cruiser tank, 1940

Photographed in England. 14.75 tons, with light armour and one 2-pounder (40mm) and one rifle-caliber machine gun. Also outclassed by German armour.

Copyright IWM, negative MH 8116.

4. British Infantry tank (Matilda), 1940

Photographed in England. 26.5 tons, with effective armour and one 2-pounder and one machine gun. The best available British tank, but extremely slow: 15mph, half the speed of the Light and Cruiser models.

Used by some British units in France and North Africa and considered successful there until the arrival of the German Panzers. However, it was never used by the 2nd Armoured Brigade.

Copyright IWM, negative MH 9264.

5. German 88mm anti-tank gun, 1942

Knocked out and photographed in North Africa. The 88mm was an anti-aircraft gun engineered to fire horizontally. First used in 1940 and operated with deadly effect against British armour in North Africa. The most effective anti-tank gun used by any army during the whole of the Second World War.

Copyright IWM, negative E 14520.

6. German Panzer IV tank, 1942

Knocked out and photographed in North Africa. 26 tons, with strong armour and 75mm gun. Outclassed all British-built tanks. The American Stuarts, Grants and Shermans (all introduced in 1942) were much better than British vehicles, but for various reasons they were still not equal to the Panzer IV.

Copyright MacGill Family.

7. Somme, 1940: destroyed Queen's Bay Cruiser tank

The pleasant countryside of Northern France in June 1940 was a scene of the destructiveness of modern war. The tank was battered and crippled but was not burnt, so that the crew probably managed to escape.

Copyright IWM, negative F 4605.

8. Surrender of 51ˢᵗ Highland Division, St. Valery

On 11 June 1940, most of the units in the famous 51ˢᵗ Highland Division (Territorial) were surrounded and forced to surrender. The Divisional Commander, Major General Fortune (in battledress and service-dress cap), with Major General Rommel, Commander of 7ᵗʰ Panzer Division (in uniform with decorations).

IWM negative RML 342, open copyright.

9. British Stuart tank, 1942

A vivid action photograph; note the flags. The Stuart Light tank was the first American-made vehicle to see action. Popular with the crews, who gave the vehicle the name 'Honey'. A reliable 2.23 ton tank, high off the ground. One 37mm gun plus a rifle-calibre machine gun.

Copyright IWM, negative MH 3802.

10. British Cruiser tank (Crusader), 1942

Photographed in England. Tank with an elegant design and an improvement on the Cruiser used in 1940. (Plate 3.) 2-pounder gun, which was inadequate, but later models had the 6-pounder.

Copyright IWM, negative E 18881.

11. British Grant tank, 1942

American-made, the Grant was the first tank to come near the performance of the Panzers. Unusual design, high off the ground. The main armament, a 75mm gun, was placed low and had limited vertical and lateral traverse. A second gun, 37mm, was above it in a conventional rotating turret.

Copyright IWM, negative 13533.

12. British Sherman tank, 1942

American-made Cruiser, and the most widely used Allied tank in the Second World War. The 300 Shermans provided by President Roosevelt made a significant contribution to the victory of El Alamein. The Sherman was reliable and fast, but the inadequacy of the armour caused the tank to catch fire if hit near the petrol tank and ammunition storage racks. In North Africa, the Sherman had a short (later a long) 75mm gun; heavier guns were installed in 1944 before and during the invasion of France.

Copyright IWM, negative K 6707.

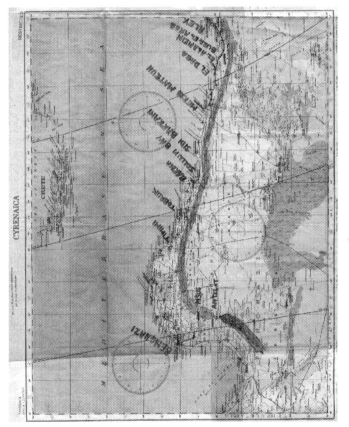

13. JSM's tactical map of Cyrenaica

This heavily marked large-scale tactical map shows Dr. MacGill's peregrinations across the desert. Note in particular the major German assault at the Battle of Gazala, May/June 1942: this led to the British retreat from Antielat to Msus, and to Tobruk and beyond. At about this time he left the Queen's Bays and joined the 1st Light Field Ambulance. (Compare with maps 3 and 6.)

Copyright MacGill Family.

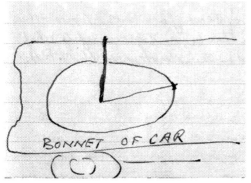

14. JSM's sketch of sun compass

A vitally important aid to desert navigation. Described in Chapter 4.

Copyright MacGill Family.

15. JSM's sketch of protection against desert sandstorm

A typical piece of effective improvisation. Described in Chapter 4.

Copyright MacGill Family.

16. JSM's sketch of a trap for rats

Imaginative improvisation again. Described in Chapter 8.

Copyright MacGill Family.

17. Strip-bathing in desert

An illustration of British ingenuity and passion for cleanliness. The photograph also illustrates the loneliness of the desert, something emphasized by the tire marks on the sand.

Copyright MacGill Family.

18. Bedouin tribe in desert

Arab nomads viewing the war fought by European armies. Note the special camel saddle for women. Also the loneliness of the desert. The Bedouins traded with both armies, selling eggs and information.

Copyright MacGill Family.

19. HAC 25-pounder gun

The best field gun of the Second World War used by any army. Robust construction; 40 degree angle of fire so that it could be used as a howitzer; range 13,400 yards on supercharge. British divisions had substantial artillery support, with field, medium, anti-tank, and anti-aircraft regiments. One field regiment per brigade; one battery per armoured regiment or infantry battalion. Units of Royal Horse Artillery (RHA) supported armour; Royal Artillery (RA) supported infantry. 11 Regiment Royal Horse Artillery (Honourable Artillery Company), abbreviated to 11RHA (HAC) supported the 2nd Armoured Brigade, and A Battery supported the Bays. The 25-pounder gun was used by 11 RHA (HAC) for its first months in the desert. However, before the Battle of El Alamein, the regiment was one of the first to be given *Priests*, self-propelled guns, with an American 105mm gun mounted on a tank chassis.

Copyright HAC.

20. HAC tank used by Forward Observation Officer, with Bays driver

Captain Gerry Chastel de Boinville mounted on 'Christchurch,' the Stuart tank 'with ninety-nine lives.' It drove 5,000 miles without a track change or major mechanical defect.

Copyright HAC.

21. Major McDermid, HAC, with Queen Elizabeth

The King and Queen visited 11 RHA (HAC) on 30 July 1941, before the regiment's departure on active service. Major John McDermid, who commanded A Battery (in support of the Bays), was wounded in the desert and captured.

Copyright HAC.

22. Cookhouse in desert for Bays' 'other ranks'

This was in early 1942. Solar topees were discarded in the middle of the year because they were clumsy and unsuitable for tanks. See Plate 40.

Copyright MacGill Family.

23. Cooking a meal with a petrol burner

This burner was crude and effective. It was no more than a patch of sand a little larger than a soldier's mess tin. It was soaked with petrol, and when lit burned long enough to cook a meal.

Copyright MacGill Family.

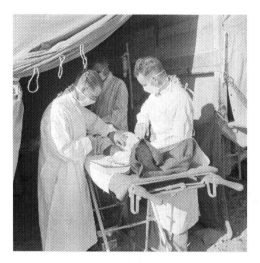

24. Emergency surgery at Field Ambulance dressing station

Despite the problems of working in the open air, the conditions in this dressing station were relatively sterile. The surgeons and nurses/orderlies wore masks and rubber gloves.

Copyright IWM, negative F 18977

25. British Army scout car

Strongly-built four-ton machine, with armour plating and the option of carrying a light machine gun. (The RAMC does not carry arms.)

Copyright IWM, negative H 16292.

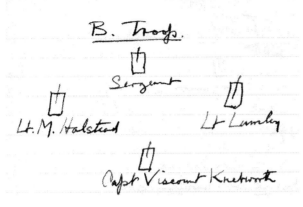

26. Tank Troop desert formation

Four tanks in diamond formation.

Copyright MacGill Family.

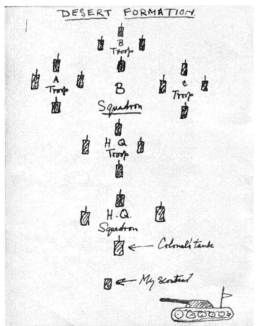

27. Tank Squadron desert formation

Five troops, each of four tanks in desert formation. Medical Officer in rear.

Small diagram illustrating the use of flags (described in Chapter 4).

Copyright MacGill Family.

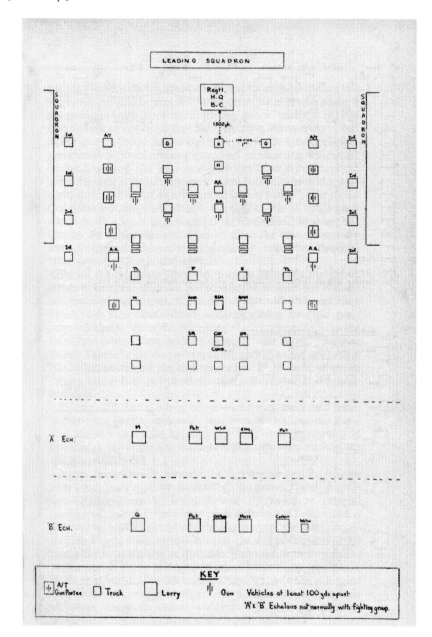

28. Tank Squadron desert formation with accompanying arms

Tanks, field guns, infantry, 'A' Echelon (some distance in rear) and 'B' Echelon (still further in rear). 'Jock' Columns (described in Chapter 6) were based on this formation.

Copyright HAC.

29. 'The Wire,' separating Libya from Egypt

This feeble barrier, erected by the Italians, was no impediment to advancing British and Commonwealth troops. The four-ton armoured car, fitted with a machine gun, belonged to the 11th Hussars (the 'Cherry Pickers'), who built a formidable reputation for aggressiveness during the whole of the North African campaign.

Copyright IWM, negative E 378.

30. Arrival at Sollum, descending the Escarpment

The port of Sollum is the most easterly town in Libya, and just short of the frontier with Egypt. The long descending road does not show adequately the steepness of the Escarpment. Not far away, at Halfaya ('Hell Fire') Pass, it was a formidable obstacle.

Copyright MacGill Family.

CHAPTER 4

A LONG WAR AHEAD

The 2ⁿᵈ Armoured Brigade – the Queen's Bays, 9ᵗʰ Lancers and 10ᵗʰ Hussars – had been reorganized in England before the end of June 1940. The numbers of killed, wounded and missing had been mercifully small, and the three regiments minus their tanks, whose hulks remained in France, made up the most important element of the 1ˢᵗ Armoured Division. The most urgent task of this division was to form part of the large but ill-equipped force defending Britain against a German invasion. At the end of the summer, the division received new tanks. Although these were similar to the ones in which the regiments had fought in France, the main job of the officers and men was to re-learn how to handle these vehicles mechanically in all conditions of ground and weather, carrying out as much field firing as possible with the limited supply of ammunition. As they became comfortable with their equipment, the regiments and the larger formations of which they formed part, the 2ⁿᵈ Armoured Brigade and the 1ˢᵗ Armoured Division, had to begin the difficult process of developing their skills in how to use armour on the field of battle. The German army had demonstrated the importance of the closest possible cooperation between armour and the other arms: infantry, artillery (particularly anti-tank guns), engineers, and air support. The British commanders should have taken to heart the lessons of the German successes, but there is not much evidence that this was done. The British army had to learn the hard way, although the 1ˢᵗ Armoured Division did receive improved tanks in August 1941, just before it left Britain for the North African desert.

Fortress Britain

Before the end of June 1940, more than 300,000 soldiers and airmen from the BEF had been evacuated from France. They were mostly British although they included small numbers from France, Belgium, Poland and Czechoslovakia. In addition, more than 100,000 French troops had been shipped from Dunkirk in early June, but the vast majority had returned to France because they believed against the odds that the battle of France had not been lost. The force of 300,000 men was bigger in total than the British armies overseas: in Africa and the Middle East and in India and the Far East. (However the British army in India was not the only force under arms. There was also the Indian army – locally recruited from Indian-born men, with British commanders, and staff and senior regimental officers – which by the end of the war had become the largest volunteer army anywhere in the world. But this took time to build up, in response to the Japanese menace.)

There was a problem with the Home Army, the name for the large body of soldiers in Britain: the former BEF plus those who had not gone to France. This was not a problem of low morale because the men were in remarkably buoyant spirits. The difficulty was that the BEF had lost their equipment. They had their small arms – rifles and light machine guns – but had left behind in France all their artillery (disabled), their tanks (also disabled) and their trucks. British manufacturers worked at a furious pace to fill the plentiful gaps. Lend-Lease supplies from the United States also began to arrive across the Atlantic, despite the attentions of the German U-Boat fleet that sent many British ships to the bottom of the sea, and even some American ones although the United States would not come into the war until December 1941.

At the beginning of the war, the Chief of the Imperial General Staff was General Ironside, who had started his army life in the Royal Artillery. He was a tall and imposing figure (with the appropriately English nickname of 'Tiny'), and had a formidable fighting reputation. He was a remarkable linguist and Russian speaker and had published two well-respected books on the Russian front in 1914 and 1919. (Ironside had commanded a British expedition to north Russia in 1919.) But in the view of many senior soldiers and politicians, Ironside was not a 'big thinker' and he also lacked a concentrated focus. Lieutenant General Dill, a corps commander in the BEF, was brought home in April 1940 as Vice Chief of the Imperial General Staff, which meant in effect that he would understudy Ironside. When Churchill became Prime Minister and Minister of Defence, he was unhappy with Ironside's lack of 'grip' and energy, and Dill replaced him on 27 May 1940.

Ironside was now given an important job, as Commander-in-Chief of the Home Army, whose numbers were being augmented by a flow of untrained conscripts, and which was being re-armed steadily although slowly. A very large number of training and other non-combatant units were decentralized and spread all over Britain. The 'teeth arms' were divided into eight military districts, equivalent to the corps of an army. Lieutenant General Brooke, following his abortive experience with the revived BEF and his return to England, was appointed General Officer Commanding (GOC) the most important district, Southern Command, where any German invasion would most likely land. The area Brooke covered stretched from West Sussex to Wales.

Churchill, who of course already knew Brooke, continued to be impressed by him because of his skill, optimism, energy and toughness. But he had a relatively small command: a single Regular division, the 4th, plus three less well trained Territorial ones. Ironside's strategy was to 'fight on the beaches' and rely on an unsupported line along or near the coast, made as strong as the limited number of divisions could make it, and fortified with strong points. However, there was no depth. Brooke moved as quickly as he could to establish a new strategy. He planned to hold a thin outpost line whose function would be to delay any invading German army, then Brooke would throw against it a *masse de manoeuvre*, a mobile counter-attack force. He assembled such a force on Salisbury Plain. When Brooke replaced Ironside as Commander-in-Chief of the Home Army on 19 July 1940, this led to a general change of strategy towards Brooke's outpost line and powerful *masse de manoeuvre*.

Brooke's long-term plan for the Home Army was to build a force of impressive size. He aimed for a fully-trained body of men large enough to fill the ranks of twenty-five divisions, including eight armoured. In addition there were coastal defences and the part-time Home Guard. There would also be the customary army services – ordnance, service corps, medical corps etc. – plus a vast structure of training units. (Before the end of the war, the armoured force alone required eleven training regiments.) One minor miracle was the way in which all these servicemen were given three meals a day that were reasonably well balanced and had enough calories for them to undertake the physical labour that is usually part of a soldier's life. Brooke realized that such a force would not be built up to this concentrated strength in Britain because trained divisions would have to be shipped overseas to join the battle. But when the British army was at its maximum size of 3,000,000 well-led and well-trained men and women in 1945, it was obvious that such a force would never have been possible unless Britain had for years been an armed camp, in effect a fortress equipped for attack and defence.

For a small country like Britain, there was an unprecedented density of army barracks and camps; and the large training areas – especially Salisbury Plain, Brecon, Stamford, Catterick and Otterburn – were scenes of perpetual activity by battalions, regiments, brigades and divisions learning their jobs. There were also enough RAF stations, some permanent but many more of them temporary, to house the independent commands – Fighter, Bomber, Coastal, Army-Cooperation, Maintenance and Training – with some thousands of aircraft and the tens of thousands of men and women needed to keep them in the air, particularly engineers and armourers, and signals and radar technicians, besides different levels of administrators. Around the coasts there were ports, docks and training establishments for the second-largest navy in the world. And in 1942, 1943 and 1944, a flow of American soldiers and airmen arrived: a number that eventually totalled 2,000,000. As a signal of the high level of activity, the British trains were always full, with the corridors crowded with service men and women. There were no motorways; no private motoring; and the existing roads were in constant use by military trucks, some of gigantic size, as well as many smaller vehicles.

In this way the British Isles were being transformed into an armed fortress, and the return of the Queen's Bays in June 1940 was part of this process. When the regiment got back from France, they immediately went into a half-finished camp at Warminster on Salisbury Plain, and were mainly housed in symmetrical lines of new white tents: rather different from their tactical deployment on the battlefield in France. On

2 July, Brigadier McCreery made his presence felt when he addressed all the officers and non-commissioned officers in the 2ⁿᵈ Armoured Brigade. The next day he held a conference of all Commanding Officers in which he laid down a training programme and summary of operational tasks that the brigade would have to be prepared to carry out.

The 1ˢᵗ Armoured Division, together with the Canadian Corps that had just arrived, made up Brooke's *masse de manoeuvre*. The Bays moved to Surrey in October 1940, and from now on worked with their newly-issued tanks, although these were to be replaced with better vehicles before the regiment left for active service. The Bays moved back to Salisbury Plain in early June 1941, and they and the rest of the 1ˢᵗ Armoured Division sailed for Egypt at the end of September 1941. They took the long route around Africa.

To return to the 1ˢᵗ Armoured Division's departure from France in June 1940, an important change took place shortly after this. The divisional commander, Major General Evans, was made the scapegoat for the débâcle south of the Somme, when the division attempted to halt the German Panzers. He had a painful interview with Brooke who told him that he could not expect any further employment. His replacement was Major General Norrie, who had commanded the 10ᵗʰ Hussars during the early 1930s. Before the division arrived in Egypt at the end of 1941, command passed to Major General Lumsden. Lumsden had led the 12ᵗʰ Lancers, the regiment of armoured cars that had performed so effectively during the retreat of the BEF. The 2ⁿᵈ Armoured Brigade also had a change of command in December 1940, when Brigadier McCreery handed over to Brigadier Briggs, who would have a long tenure and led the brigade until after the Battle of El Alamein.

The question that calls for an answer is why it took from June 1940 to September 1941 – more than fifteen months – before the 1ˢᵗ Armoured Division returned to the battlefield. Equipping the regiments with new tanks obviously took time, since they were manufactured so slowly, and the tank crews had to work hard to master their new machines. There was also the matter of armoured tactics and the gradual move towards closer cooperation with the other 'teeth arms'. But these problems were symptoms of something more deeply rooted. *British soldiers needed much more training to enable them to face the German army.* This was particularly true of the Territorials who were mobilized in September 1939, and the large numbers of conscripts who were being continuously fed into the military machine. Even elite Regular cavalry regiments like the Bays needed to be shaken free of their innate conservatism.

The British army was on the defensive after the return of the BEF. Very few drafts were sent abroad in 1940, and the pace only increased at the end of 1941, when divisions were sent to Egypt. In 1942, troops were drafted both to North Africa and to the Far East; and in 1943 to Italy and the Far East. But the largest dispatch of divisions to the battlefield only took place before and after D-Day, 6 June 1944. After D-Day, the majority of the soldiers who fought in north-west Europe had been trained in Britain for four years. The lesson had been learned by the military planners that non-Regular soldiers needed years rather than months of military discipline and training – if possible realistic and imaginative training – before they could be sent into battle.

A New Generation of Tanks

The 2nd Armoured Brigade had gone to war in May 1940 mounted in Light and Cruiser tanks. The Queen's Bays had fifty machines which they had barely learned to operate, and there were no reserves to replace tanks that were knocked out in battle or otherwise disabled. Of the fifty, twenty-one were Light tanks, thin-skinned and armed only with machine guns. (**Plate 2.**) These were effective against infantry, but useless against strong points and particularly German armour and anti-tank guns, both of which were superior to anything possessed by the British. The remaining twenty-nine tanks were the somewhat larger Cruisers. (**Plate 3.**) These had similarly thin armour, and mounted a single machine gun and a relatively feeble 2-pounder gun to fire shells. These were also outclassed by the Germans. The two units of the Royal Tank Regiment that made up the 3rd Armoured Brigade were equipped with the slow, heavy Infantry tanks (**Plate 4**), but these were early models equipped only with machine guns and therefore no match for the Panzer III and Panzer IV tanks. By the end of the campaign, the five regiments of the 1st Armoured Division had lost 120 tanks: almost half their original strength. The surviving vehicles were disabled and dumped when the troops in the division were evacuated to Britain.

Before 1939, the War Office in London had ordered the manufacturer of 2,000 tanks, and these began to roll off the production lines in 1940. The French and German army each had slightly more than 2,000 vehicles. But it is misleading to compare different armies on the basis of any fixed number of tanks. What matters most is the quality and also the rate of obsolescence of the vehicles, and in 1940 the obsolescence of British tanks was governed by the superior performance of the German machines. In the battle of France, the Panzer III and Panzer IV tanks were from every point of view better, especially the Mark IV with their 75mm guns. (**Plate 6.**) British tank production continued non-stop, with the aim of equaling the quality of the Germans, but while this was happening the Panzers in turn were being improved. During the whole course of the war – to the chagrin of the British and Americans, but not the Russians whose T34 tanks were always feared by their opponents – the German army kept its edge.

What the British army of course needed was an uninterrupted flow of tanks that were being significantly and continuously improved. Quality always mattered, but so did quantity. There were two reasons for this. First, in addition to the basic number of tanks needed to fill the squadrons, many more were needed in each regiment as reserves to replace those that had been put out of action. The second point was that General Brooke, as Commander-in-Chief of the Home Army and later CIGS, had ambitions to increase greatly the number of armoured divisions in the British army. This was a transformational plan that was substantially carried into effect.

In 1942 in the North African desert, the British army began to receive large numbers of American tanks, the most important of which were the Sherman Cruisers. (**Plate 12.**) Also during the desert campaign, an imaginative organizational change took place when a new regiment, the Royal Electrical and Mechanical Engineers (REME), was splintered off the Royal Engineers. The REME provided skilled technicians and heavy equipment to repair disabled British tanks and in many cases was able to return them to action. A REME officer and a group of technicians, called a Light Aid Detachment (LAD), soon formed a part of every armoured regiment. The REME sprang quickly into existence because, in many cases, the first REME technicians were the fitters who were already in the regiment, and who remained in their jobs but with new regimental badges.

Between June and October 1940, the 2nd Armoured Brigade possessed no tanks and the troops had to march and be prepared to fight on their feet. This regime made the regiments concentrate on improving the basic military skills of the officers and men in the ranks. But in October 1940, the brigade began to receive tanks that were leaving the factories. The Bays soon had their full establishment of Cruiser tanks, although these were no better than those in which they had fought in France. But despite their obsolescence, the tanks were good enough to be used for tactical training and also developing the basic skills needed by tank crews: driving and maintenance, gunnery, and signals. The training increasingly focused on preparation for the open spaces of the North African desert (insofar as these could be duplicated in Britain), because it was an open secret that this was to be the destination of the 1st Armoured Division. The division also began to spend much time on tactical exercises in the field, including a particularly ambitious scheme in April 1941. As a foretaste of the future, the division for this exercise came under the command of Lieutenant General Montgomery, at the time GOC of V Corps in the Home Army.

More than a year passed since the Bays and their sister regiments had arrived back in Britain: a period during which their main task was intensive preparation to go to war. As a result of this and new tanks they received in August 1941, the regiments of the 2nd Armoured Brigade were in far better shape than when they had first gone to France in May 1940.

The new tanks were two types. The Bays received a total of fifty-two. Sixteen were the American M3 Stuart Light tanks, the first armour that the British had received as a result of Lend-Lease. Stuarts were popular with their crews and were given the nickname of Honeys. (**Plate 9.**) Although they were not particularly comfortable, they were mechanically very robust. Stuarts were not a new design and were high off the ground, which was a disadvantage because the tanks were too visible in the open desert. They were armed with a 37mm gun and a machine gun, which made them in effect what the British called Cruisers. They did not fight for long in 1942 because they became outclassed. The Bays also received thirty-six of the relatively new Cruiser tank, the Mark VI Crusader. (**Plate 10.**) These had breakdowns, but they had a low profile and a very businesslike appearance. The vehicles that the Bays used during their early experience of the desert had the unsatisfactory 2-pounder gun and a machine gun. These were no match for the German tanks and anti-tank guns. Later in 1942, upgraded Crusaders arrived with 6-pounder guns, but even when they faced these, the Germans still retained their advantage.

Dr. MacGill was not an officer who commanded tanks, although he lived in the midst of officers who did. However, since his job was to treat men who had been wounded in tanks, he was able to give a commonsense description of how the Crusaders actually operated in early 1942. A non-technical description like this is unusual in works of military history.

JSM Journal

> Each tank has four men: a driver, a gunner, a wireless operator and a commander. The commander gives the orders and the others do what he tells them. The commander is an officer or senior NCO. Each tank has a wireless aerial and on it a flag. This flag is called a *Recognition Flag*, and each tank has two. Each day the flags are moved and they are of course to enable our tank commanders to recognize each other. One day there would be one flag at the top of the aerial, next day it might be half way down for both, next day one half way down, next day two at the top, and next day one at the top and one half way down. As all our tanks in the regiment were the same, one soon got to recognize them from their shape without any prompting from the flags. Because of this, any tank of a different shape, however slight, must be enemy. But when the tanks were close together and milling around in a lot of dust and exhaust and gun smoke, the flags were useful. (**Plates 9, 27.**)

> The petrol tank of each vehicle would hold one hundred gallons, and a tank did one mile to the gallon so that

it could do one hundred miles on a full tank. The journey by road, or over the desert, all of 750 miles from Alexandria to Benghazi, played havoc with the tank tracks, and so tank transporters were used to carry the tanks to the battle area.

At first we had Crusader tanks, which were not much use. The German tanks had bigger guns, with longer range and thicker armour. They could therefore sit back out of range and pound our tanks to pieces. And even when our tanks got close enough, their shells could not penetrate the German armour and just bounced off. At El Alamein we got Sherman tanks and the position was reversed. We had bigger guns and thicker armour. That had a lot to do with the advance from then on, although General Montgomery takes all the credit.

JSM did not dwell on the difficulties that were to be encountered with the Sherman tanks. They were used by both the American and British armies until the end of the war, and in the North-West Europe campaign many Shermans were fitted with heavier guns, although again these were no match for either the German 88mm anti-tank guns or the largest of the German tanks that were also equipped with this weapon. The problems with the Shermans were that they had a high profile that made them vulnerable, and a frightening tendency to catch fire when they were hit. This is something that often weakened the morale and aggressiveness of the tank crews.

Getting the Balance Right

As explained earlier in this book, the ability of an army to carry out and win a tank war depends on three factors: first, the basic strategic decision governing the number of armoured divisions in comparison with infantry; second, the tactical composition of each armoured division, with the right balance of armour, infantry and artillery. The third point is the quality of the tanks themselves. How well did the British army meet these challenges during the early years of the Second World War?

Brooke, as CIGS, made the key decision to allocate a large slice of the army's scarce resources to boosting its armoured strength. He had made considerable progress in this before the battle of El Alamein in October 1942: a progress that continued with increased momentum during the following years. The second factor – and the subject of this discussion – the best balance of the 'teeth arms' within an armoured division, took time and the British army only got it right in 1944, when the armoured divisions had enough motor battalions to fight enemy infantry and also occupy ground, and plentiful artillery to support the armour and infantry in attack and defence. The third factor, the quality of the tanks themselves, became a hostage to the long lead times demanded by industrial manufacture in Britain and America. As a result, the military planners deserve a barely passing grade. The German army did a better job; until the end of the war, the German tanks kept up with American and British improvements and generally exceeded them.

For three years following the outbreak of war in 1939, British armoured divisions were structured on what to the British army were traditional lines. They were heavy with two armoured brigades (armed with generally inadequate tanks), plus a support group of infantry and artillery. The unhappy experience of the 1st Armoured Division in the French campaign of 1940 was a result both of the inadequacy of the tanks and the lopsided divisional organization: an imbalance that had been exacerbated by the transfer of three important units to other divisions. But even if the various components of the division had remained intact, the balance was still skewed towards armour. Although the official establishment changed in May 1942 to reduce the amount of armour and increase the infantry, the 7th and 10th British Armoured Divisions that fought at El Alamein in October/November 1942 had the traditional organization based on two armoured brigades. However, the 1st Armoured Division, although strengthened, was based on a single armoured brigade, balanced with heavy infantry and artillery.

During the 1st Armoured Division's fifteen months in Britain following their return from France, the support elements were given much more muscle, with two motor infantry battalions: 2 Rifle Brigade (RB) and 2 King's Royal Rifle Corps (KRRC). There were also three artillery regiments: a Royal Horse Artillery (RHA) unit for close support of the individual armoured regiments, and an anti-tank and an anti-aircraft regiment. The RHA regiment was part of the oldest organization in the British army, the Honourable Artillery Company (HAC), a unit that had infantry and artillery components, both of which produced large numbers of officers for other regiments. The official title of the regiment supporting the 1st Armoured Division was 11th Regiment RHA (HAC). It was to engage in much hard fighting in the desert and in Italy, and out of the original forty-five officers, thirteen were to lose their lives in battle or on other active service.

The regiment had three batteries. The two original batteries that preceded the major expansion before the outbreak of war were 'A' and 'B'. 'A' Battery was now affiliated to the Queen's Bays, and the Battery Commander and his Forward Observation Officers (FOO) were mounted in tanks and accompanied the Bays' regimental headquarters. (**Plate 20.**) 'E' Battery was attached to the 9th Lancers, and 'B' Battery to the 10th Hussars. Each battery of eight guns was composed of two four-gun troops. The weapons were the magnificent 25-pounder gun-howitzers (**Plate 19**), which were towed by QUAD four-wheel-drive tractors. The troop commanders acted as FOOs and showed great skill and coolness under fire.

Armoured and infantry regiments worked closely with the batteries and even before they were all in the desert, a strong mutual trust and understanding had been built. The time spent in Britain from the summer of 1940 to the autumn of 1941 made it possible for the senior officers in the 1st Armoured Division to knit together the armoured regiments and the supporting arms. As a result of all this, the 1st Armoured Division was a more efficient formation – in whole as well as in parts – than it had been in June 1940. As early as February 1941, the division laid on a field exercise followed by an inspection by Winston Churchill, who was accompanied by the émigré leaders of two European countries that had been subjugated by the Germans: General de Gaulle of France, and General Sikorsky of Poland. JSM was introduced to the distinguished visitors. He was also presented to the Queen (subsequently the Queen Mother) before the Bays departed for Africa.

Before the 1st Armoured Division left on active service, the 3rd Armoured Brigade had been transferred. The 22nd Armoured Brigade took its place and departed for Egypt before the rest of the division, but when it arrived it was added to the strength of the 7th Armoured Division. The 1st Armoured Division therefore went into battle with only its original armoured regiments, the Bays, 9th Lancers and 10th Hussars, plus its strong supporting arms. This general structure was to point the way to the shape of future British armoured divisions.

All the British armoured divisions were strengthened before the battle of El Alamein, and the Order of Battle (ORBAT) of the 1st Armoured Division was then as follows:

- 2nd Armoured Brigade: Bays, 9th Lancers, 10th Hussars, Yorkshire Dragoons (infantry motor battalion).

- 7th Motor Brigade: 2 RB, 7 RB, 2 KRRC.

- 12th Lancers (armoured cars).

- 2 RHA, 4 RHA, 11 RHA(HAC), 78th Field Regiment RA, 76th Anti-Tank Regiment RA, 42nd Light Anti-Aircraft RA.

- 'Hammerforce': Artillery and armoured cars.

- Engineers, Signals, and various supporting corps troops.

It had taken nine months for the division to be brought up to this strength and balance, with more than four armoured regiments mostly mounted in Sherman tanks; four motor battalions; and more than six artillery regiments. This was to be the approximate shape of the British and Canadian armoured divisions that fought their way across North-West Europe between June 1944 and May 1945.

Although in Africa the desert air force provided very effective support to the troops on the ground, in North-West Europe the battlefield had many more soldiers per square mile, and this demanded that the British and American armies had to be supported by dominating airpower. The newly-organized Tactical Air Forces were equipped with fighter-bombers, especially the deadly rocket-firing Typhoons that brought fire down under the orders of observers on the ground, who were Royal Air Force officers marching with the troops. This type of tactical support was a crucial extra ingredient in a moving battle: just as the Germans had discovered when they developed their Panzer divisions before the Second World War. And this was not all, because before and after the invasion of Normandy, British and American strategic bombers carried out a vast amount of interdiction, attacking transport centres and sources of German oil.

The Desert Ocean and the Marauding Battle Fleets

The first biography of Field Marshal Rommel was written shortly after the end of the war by Desmond Young, a British army officer who had served in the North African desert and had been captured. The book, which was a best seller, showed Rommel to be a tactician with a sixth sense and ferocious drive, and also an honourable man with great charisma, even in the eyes of the British.

In his book, Young presents a striking image of the desert as an ocean. Although it was not totally flat, it had few natural or man-made features, and this made navigation particularly difficult and vitally important. The desert ocean covered a huge area, and the formations and units of the opposing armies were out of touch with the other side for long enough periods to make it difficult to draw up careful plans for attack and defence. The desert was far less densely populated than the European battlefields. The battle fleets in the desert – tanks, mobile infantry, and towed artillery – were only able to move if the ground had been carefully reconnoitered. The Western Desert Force (renamed 8th Army in the summer of 1941) gave birth to a unique reconnaissance organization, the Long Range Desert Group (LRDG), which cautiously roamed over enemy-occupied territory, mounted in small trucks carrying machine guns. It was only when opposing lines had at last been established, before the Battle of El Alamein, that a conventional set-piece clash became possible. After twelve days of hard fighting, controlled by Lieutenant General Montgomery's 'grip' on the action, El Alamein became a decisive victory.

I shall do my best to describe the North African desert. But as a prelude, Dr. MacGill has a story to tell of the Queen's Bays' departure from Britain, their long voyage around Africa and their arrival in Egypt, two months after they had embarked from Gourock on the Clyde. The 13,000 mile journey was necessary because very few convoys sailed through the Mediterranean because of enemy airpower and submarines. Tanks were sometimes shipped from Gibraltar to Egypt, because they were urgently needed.

JSM Journal

On 28 September 1941, the whole regiment left Marlborough railway sation and travelled non-stop by train to Gourock on the Clyde, where we went aboard the troop ship *Empire Pride*. It was to be its maiden voyage and there were about 1,000 troops on board. On 30 September we sailed in a convoy of forty-seven ships, with six warships to escort us. For the nine weeks we were at sea, I shared a small cabin with the Quartermaster of the Queen's Bays and another officer. The Quartermaster was a fat jolly chap aged about forty, and his nickname was 'Fruity'. He was fond of his beer and used to come to bed at 2:00AM, switch on the light and wake me up.

The convoy sailed due west for four days, and then turned south. The nearest ship to us was only about 100 yards away, and there were ships all round us as far as the eye could see. We sailed a zigzag course to avoid the U-boats, and every five minutes a bell would sound and the ship did a ninety degree turn, and five minutes later ninety degrees back. This meant that the boat sailing alongside us would be behind us, and the next change of direction in front of us.

During the first three weeks we had ten action stations when U-boats were close, and I had to go up to the bow of the ship to a large room which was to be my dressing station. I used to pass the time playing Patience while the other doctor there was a seasick expert. Twice the action stations came in the evening and I was in Blues (regimental 'undress' worn by officers in the evening). There were about ten doctors on the ship at other dressing stations. I am a very good sailor and have never been seasick, but I couldn't smoke my pipe because when I did, it made me feel sick. After the first ten days the sea calmed down. The only exercise we did was what we called 'running on the spot' or marking time. However, I strained my Achilles tendon and could not do any more.

All the Bays' officers had Blues and so did I, so we changed every evening for dinner. The food was excellent, with soup, curry (we had Indian cooks), main course and pudding. After dinner we played Bridge. We called at Freetown, but we did not go ashore. Then we crossed the Equator. The captain of the ship said 'King Neptune wishes to drink a toast with you' and we all drank to King Neptune, and found it was sea water. The men had a boxing tournament in a ring fixed up on deck and all the officers went to watch. One officer went and shot himself in the toilet; he was not a Bays officer. Earlier, the Padre and I were having tea with him and another officer when he got up and said 'I know what you are thinking' and walked off. I said to the Padre 'he is going to do something, you will see.' And a few days later he shot himself. I went to the Padre and said 'he has done it.' I should have done something to stop him, but I don't know what could have been done short of locking him up somewhere.

We arrived at Cape Town and were four days there and we went ashore. When we landed, ladies with cars took men for rides. We went up to the top of Table Mountain. We went to the cinema. We stood for a minute's silence at 12:00 noon every day in honour of the war dead. We drank the drink of the country.

We sailed on, and in the Indian Ocean, an aircraft carrier *The New Australia*, left us, sailed past with all its 1,000 sailors lining the deck. We heard later that it was sunk with all hands. We called at Aden but were not allowed ashore. We looked at the land and were reminded of *The Barren Rocks of Aden* (a famous bagpipe tune); by gum, it was barren! We sailed up the Red Sea, which was not red, and arrived at Suez. We saw the sunken wreck of *The Georgic*, a fine passenger ship. I had last seen her at Liverpool. We landed at Suez, after nine weeks at sea, almost a whole term at school. We went by train to Alexandria, and then when the tanks arrived (they had arrived by the risky Mediterranean route), we set off for the Western desert. (**Map 3.**) When we arrived at Sidi Barrani, we were told that the Japs had bombed Pearl Harbor and America was in the war. So it must have been 7 December 1941.

The most striking characteristic of the North African desert is its size. The main British base at Alexandria, in the east, is 1,100 miles distance in a straight line from Tripoli in the west. Tripoli was the capital of the Italian colony of Libya, and the British army's ultimate objective. The route taken by the troops in trucks and tanks and on foot was longer than 1,100 miles because there is a large bend in the Mediterranean coast. About half way between Alexandria and Tripoli, the coast changes direction slightly to the northwest, and then south round the coast of Cyrenaica for 150 miles, before returning to its westward course. The fighting all took place within sixty miles of the Mediterranean. This means that the long narrow strip of desert that saw all the military activity covered an area larger than the Indian sub-continent. This field of battle was sparsely occupied: far more so than the European battlefields. Many units found that the desert was often an empty place. (**Plates 9, 17, 18, 19, 34, 37, 38, 39.**)

The narrow metalled coast road west of Alexandria passed through a number of coastal towns of varying sizes that were to become famous during the course of the campaign: a series of battles that lasted for thirty-four months. Since the Queen's Bays only arrived at the end of 1941, they had missed more than a year of fighting before their arrival. The main towns or settlements that became famous are as follows, with their approximate distances in miles from Alexandria: El Alamein (60), Mersa Matruh (180), Sidi Barrani (230), and Sollum (295). Then there was the 'Wire', the flimsy barrier separating Egypt and Libya, about 300 miles from Alexandria. (**Plate 29.**) The Libyan towns west of the 'Wire', again with their approximate distances from Alexandria, are Bardia (320), Tobruk (400), Gazala (450), Benghazi (750), El Agheila (870), and Beda Fomm (880). Tobruk and Benghazi were ports that could handle cargo ships. Supplies could be landed by sea, something that made it much easier to unload ammunition and all the other things an army needs to conduct war. When this could not be done, advancing troops had to rely on trucks driving along indifferent roads for hundreds of miles from the German base in Tripoli or the British base in Alexandria. (**Map 3.**)

The desert is actually on a plateau, with an escarpment leading down to the Mediterranean. This is only about 200ft. from escarpment to sea level, but the passes were the scenes of hard battles. The most important was the winding Halfaya ('Hellfire') Pass, four miles south of the town of Sollum. (**Plate 30.**) The pass itself was exceptionally difficult for tanks to negotiate. The terrain of the desert is monotonous and from the air seems featureless. But this is a misleading impression, since there are large sand dunes, and various areas of difficult 'going', where the wheels and tracks of vehicles could sink into the soft sand. There were also open rock surfaces that were hard on tank tracks, and rocky surfaces coated with fine sand. Worst of all are salt pans that are in danger of collapsing and causing a vehicle to sink. These features were not marked on the maps that the armies used, and they emphasized the need for reconnaissance before tanks and trucks moved forward. The REME detachments in the armoured regiments became adept at towing ditched vehicles out of the sand. Another unpleasant complication became worse as the desert war proceeded. These were anti-personnel and anti-tank mines sown in clusters, in 'fields' nicknamed the 'devil's gardens'. They were a great hazard when British infantry began their attack during the Battle of El Alamein.

The desert during the war was home to a small number of nomadic Bedouin families, who moved from place to place in search of water and places during the spring where there were patches of greenery where their animals could graze. The Bedouin families possessed a few camels and other livestock, and their womenfolk were secluded from any outsiders who were encountered. (**Plate 18.**) These nomads occasionally offered information about enemy positions: a task that they carried out for both the British and the German/Italian armies. The Bedouin also accepted canned or dry army rations in exchange for eggs, which the troops on both sides could fry on the sun-baked metal of their tanks. The bartering was of course carried out in sign language.

The desert was the home of gazelle and the Jerboa, the desert rat (who gave its name to the 7th Armoured Division). There were also beetles, scorpions and flies that clustered densely around food and did an excellent job of spreading bacteria. These were the cause of serious digestive problems as well as the desert sores that seemed to take forever to heal. The summertime temperature was often 120 degrees Fahrenheit. This temperature made tanks extremely uncomfortable homes, and they were often referred to as permanent dusty ovens. The effect of the heat was made even worse by the frequent *Khamsin*, the desert sandstorms that reduced visibility to zero and made flying and driving extremely hazardous, not only because it was difficult to see one's way but also because engines became clogged. All vehicles had sand filters, but although these were effective for normal desert driving, they could not handle sandstorms. The fine sand permeated fabrics and coated everything in sight, especially food, and irritated unprotected skin. (**Plate 15.**) The sandstorms tended to depress morale. The weather was also variable. It was occasionally wet, and nights in the desert were very cold in winter and sometimes also in summer. This is why so many photographs exist of British soldiers in serge battledress and winter overcoats more commonly worn on active service in Europe.

The worst problem in the desert was water. The ration per head was half a gallon per day, and this had to provide for a man's personal use and also his contribution to the radiator of the vehicle in which he travelled. Soldiers in the 8th Army showed considerable ingenuity in recycling water, to fill radiators. Soldiers newly arrived in the desert soon discovered that it was extravagant to drink water out of their bottles. It was normally consumed as tea, the standard British army beverage. (They would have been mystified by the plentiful numbers of over-size bottles of purified water that the American soldiers carried during the Iraq campaign of the 21st Century.)

There were two important reasons why soldiers had to learn to navigate in the desert. The first was to manoevre to seek out and engage the enemy, who was not necessarily visible. The second was to ensure a regular supply of the stores that troops need to fight battles: food, water, ammunition, and POL (petrol, oil and lubricants), and also to find ways of evacuating the wounded and sick. Disaster was always possible if sub-units or individual vehicles became separated from their main columns. When the regiment or the squadrons were concentrated, there were separate messes for the officers, the senior NCOs and the rank-and-file. (**Plate 22.**) In the desert, the crew of each tank or vehicle was responsible for their own cooking, and they usually cooked their rations on improvised petrol stoves. (**Plate 23.**) Because the number of vehicles was so large and their demands for fuel so enormous, the troops were not as frugal about conserving petrol as they were about economizing on water. British petrol cans were square with sharp edges, and tended to leak. The German five-gallon ones, nicknamed 'Jerrycans', were better from every point of view. Before long, the 8th Army was using Jerrycans, either 'liberated' German ones or similar ones of British manufacture. The British army in the 21st Century still uses Jerrycans.

JSM Journal

For desert navigation you require: (i) a map; (ii) a pencil; (iii) a ruler; (iv) an India rubber; (v) dividers or compasses; (vi) a protractor; (vii) an odometer; (viii) a prismatic compass; (ix) a means of transport; (x) a navigation ledger or log book. The log book has a number of columns, each devoted to: the starting map reference, the starting odometer reading, the date, the time, the distance to travel, the compass bearing, the final odometer reading, and the final map reference.

On the log book, you indicate the date and time, and the initial odometer reading. You mark the destination with a dot on the map. You then connect the destination from your present position with a pencil line. You measure the exact distance with the dividers. With the protractor, you find the compass bearing on which you have to travel, and the distance to be travelled. You then proceed on the compass bearing until you reach the place calculated to be the final odometer reading. You are now at your new destination.

The sun compass (Gnomon) is very useful when there is sunshine most of the time. (**Plate 14.**) It is more accurate than an ordinary prismatic compass in a car or truck, because it is not influenced by the metal of the vehicle which always causes the needle to point north. (The tanks have large compasses which are insulated from the metal.)

The sun compass is a metal disc which is placed on top of the bonnet of the vehicle so that it can be seen by the driver or a passenger. A metal rod sticks up out of the centre of the disc, and another metal disc lies on top of the first one and can be rotated and fixed with a small screw. It is white metal and has a dark groove at one point from the centre of the perimeter. To use the sun compass, first you have to use an ordinary prismatic compass to line up the vehicle on the compass bearing established for the direction you have to go. To do this, one man stands ten yards behind the vehicle, telling the driver to move slowly forward, turning the vehicle until it is facing precisely the right way. Then the disc of the sun compass is turned until the shadow of the metal rod lies on the groove, and the disc is fixed in that position.

The driver (or passenger) then keeps the shadow of the rod on the groove, and he can thus travel for five miles or twenty minutes before he has to take a fresh bearing, by which time the sun will have moved a degree or two to the west.

I used the sun compass when we were near Tobruk. One morning, the Colonel asked me to go to the Tobruk hospital and see how one of our men, who was wounded, was doing. He also said the regiment was moving in twenty minutes, travelling thirty-five miles south-west, on a bearing of 240 degrees. I had to follow later. After leaving the hospital, my driver and I in my scout car were alone in the desert. Following my instructions, we hoped to find the tanks at the end. We relied entirely on the sun compass (on which I had very little faith!) but we were soon to find out how efficient it was. We never saw a sign of man or beast for about three hours when we sighted the tanks, and we gave a sigh of relief. Maximum speed in the desert was 26mph.

The 1st Armoured Division was from most points of view well prepared for war. It had an appropriate balance of fighting arms, and the men were well trained and as well equipped as was possible with the generally inferior British tanks. Morale was high. The rest of the 8th Army, who had spent the whole of 1941 in the desert, had experienced a war of movement. It had first made a long advance to the west, then a similarly long retreat to the east, and two abortive attacks followed by Operation *Crusader*, which made strong initial progress. 1st Armoured Division arrived in December 1941 shortly after *Crusader's* forward movement had lost steam, and Rommel was beginning his riposte. This was to herald six months of fierce battles across the desert. The to-and-fro of fighting in North Africa had already become known, using an appropriately British horse-racing metaphor, as 'the Benghazi Handicap' which eventually had five laps: east to west, west to east, east to west, west to east, and finally (after the Battle of El Alamein) east to west again. The Afrika Korps, experienced, well-armed and well-led and relying on quality rather than quantity, had been renamed in August 1941 and was now known as the Panzergruppe Afrika since the German troops were actually in a minority, although a substantial one. The 1st Armoured Division had not yet encountered them, and it is not surprising that the inexperienced British division would make little impact on the forthcoming battle, which was the beginning of the fourth lap of the desert war, Rommel's fierce assault from the Benghazi sector.

CHAPTER 5

TOTAL WAR ON THREE BATTLEFRONTS

The Second World War, the most monstrous conflict in history, was fought worldwide on three battlefronts, sea, air and land. In 1940 the sea battlefront was the Atlantic. The air battlefront was the skies over Germany, where Britain felt strong enough to take the initiative in bombing German targets, most (although not all) of which were militarily important. The British army had no obvious battlefront in Europe since it had been ejected from France, but it nevertheless carried out Commando raids on the coast of the occupied countries: sharp pinpricks that irritated the Germans and caused them to spread their defences. The only substantial battlefield for the British army was the North African desert. The enemy was Mussolini, Germany's junior partner; and Italy's colony Libya became the cockpit of the desert war. Churchill spoke for the British people in their attitude to the war. He and they refused to consider inaction such as had led to the Phoney War of 1940. The British war effort on sea, air and land was uncompromisingly aggressive, despite the weaknesses caused by years of inadequate rearmament during the 1930s, not to speak of all the military equipment lost at Dunkirk.

The Benghazi Handicap

Mussolini was fixated on Egypt. If, by using Libya as a springboard, the Italian army managed to crush the British and capture the Suez Canal, Mussolini would emulate the *Wehrmacht's* achievement in slicing through Northern France in 1940.

But this was not to be. The Italian army was no *Wehrmacht*. It was not well-led, nor were most of the soldiers well-trained and well-equipped (although a few were). Most important of all, the soldiers' hearts were not in the fight. Latins were perhaps more cynical than Teutons in their attitudes to grandiloquent political leaders, and the evidence of poor morale was the tens of thousands of Italian soldiers who were captured by the British during their successful advance in January 1941: the first lap of the Benghazi Handicap. Newsreels of the long lines of Italian prisoners brought great cheer to the beleaguered British population.

The British army worldwide was organized in three Commands: Home, Middle East, and India. Middle East Command, based in Cairo, was responsible for a number of regions, the most important of which were Egypt (on the Libyan frontier); East Africa (the battlefront formed by the Italian colonies of Ethiopia and Eritrea); and the Arab countries of the Middle East. As 1941 progressed, so did the number of trouble spots, and military forces also had to be deployed in Greece, Crete, Iraq and Syria. As a result, the military resources of Middle East Command soon became seriously stretched: a difficulty that affected directly the fortunes of the British army in the North African desert.

The Mediterranean and the Middle East were critically important to Britain. The Mediterranean was the sea route to Britain's most important possession, India, and because of this the Suez Canal was sometimes called the carotid artery of the British Empire. In the middle of the Mediterranean, the island of Malta stood like an unsinkable aircraft carrier, a constant threat to the supplies and reinforcements sent to the Axis forces in North Africa, and for that reason subject to punishing air attacks from Italy. Aside from the Mediterranean as a route to the east, Iran and Iraq were crucial sources of oil, transported mainly through the Persian Gulf. Without this supply it was impossible for Britain to wage war. The sinking of large numbers of tankers carrying American oil across the Atlantic continued to be one of the greatest hazards to the Allied cause, and this emphasized the importance of oil from the Middle East: a situation that is much the same during the 21st Century.

Middle East Command was headed by General Wavell, who had been appointed just before the war began. He was one of the top men in the British army. After the fall of France he was considered one of three senior commanders – the others being Dill, the CIGS, and Brooke, Home Army C-in-C – who would have to carry the strain of conducting the war on land. Wavell was a recognized leader and strategist. As a product of Winchester, the most intellectual of the British public schools, he had a speculative mind. He published books about the 1918 Palestine Campaign in which he had served as a staff officer; he delivered a series of celebrated lectures on Generalship at Cambridge University (which were later translated into German by Rommel); and like few other generals he was a connoisseur of poetry. But Wavell also had an unusual personality: extremely taciturn, he did not enjoy debate and kept his own counsel. Discussions with Wavell sometimes meant long silences. These qualities were to cause considerable problems with Winston Churchill, who thrived on the cut-and-thrust of vigorous argument. The Prime Minister was also Minister of Defence and directed British military strategy, with close advice from the Chiefs-of-Staff Committee, whose counsel he ultimately had to accept, normally after a fight. Churchill had the habit of writing sharp memoranda demanding action, and a number went to the Commanders-in-Chief in the field. Wavell was to be the target of many of these.

During the course of the war, Wavell worked more continuously on all cylinders than most generals. He held four top commands: Middle East, India, ABDA (the ad hoc alliance of American, British, Dutch and Australian forces aimed at blocking the ferocious assaults of the Japanese), and in 1943 the political leadership of the Indian Empire, as Viceroy. From a historical perspective, none of these commands was successful, and there was a reason. Despite his many talents and although he became a Field Marshal, Wavell lacked the gift that was so highly esteemed by Napoleon: *luck*. He was usually in the wrong place at the wrong time.

The Italians entered the war in June 1940. But the 150,000 men in the Italian 10th Army made very little progress during the following months, despite Mussolini's ambitious posturing. The Italians eventually breached the 'Wire' separating Libya and Egypt and reached fifty miles beyond it to the small Egyptian port of Sidi Barrani. Here they sat on their hands behind fixed defenses. It did not take Wavell long to realize that the Italians at Sidi Barrani offered a great opportunity for a counter-stroke. (**Map 3**.) What Wavell had in mind was a five-day raid into Libya to establish a psychological advantage over the Italians and keep the upper hand. Wavell gave the job to Lieutenant General O'Connor, an energetic tactician whose 'grip' was as strong as that of a German opponent who would shortly appear on the scene, Lieutenant General Rommel. O'Connor commanded a formation shortly to be called XIII Corps. It was made up of the 7th Armoured Division and a division of infantry, which included some Matilda tanks: 30,000 men in all.

The raid began on 9 December 1940, and cut through the Italians who offered very little resistance. The British advanced along the coast, taking the port of Tobruk (a place that was later to become important). Then the 7th Armoured Division charged across the desert through the large 'bulge' of Cyrenaica (eastern Libya), and reached the road at Beda Fomm, south of Benghazi, and in doing this surrounded the Italian troops to the north. The capital of Cyrenaica, Benghazi, quickly fell. The expedition had become a much bigger operation than a raid. Benghazi is 300 miles west of the 'Wire', and 700 miles short of Tripoli, the capital of Libya. O'Connor then moved along the coast beyond Beda Fomm and occupied advanced positions at El Agheila, 150 miles beyond Benghazi. He was naturally anxious to surge forward to capture Tripoli, but unfortunately urgent alternative calls on Wavell's resources made this an impossible plan. Nevertheless, the first (east to west) lap of the Benghazi Handicap had been an unexpected triumph, with the Italian 10th Army destroyed and with 130,000 prisoners 'in the bag'. (**Map 4.**)

During this unexpectedly successful venture, Wavell was facing mounting problems. He commanded a total of 300,000 men, a force that seemed to Churchill to be large enough for all the jobs – many of which were occupying static garrisons – for which Wavell was responsible. A barrage of messages had arrived from London during the autumn of 1940, and these all urged Wavell to be aggressive. However, he was at the time making plans for O'Connor's raid, and everything was being handled with professionalism and in total secrecy. Churchill greeted the victory with enthusiasm. But he still thought that Wavell had men to spare. During the whole course of the war, and in particular when the Americans came on the scene, Churchill never appreciated the need for a long administrative 'tail' to wage with total success mechanized warfare covering long distances. Another reason why Churchill's view was flawed was that the Middle East command was a predominantly infantry force. There was only one fully-trained armoured division, the 7th, the 'Desert Rats', who had done so well under O'Connor. The 2nd Armoured Division was in Egypt and untrained, and the 1st Armoured Division was not to arrive until December 1941. As was soon apparent, the war in the North African desert was going to be an armoured conflict, with the Germans making the running.

Even when O'Connor's operation was under way, Wavell removed one infantry division and replaced it with a less experienced one. The division that came from O'Connor was sent to East Africa, where it contributed to the totally successful campaign that drove the Italians out of Ethiopia and Eritrea. However, O'Connor's force was shortly to be weakened in an even more serious way.

The German army was active in the Balkans, providing support for the Italians after their not very successful invasion of Albania and their tentative attack on Greece. It was inevitable that the Germans would move on Greece in order to strengthen their position in the Mediterranean. The German invasion began on 6 April 1941, but before this had happened a substantial force of Australian and New Zealand troops had arrived in Greece, implementing Churchill's decision that Britain's position in the Mediterranean had to be protected. He also felt an obligation to the Greeks who were being attacked by a much stronger enemy. The troops who were sent to Greece naturally came from Wavell's command. As a result, keeping up the strength of XIII Corps in Libya became a matter of improvisation. Across the Mediterranean, the Commonwealth force was expelled from Greece with considerable losses. A number of the men reached Crete, where they were overcome by a German airborne assault. Wavell soon had two losers on his hands.

After O'Connor's triumph in Cyrenaica, XIII Corps was faced almost immediately by a dangerous threat. In the first week in February, units of the German Afrika Korps began to arrive in Tripoli. The force was commanded by Lieutenant General Rommel, fresh from his dramatic victories during the campaign against France in May/June 1940. Rommel quickly made his presence felt, and his dramatic successes on the desert battlefield made him a hero to his own men and the German public. At the same time the British gave him grudging admiration and caused some to question the capacity of their own leaders.

The Afrika Korps had been sent to the desert for a broader reason than Hitler's wish to shore up Mussolini's African empire. Hitler and his senior officers visualized enormous advantages if the German army managed to capture the Middle Eastern oilfields. At the back of many minds in the German High Command was the possibility of cooperation between the Afrika Korps and German forces attacking east from German occupied territory and then changing direction south through Turkey or Russia. As was obvious from *Mein Kampf*, Hitler saw Russia as Germany's ultimate enemy. This was to become only too apparent in June 1941 when he launched Operation *Barbarossa*, the massive German assault on Russia.

Rommel was subordinate to the Italian Commander-in-Chief since the Axis Force of 165,000 men was two-thirds Italian. But despite Rommel's lower position in the hierarchy, he exercised *de facto* authority over the Germans and Italians from first to last. The German formations were better led, better trained and better equipped than the Italians. Nevertheless under Rommel's leadership, the Italians became doughtier fighters than they had been during the months before the arrival of the Afrika Korps. The Afrika Korps itself was made up of armour and infantry, with a strong air component of Stuka dive bombers and Messerschmitt fighters. (**Plates 36, 35.**) On 4 March 1941, the first armoured regiment (equivalent to a British brigade) arrived in Tripoli, with 155 tanks, 108 of them the Panzer III and Panzer IV models. These all decisively out-gunned the British armour, a situation that continued for more than a year until American Grants arrived. These were a match for the German tanks although not for the 88mm anti-tank guns.

Before his arrival in Africa, Rommel knew nothing about the desert and spent days exploring it from the air, using a low-flying spotter aircraft. 700 miles separated Tripoli from the foremost British positions, so that before battle an enormous approach march would be needed through a difficult desert environment, with heavy demands on gasoline and other supplies. With his characteristic drive, Rommel forced the pace. Parties of German reconnaissance units were soon moving into Cyrenaica.

As early as January 1941, a group of armoured cars and motorcycles suddenly came across a sub-unit of XIII Corps: an alarming surprise for the British. In order to provide a base of further operations, on 24 March 1941 the Afrika Korps captured and fortified El Agheila, although by then the battle with XIII Corps was under way. XIII Corps had been significantly weakened when the untried 2nd Armoured Division had arrived to replace the veteran 7th Armoured Division, sent back to Egypt to lick its wounds.

Rommel was now helped by a remarkable stroke of luck. The expedition to Greece was commanded by the GOC of the army in Egypt, Lieutenant General Wilson. O'Connor was brought back to take his place and was replaced at XIII Corps by a brave but much less competent officer. With the Afrika Korps acting with dangerous aggressiveness, O'Connor returned to XIII Corps in the hope of pulling chestnuts out of the fire. In a brief situation of confusion on the battlefield, O'Connor and his replacement were caught by German units on 7 April and put into a prisoner-of-war cage. Shortly before this the same had happened to the commander of the 2nd Armoured Division.

There was now no stopping Rommel. It had taken him six weeks – from his arrival on 12 February to 24 March – to occupy El Agheila. He then took Benghazi on 3 April and reached the port of Tobruk on 10 April. He attacked it unsuccessfully, but he cordoned it off and began an epic siege that was to last until 10 December 1941. On 15 May 1941, Rommel reached the 'Wire' and entered Egypt at Halfaya and Sollum. The second (west to east) lap of the Benghazi Handicap had become a considerable although not decisive German victory. (**Map 4.**)

Wavell knew very well, without the regular and increasingly urgent prompting from London, that Rommel had to be stopped. With his attenuated force, Wavell wasted no time on attacking the Halfaya/Sollum position. The operation, codenamed *Brevity*, was swiftly defeated by German counter-strokes. *Brevity* was followed on 15 June by a more ambitious operation in the same sector, Operation *Battleaxe*. By this time, the British and German armies had received many new tanks to replace losses, and the British assaulted with an unprecedented weight of armour: 400 machines. Rommel was helped by his army's ability to intercept British signals traffic, and he met the British assaults instantly. Mobility was always an impressive characteristic of the Afrika Korps. The high level of activity on both sides had been self-cancelling, and on 19 June both armies were back at their starting positions on the Egyptian frontier. *Brevity* and *Battleaxe* lacked the punch to overcome the opposition. There was for the moment no third lap of the Benghazi Handicap.

By the end of May 1941, Churchill was becoming totally disenchanted with Wavell. There had been too many failures, and Churchill had little understanding of the difficulties that Wavell had faced. The Commander-in-Chief's attitude also continued to irritate, since the peremptory messages from London did not stimulate equally vigorous responses. Wavell just got on with the job. On 5 July 1941, he was replaced by General Auchinleck, who was at the time Commander-in-Chief, India. There was a direct exchange of appointments, and Wavell flew to New Delhi, where he was shortly going to encounter a new raft of troubles: the outcome of the Japanese entry into the war in December 1941.

'Like a Noble Stag'

Auchinleck was in his late fifties and was an Indian army officer with considerable experience of command. Before the war he had been known as a military reformer stemming from his knowledge of both the British and Indian armies. There were differences between the two: barriers in the minds of many officers. The Indian army attracted many of the best cadets from the Royal Military College, Sandhurst, because India offered higher pay and a lower cost of living. The British officers commanded native-born troops and gained valuable experience in fighting frontier wars. The 4th Indian Division fought splendidly in the North African campaign and in Italy, and during this time the Indian and British armies fought closely together.

With the coming of war Auchinleck (nicknamed the 'Auk') was appointed to lead a division, and then – most unusually – was posted to England to command IV Corps, which was made up entirely of British units. In May 1940 IV Corps was dispatched to Norway, and after a confused campaign Auchinleck and his men were forced to evacuate the country. This débâcle was the result of a flawed overall strategy (something that had been established before Auchinleck's arrival), made worse by too few men and much obsolete equipment (e.g. biplane aircraft).

After his return to Britain, he commanded a sector of the English coast to guard against a German invasion, where he had severe disagreements with Montgomery. Auchinleck then returned to India as Commander-in-Chief. This was a very important appointment although it only became critical after the seemingly-unstoppable Japanese assaults in the Far East. Soon after Auchinleck's return to India, he moved very quickly to squash a German-inspired insurrection in Iraq. This was in May 1941, and it greatly impressed Churchill. The fact that he was successfully commanding soldiers in action in the Middle East was persuasive in Churchill's eyes, and led to Auchinleck's move to Cairo to take over from Wavell. During his command of the 8th Army, Auchinleck was associated with two successes and one serious failure, when the 8th Army was pushed all the way back to El Alamein. He had to take responsibility for the latter although the blame lay equally with his subordinates. In August 1942, Churchill realized that Auchinleck had to be relieved. He hated doing this, and said afterwards that it was like shooting a noble stag. All that was in the future.

Shortly after Auchinleck's arrival in Cairo in May 1941 Churchill resumed his game of applying pressure on his Commander-in-Chief to go after Rommel. Britain still lacked allies who could provide material and moral support, although this situation unexpectedly changed in June 1941, when Germany invaded Russia. This should have relaxed some of the load that Britain single-handedly had been carrying, but Stalin very soon started applying pressure of his own for the British forces to get to grips with the enemy in every way possible, and at the same time ship to the Soviet Union aircraft, tanks, guns and all types of supplies that the British also desperately needed.

At this early stage, because Auchinleck was an experienced professional and did not lack moral courage in standing up to his political masters, Churchill was unable to force him to take action. Auchinleck insisted that his force (formally established as the 8th Army on 18 September 1941) should be properly trained and equipped. Rommel had serious logistical problems because consignments from Europe of equipment and supplies, particularly oil, were being impeded by attacks on his shipping by the Royal Navy and the Royal Air Force. Wavell's unsuccessful advance against the Afrika Korps, Operation *Battleaxe*, had foundered on 17 June and it was two months after this that Auchinleck took the offensive with Operation *Crusader*, launched on 18 August. The third phase of the Benghazi Handicap was about to begin. Rommel, despite his lack of reinforcements, was actually on the point of assaulting the Tobruk garrison just before Auchinleck struck.

The *Crusader* plan was to demonstrate a serious flaw in Auchinleck's military capacity. He correctly realized that the (newly titled) 8th Army had to have a leader with the ability and the freedom to make his own tactical plans. The problem was that Auchinleck picked an unsuitable commander in Lieutenant General Cunningham, who had just won a decisive victory over the Italian army in East Africa. Unfortunately this did not qualify him to conduct a successful armoured campaign in the desert against Rommel.

Cunningham had been allocated two corps, XIII and XXX, with a total of 118,000 men in five divisions. The armour was made up of 7th Armoured Division (in XXX Corps) and 22nd Armoured Brigade (in XIII Corps). The plan of attack was admirably simple, but it was rigid. The general direction of the advance was from east to west. On the right, XIII Corps was ordered to invade Libya and take up strong defensive positions of both sides of the Frontier, at Sollum and Halfaya Pass, the 'Wire' and Sidi Omar. Later it was to advance on Tobruk. XXX Corps was ordered to protect the left, and sweep around to approach Tobruk from the south, at which stage the Tobruk garrison would break out. Cunningham's plan aimed for one of two objectives: to push Rommel back to Benghazi, or else to encircle the Afrika Korps, and with its divisions enclosed in a pocket to bring them to battle on ground that Cunningham chose. (**Map 5.**)

7th Armoured Division had 491 tanks, twice as many as the two Panzer Divisions opposing it. Most of the German tanks outclassed the British. A similarly serious problem was that British commanders suffered from complete misunderstandings about their enemy. While Rommel had a good deal of faith in the Italian divisions, Cunningham and his senior subordinates made the mistake of not taking them seriously. The British also had no understanding of German tactics, which were not based on fighting tank-on-tank, but directed at luring British armour into nests of 88mm anti-tank guns closely supported by infantry. All ranks of the German army were rigorously drilled into using their own initiative and automatically moving *upward* to take responsibility from men who had been knocked out in a fluid battle which was typical of desert conditions. In this respect they were superior to the 8th Army, although Auchinleck had laid great emphasis on conventional training during the months he had been in North Africa. The 8th Army adhered to the traditional rigid 'top down' system, like Cunningham's tactical plan for the invasion of Libya.

Operation *Crusader* completed the third lap of the Benghazi Handicap, but it was very hard going for the 8th Army and took six weeks of sometimes brutal fighting. The operation covered the whole length of Cyrenaica, 300 miles in a direct line from the frontier 'Wire' to Benghazi. The action took place within sixty miles of the North African coast, making an area of 18,000 square miles. This is the battlefield in which about 240,000 soldiers fought (i.e. thirteen men per square mile), so it was not surprising that the scenery often looked empty to many of them. The main scenes of individual battles were as follows, moving from east to west: Sollum and Halfaya Pass; the 'Wire'; Fort Capuzzo; Sidi Omar; Sidi Rezegh airfield; Tobruk; Gazala; Benghazi; Msus airfield; El Agheila.

Rommel commanded an army of about the same size as the British. Surprisingly he did not immediately react to Operation *Crusader*. He believed that it was a feint. But he soon saw what was going on, and his counter-attacks began. 7th Armoured Division was vulnerable because it had become dispersed, and the Italians had been underestimated by the British. Under Rommel's personal command, German and Italian divisions hit the 7th Armoured Division at Sidi Rezegh, twenty miles south-east of Tobruk, in the hottest armoured clash ever seen in the desert. The Germans had better tanks, and used them more effectively in cooperation with their infantry and artillery. The British, whose vehicles had insufficient armoured protection and whose guns were too light to outfight the Germans, were reduced to making 'hell for leather' charges in the ancient cavalry tradition. This was not a hopeless tactic although it was an expensive one. Such charges brought the British tanks close enough to the enemy for the British 2-pounder guns to have some effect.

Rommel's speedy reaction to the British invasion of Libya meant that he had acquired something of priceless importance: the initiative on the battlefield. Cunningham still kept to his original plan, which was becoming less and less relevant because Rommel was a supreme opportunist. The British defeat at Sidi Rezegh, with the loss of half the 8th Army's tanks, had a devastating effect on Cunningham. This battle was a supreme example of a to-and-fro engagement, with maximum confusion.

> *Peter Lovegrove, 'Not Least in the Crusade'*
>
> Some of the personnel had the extraordinary experience of serving both sides as the tide of battle ebbed and flowed. At Sidi Rezegh during the confused fighting of October 1941, one advanced surgical center was 'captured' and 'recaptured' four times, and was even visited by Rommel, the German commander.

On 23 November, Cunningham asked Auchinleck to come up from Cairo, and when they met Cunningham proposed a retreat back to Egypt. The Commander-in-Chief demonstrated his usual coolness and strength in order to stiffen Cunningham's resolution, and ordered the 8th Army commander to continue his offensive.

But things were taking place on the other side of the hill. On 24 November Rommel, brimming with confidence, assembled his Panzers and charged east, in a manoeuvre that became immortalized with the name 'The Dash for the "Wire"'. By doing this, he was weakening the force holding the Sidi Rezegh battlefield, which the British were slowly reoccupying, and removing disabled tanks for repair. The 8th Army was still a force to be reckoned with (as Rommel was soon to find out). Nevertheless in Egypt, with the news that Rommel was pushing in the direction of Cairo, panic broke out. Convoys of soft-skinned vehicles began rushing east, with Rommel not far behind. The positions on both sides of the 'Wire' that XIII Corps had so recently fortified were taken back by Rommel, and British, German and Italian units and small parties of troops became mixed up in bizarre confusion.

Rommel received no reward for his audacity. His extended line of communication had lengthened, increasing the difficulty of keeping up his flow of supplies. Rommel himself was isolated for many hours and lost control of the battle. Auchinleck was not in the least fazed by Rommel's remarkable initiative and forecast correctly that the advance could not be sustained. Cunningham however became increasingly jumpy, and this led Auchinleck to decide that he had to be relieved. This was done immediately. His successor was a most unexpected man, Major General Ritchie, who was Deputy Chief-of-Staff at General Headquarters in Cairo and a competent and experienced staff officer. But he had not commanded many troops, having only led an infantry division for a brief period after Dunkirk. He was solid and unhurried, and in this respect was different from the more febrile Cunningham. Ritchie's appointment was the second time that Auchinleck had chosen an inadequate commander for the 8th Army. He was soon out of his depth, and Auchinleck had to spend time with him giving support and advice. The Commander-in-Chief was forced in effect to take control of the 8th Army.

On 27 November 1941 good news arrived. The Tobruk garrison, after an epic siege lasting eight months, managed to break out of its perimeter, and on 10 December the 8th Army was in possession of the port. Rommel now received the bad news that tank reinforcements from Europe that he was expecting would not arrive in Tripoli for some weeks. He decided on an orderly retreat by the complete Panzerarmee Afrika, in the firm expectation that he would soon regain the initiative. By Christmas 1941 Rommel's force was back at El Agheila, which meant in turn that the 8th Army's line of communication was so extended that the flow of supplies would be extremely difficult. In January 1942, four Panzer companies (approximately equivalent to a complete British armoured regiment) arrived in Africa. This meant that Rommel felt ready to attack.

The third lap of the Benghazi Handicap was now over. The Germans and Italians had lost 38,000 killed, wounded and missing; the 8th Army, 17,500. The general rule of battle is that attackers virtually always suffer more casualties than defenders, often in the ratio of three to one. Operation *Crusader* was planned as a British offensive. But the greater losses on the enemy side were proof that over the course of the battle the British were actually the defenders and the Germans and Italians held the whip hand. Rommel now prepared his men for a resumption of battle, spending his time reorganizing and collecting all the reinforcements that he was able to bring out of a pretty empty cupboard. In January 1942, the fourth lap of the Benghazi Handicap was launched. It was to be another hard-fought struggle. It was at the beginning of this battle that the Queen's Bays arrived to play their part. (**Map 6.**)

The Queen's Bays Return to War

Although the Bays and the rest of the 2nd Armoured Brigade had landed in Egypt in early December 1941, they were not yet ready for battle. The engines of the tanks and trucks had to be inspected and overhauled, sand filters had to be installed, the exterior of the vehicles had to be sprayed with 'Desert Yellow' camouflage, and the guns had to be mounted, tested and fired. The Bays had forty-eight tanks, all with inadequate 2-pounder guns. There were thirty-one Cruisers, mainly Crusaders, which were allocated to 'A' and 'B' Squadrons. (**Plate 10.**) These were plagued by breakdowns. 'C' Squadron received seventeen of the American Stuarts, which were light tanks and were mechanically reliable. (**Plate 9.**) Stuarts were popular with their crews, who nicknamed them 'Honeys', although they were unfortunately no more heavily armed than British-built machines. The much better Grant tanks, with their 75mm guns, began to arrive in spring of 1942. (**Plate 11.**) The 75mm gun at last enabled the British armour to stand up to the Panzers.

The officers and men of the 2nd Armoured Brigade had to be indoctrinated into desert fighting because the 8th Army had by now developed its own way of living in the inhospitable desert environment, at the same time remaining constantly alert for aggressive German activity. All ranks had to learn how tanks and other vehicles should be clustered – not too close and not too distant – when they moved over ground, and how they should leaguer in defensive positions at night. These tasks were completed rapidly, and the regiment was on the move in mid-January 1942. (**Plates 26, 27, 28.**)

Although Britain had now been at war for more than two years, when the Bays went to Africa they were still an essentially pre-war Regular regiment. (Some of the officers and men had served when the regiment was still mounted.) The officers and soldiers in the ranks handled their tanks with great skill. They were highly trained for the field, within the limits of the tactical doctrine of the British army at the time. Morale was universally high. But the regiment was shortly to discover serious problems with their tanks, and for some months the regiment was handicapped for this reason.

An armored regiment was made up of about 660 all ranks, of whom five percent were officers. (The actual numbers at any time varied according to the numbers of casualties and reinforcements.) Dr. MacGill wrote word portraits of half the officers. Of these fifteen men, six were later to be killed, three others wounded, and one became a prisoner-of-war: a loss rate of two-thirds, only too typical of units of all British 'teeth arms'. During the war the Bays received many reinforcements to replace losses, and during this whole period twenty-four officers and 152 soldiers in the ranks lost their lives. Captain Lewis, the young doctor who replaced JSM before the Battle of El Alamein lost his life. Although more soldiers were killed than officers, the officers were more severely hit because of the higher proportion of fatalities out of the total officer strength. This was a normal pattern in armored, artillery and infantry units.

JSM Journal

> The reason my pen portraits are all about officers is because I was an officer and I lived with them all the time and got to know them all very well. I can even remember most of them individually after all this time. I did not see so much of the men and so did not get to know them, except for a few.
>
> **Colonel Tom Draffen.** (*JSM remembers him as – perhaps temporarily – a full Colonel. This was unusual because the virtually universal pattern was that units*

of all arms were commanded by Lieutenant Colonels.)
Colonel Draffen was a small dark man with a small
black moustache. He looked like Charlie Chaplin in
fact. No one dared mention Charlie Chaplin in the mess
in case he thought they were taking him off. Well, if
the tanks were stationary and not in action, sometimes
a man would come up with a message to the Colonel
when I was standing beside him, and if he did not know
the Colonel by sight he would stop in front of me and
salute me. I would have to tell him that I was *not* the
Colonel and point him out. We both had three badges
on the shoulder: I had three stars/pips, and the Colonel
had a crown and two stars. The Colonel was treated
like a king. Everyone stood up when he came into the
mess and no one spoke to him unless he spoke first. I
was in a unique position because I was only attached to
the Bays. I was not one of *his* officers. He could not get
too friendly with any of them or it might be thought he
was a favourite. He had to treat them all alike. But with
me it was different: he could chat with me as much as he
liked and not be accused of favouritism. We had a lot of
conferences and he confided in me often. We were both
keen on Bridge and played every night before the battle
of Msus. The Colonel of the Bays was looked up to and
obeyed at all times. He and I were about the same age.
I was Jimmy when I was with the Bays, and I looked
more like a Colonel than the Colonel did.

Major Barclay. He commanded 'B' Squadron in late
January 1942, during one of our early engagements.
His tank was hit and set on fire: 'brewed up', as it was
called. He and his crew got out and hid in some scrub
a hundred yards away. After the Germans had gone and
all was quiet, he proceeded to walk to Benghazi, thirty-
two miles away. But all he had on the way was some
goat's milk from an Arab they came across with a herd
of goats. Major Barclay rejoined the regiment, and last
time I visited him he was the Colonel, replacing Colonel

Draffen. (*In late August 1942, Colonel Draffen was posted as Second-in-Command of 9ᵗʰ Armoured Brigade.*)

Major Peter Sykes. He was Second-in-Command in the desert and was a grand chap. When he was in France he was acting Colonel for a time, and it was he and I who sat on the two-seater loo in the open in the French village. In the desert he did the navigating, and I never saw him without a map case. He was badly wounded in the hip and I last saw him when he was being taken off in the ambulance.

Captain Dance. 'C' Troop of four tanks was commanded by Captain Dance, whose two subalterns were Lieutenant Glynn and Lieutenant Frankau.

Captain Godbold. He was the Quartermaster and named 'Fruity'. (*He had shared a cabin on the troop ship with JSM on the long voyage from Scotland to North Africa.*) He was fat and jolly and commanded 'B' Echelon and came up each night, navigating by compass, in the leading lorry. (*'B' Echelon is described later.*)

Captain Viscount Knebworth. He commanded 'B' Troop, and his subalterns were Lieutenant Halstead and Lieutenant Lumley. Lord Knebworth was 6 feet 8 inches tall, far too big for tanks. You want small men. He could hardly get into it. He was very friendly. I had to vaccinate him once in Britain. He was sitting on a chair, and when I was in the middle of doing it he keeled over in a dead faint! One day I had to go to his tent to get him to sign a document. This was at Warminster. He put his signature on it, with a single letter 'K'. I said 'Is this your signature?' He said 'Yes'. I said 'Well I could have signed it myself. Don't you think you should make it more difficult to copy?' He said 'I never thought of that. You are quite right'. When we were in the desert after I had left the Bays, when we were retreating from Tobruk, the Colonel came to me and said Lord Knebworth had been brought it and was running a temperature and would I look after him as I knew him well. So I travelled with him in the ambulance from Tobruk to Sidi Barrani. He lay on the stretcher on one side and I sat on the stretcher on the other and had a long chat, but he slept most of the time. He was kept for a few days at Sidi Barrani when he recovered from his 'flu or whatever it was. He returned to the regiment, and it was not long after that I heard that he was killed.

Captain Patchett. 'A' Troop was commanded by Captain Patchett, whose two subalterns were Lieutenant Rich and Lieutenant Pollock. Patchett was captured in January 1942.

Captain John de G Tatham-Warter. Captain Tatham-Warter was the regimental Adjutant. He was killed after he had been transferred to one of the squadrons as a Major to take command. When that happened, he was standing up on top of his tank looking at the enemy through his binoculars. He must have thought he was back at headquarters where he could have done that fairly safely.

Lieutenant Baker. He was in Major Barclay's Headquarters Troop, and was called Josephine, or JoJo. At that time on the London music hall stage there was a coloured singer called Josephine Baker (*who died in 1975*). Jo-Jo was killed in the desert five months later.

Lieutenant Frankau. Lieutenant Frankau was wounded and I was sent for. When I arrived in my scout car, he was sitting on the ground beside his tank. He did not look too bad, so I said 'Can you get into the scout car?' He said 'No'. I looked up and saw four German tanks coming towards us firing away. I said 'Here are four German tanks coming this way' and he was in the scout car before I could turn round! I had to cling to the front of it while I took him to the ambulance, since there is only room in the scout car for the driver and one passenger. All I got was a dent in my steel helmet where something must have hit it.

Lieutenant Glynn. Lieutenant Glynn trained with the regiment in England at Marlborough. He then travelled by train and ship with the rest of us and eventually reached North Africa. When in January 1942 the regiment reached Antelat, we came face-to-face with the German 21st Panzer Division. The first day we were in action and within two hours of the first shot being fired, Lieutenant Glynn was killed. He was the first officer to lose his life, after travelling all the way from Marlborough.

Lieutenant Michael Halstead. Lieutenant Halstead was wounded in June 1942 and badly disfigured. He lost an eye. When I arrived in Washington DC, one year later on my American lecture tour, I walked into the British Army Staff office, and there was Michael behind the desk. We were friends and he was a big help on my tour of America.

Lieutenant Michael Pollock. Lieutenant Pollock was killed in May 1942 and the Colonel wrote to his mother, who replied: 'To Michael it is a great awakening, to us a great loss.'

Lieutenant Rich. Lieutenant Rich was small and sunburnt brown. He looked just like a jockey. Seeing him walking, you thought that he ought to be on a horse.

Lieutenant Taylor. When we were static behind the minefield at Knightsbridge, an officer was sent up from the base who demonstrated how to pinpoint our position on the map by means of the stars. Lieutenant Taylor thought that this was wonderful and went around telling everybody about it. So when soon after orders came that an officer was to be sent to the base on a course to learn this, he was sent. Three weeks later he returned with the instrument, and he was doing it himself! He was killed at El Alamein.

Before the Bays moved forward towards the fighting, they had to learn the proven way of moving across a featureless desert. Each troop of four tanks proceeded in a diamond formation, with the forward tank, two on the flanks, and the troop commander's tank behind. (**Plate 26.**) When the troop joined the other three troops in the squadron, they became part of a similar diamond-shaped formation. (**Plate 27.** This shows 'B' Squadron, followed by Regimental Headquarters, and JSM's small scout car in the rear.) The distance between tanks varied with battle and weather conditions. They had to be able to see one another, but they tended as a rule to spread out because tight grouping made them vulnerable to enemy fire.

All the tanks maintained good radio contact, although some tanks had different radios from others. The two pennants on each tank's aerial were also used for identification. (**Plates 9, 27,** explained in Chapter 4.) Many tanks had telephones fixed at the rear so that the infantry with whom they were cooperating could get in touch with the tank crews. Artillery regiments had very good radio communications between Forward Observation Officers and the gun positions, which was one of the reasons why British gunnery was so excellent. However, infantry battalions had light and unreliable radio sets, something that caused constant problems during the whole of the war.

JSM Journal

The Bays had six scout cars used as dispatch riders to take messages. (**Plate 25.**) They all had Bren guns mounted (except mine), in case they were attacked. A scout car had a Daimler engine with four gears forward and four gears reverse, so that one could reverse at speed if meeting the enemy. Armour was 15mm at the front and 5mm on the sides and back, which was the reason for keeping the front towards the enemy. Engine at the rear. Weight three tons. 'Run-flat' tires. I had to climb over the top to get in and 5mm armoured lid covers top. Escape door low down on left. No spare wheel (a mistake in my model). Racks on both sides for twenty gallons of water, and also carried twelve large packets of biscuits, thirty-two tins of corned beef. For my whole six months in the desert with the Bays, my scout car was my *home*. There was me and my driver, our kit and bed rolls, masses of medical equipment, besides the petrol, water, biscuits and corned beef. We spent the day in it or beside it, sat on the sand beside it to eat, lay on the sand by it to sleep. Anywhere we went, we went in it. My driver was a hairdresser in peacetime, so it was very convenient when I wanted my hair cut. The only thing was often when I wanted him he was missing – cutting someone else's hair.

When darkness fell, which was usually about 6:00PM, the tanks broke off the action with the enemy, and retired a mile or two and formed a close leaguer, so that all the tanks were together in squadrons and only about five yards between tanks. By 6:30PM it was pitch dark, and unless there was a moon it could be *very* dark. No lights of any sort were allowed so there was nothing to do but to get bedded down. It was at this time I wrote home and said that Daddy was going to bed at the same time as Neil (aged seven). As soon as it began to get light in the morning, around 4:30AM, the tanks were started up and separated again and moved forward.

My first thought on waking each morning was: 'I wonder if *this* is the day I get killed?'

Of course, about 200 men and fifty tanks were not the whole of the Queen's Bays. There is also 'B' Echelon of 400 men and about fifty lorries, trucks and other vehicles. Altogether there were at the time 600 men in the Bays. It is said that for *every man* on the battlefield, there are *ten* men at the rear. This is probably true because in the Bays alone, for each man in the tanks there were two at 'B' Echelon, and so if you take all the men and staff at Brigade, Division, Corps and Army Headquarters, all the transport, engineers, catering, supplies, mechanical personnel and all the others, there could easily be ten men to every one at the front line.

'B' Echelon means those in the supply line. The forward troops could be called 'A' Echelon but they never were, I don't know why. (*In the infantry, battalions had an 'F' or Fighting Echelon which contained only a few Jeeps; then an 'A' Echelon to provide immediate supplies to the front line. 'B' Echelon was for replenishing heavy supplies. In the armour the greatest weight of all was accounted for by the shells needed for each of the fifty tanks in a regiment.*) 'B' Echelon of the Queen's Bays was stationed in the vicinity of Brigade Headquarters in battle. It was composed of three-ton lorries, fifteen-hundredweight trucks, tank transporters and breakdown lorries. They had to keep the tanks supplied, and had to tow away and as soon as possible repair any tanks that could be repaired. They do this after the battle is over and the fighting has advanced. Of course if the tanks are retreating there is nothing they can do. So when the tanks are in close leaguer every night, a convoy of three-tonners comes up to them in the darkness and supplies the tanks with POL (petrol, oil and lubricants), ammunition, food and water.

Captain Godbold, the Quartermaster, came up each night, navigating by compass in the leading lorry. He had a huge ship's compass fixed to the front of his lorry and illuminated inside so that he could see it. No lights were allowed at all except that each lorry had a small red light underneath in the centre at the back so that it would be seen only by the lorry directly behind. 'Fruity' Godbold would get our position on the wireless in code and had to work out on the maps where we were and navigate his trucks to us.

The arrival of the 1ˢᵗ Armoured Division – fresh and at full strength – was particularly important because it represented a fifty percent increase in the armoured strength of the 8ᵗʰ Army. But its move west to the seat of war demonstrated the truth of the aphorism that the desert was good country for the tacticians but a nightmare for the officers who had to run the supply lines. They had to move forward huge quantities of water, food, POL and the heaviest things of all, shells for the tanks and artillery and limitless quantities of small arms ammunition.

The men in the 2ⁿᵈ Armoured Brigade arrived in Africa and spent what time was needed to prepare their tanks for the desert. They then began their trek west to Cyrenaica, with interruptions until supplies came up. Major General Lumsden, commanding the 1ˢᵗ Armoured Division, made his presence felt and communicated some of his enthusiasm. However, before the division encountered the Panazerarmee Afrika, Lumsden was temporarily disabled in an air raid. He was replaced by Major General Messervy, a horsed cavalryman from the Indian Army, who was to prove later in the war that he was more comfortable in Burma than in the North African desert (where on one occasion he was captured and only escaped by removing his badges of rank). JSM summarizes the progress of the Bays until 22 January 1942. (**Plate 13.**)

JSM Journal

> Then we took the train from Suez to Ikingi and so to camp at Amyrrhia, near Suez. The tanks arrived after about a week and we proceeded west on the coast road through Burg-el-Arat, El Alamein, El Data, to Mersa Matruh. There at Mersa Matruh was a hospital all underground. Four large dugouts with tents communicating them. It took about fifty patients. Had nurses and a matron. When I went to look and said: 'I am the Medical Officer of the Queen's Bays', the matron nearly fell over herself to show me round, she was so impressed!

> Many of the men of the Queen's Bays were Regular soldiers and had been in the army before they were mechanized, and so were very keen on horses. When

they were in the tanks on the road, and passed a horse or horses, they got very excited and shouted and waved! They were much more interested in a horse than a girl.

On we went to Sidi Barrani where we arrived on 7 December 1941 and heard the news that Japan had attacked Pearl Harbor and America was in the war. Next we came to Sollum Bay – absolutely fantastic. (**Plate 30.**) Beautiful white sand and a long curve around the bay, water clear as crystal so that you could see the bottom far out, and the deep purple of the Mediterranean Sea far beyond. We were all sweating hot and wanted to jump out of our vehicles, strip off, and plunge into the water. But we had to keep going through the 'Wire' dividing Egypt from Libya – to Bardia, and on to Tobruk, Tmimi and then south to Msus, and so to Antelat where we came face-to-face with the 21st Panzer Division and were in action. (*It was two months since the regiment's arrival in Africa.*)

The Preface describes how JSM, an experienced amateur photographer who used sophisticated equipment, was (like everybody else) forbidden from taking photographs on active service. But he interpreted the rule liberally, and with a snapshot camera he took many photographs of his experiences in the desert. Twenty-four are reproduced in this book, and their immediacy and historic value compensate for their technical shortcomings.

CHAPTER 6

THE NADIR OF BRITISH FORTUNES

At the beginning of 1941 British morale was surprisingly strong. The defeat of the army in France had left the country isolated from the Continent, something that paradoxically boosted both patriotism and confidence. The Blitz affected everybody in the bombed areas (including the Royal family), and this drew people together. There was also the stunning victory of the Battle of Britain. The country lacked armaments, but men in the Home Army were being intensively trained. However a year later, the beginning of 1942, things were different and much worse. Britain was now part of an alliance with Russia and the United States, and was fighting a global war in which so far there were few victories and many defeats. The Germans were continuing to devour enormous chunks of Russian territory, killing or capturing whole Russian armies. The Japanese were rampaging through the Far East and with extraordinary speed seized Hong Kong, Malaya, Singapore, Siam, French Indo-China, the Dutch East Indies, and the Philippines. The symbols of British naval power, HMS Prince of Wales and HMS Repulse, which had been sent from Europe to deter the Japanese, were at the bottom of the ocean east of Malaya. In the Atlantic, the U-boats were causing vast destruction. In the skies over Europe, large numbers of brave and highly-trained aircrew in the Royal Air Force were being lost, doing surprisingly little damage to the enemy war machine, despite the great devastation from their bombing. The Mediterranean was still a battleground, with Malta under siege. In the North African desert, Rommel was preparing to spring his counter-attack that would begin the fourth lap of the Benghazi Handicap. Facing him was the 8th Army, with its tough and experienced soldiers but inadequate tanks, all in the hands of an inexperienced and relatively junior commander. But miraculously during the arduous course of 1941, British prospects were gradually but significantly improving. Few observers at the beginning of 1942 could have forecast that the fortunes of the alliance would change radically for the better within a period of twelve months. At the beginning of 1943, victories were at last beginning to outnumber defeats.

Battles in an Empty Desert

Rommel, purposeful and energetic as ever, planned his counter-attack for 21 January 1942. His newly-arrived tanks were an important element of his fighting strength. The British, who were understandably respectful of Rommel, had been expecting him to attack, although 8th Army intelligence was not good enough to predict where and when he would strike. Auchinleck, who had been misled by badly interpreted Signals Intelligence, remained totally confident that Rommel's army was a spent force. In fact the German assault caught the British by surprise because of its strength and violence.

At the time of the German attack, the 1st Armoured Division had moved up to the front. The forward German positions at El Agheila were covered by two British formations: the 201st Guards Brigade on the right, and the Support Group (i.e. the infantry and artillery) of the 1st Armoured Division on the left. When the enemy attacked these two formations on 21 January 1942, the 2nd Armoured Brigade was ordered forward in support. (**Map 6.**) The next few days were to demonstrate a characteristic of desert fighting that was totally new to troops who had only recently arrived. The enemy always appeared out of nowhere in the empty desert, and British units large and small often found it difficult to locate their own friendly forces. The fog of war was a result mainly of the emptiness of the battlefield, but sometimes also because of real fog and occasional desert storms.

On 22 January, the Support Group found it difficult to draw back because of the rough 'going' of the desert tracks, and a number of groups of soldiers were overrun. Meanwhile the advance of the 2nd Armoured Brigade was interrupted by shortage of fuel. The crews also had reduced rations. Vague reports were coming in of strong enemy advances. The brigade therefore moved in the supposed enemy direction, to Saunnu, and then ordered north-west. Night was now falling and the tanks had to go into close leaguer.

The following days saw a number of uncoordinated engagements to the east of the forty-mile track running north from Saunnu to Msus. The Germans had better tanks, greater skills in desert tactics, in particular the close cooperation between all arms. They also had greater strength and – the most priceless asset of all – the initiative. The British were unbalanced and were forced to respond to enemy moves. The commanders of the 1ˢᵗ Armoured Division and everyone in the ranks learned hard lessons very quickly, and the arrival in May 1942 of the American Grant tanks with their 75mm guns gave the soldiers a far more effective weapon than anything that they had had to date. (**Plate 11.**) However, on 24 January the German advance north-east was unstoppable. Fog fell early on the battlefield and radio communications became erratic. It was not long before the Bays realized that the 9ᵗʰ Lancers and 10ᵗʰ Hussars, the other two regiments in the 2ⁿᵈ Armoured Brigade, were in action. Umbrellas of black smoke were rising from the explosions of tanks and petrol lorries and dumps. The 10ᵗʰ Hussars lost many tanks and had to withdraw to rescue their wounded and recover any tanks that were repairable. To make matters worse, German Stuka dive bombers now appeared on the scene. (**Plate 36.**) The Bays could not help because they had to stay in their leaguer to wait for supplies. Early on 25 January, small battles continued. But orders finally arrived for the withdrawal of the 2ⁿᵈ Armoured Brigade. There were only enough tanks to form a single regiment. This was based on the 9ᵗʰ Lancers, and included a composite squadron of the Bays and 10ᵗʰ Hussars. Colonel Draffen, with 100 men, was given the difficult job of salvaging as many tanks as he could from the battlefield.

Typical examples of small battles in which the Bays were engaged were 'C' Squadron actions, described by Trooper Jack Merewood who had been a baker in Huddersfield before the war. He was the gunner in a tank commanded by Captain Patchett, newly appointed Second-in-Command of the squadron, a popular officer. All ranks received exactly the same rations, but in the Bays the officers supplemented their rations with canned provisions they bought and had shipped from Cairo. These meant a more comfortable life in the officers' mess. Captain Patchett often brought some of these provisions to his tank crew. And on one occasion he bought a live sheep from a party of Bedouins. (One of the tank crew was a trained butcher.)

Merewood and his comrades were involved in a brief action on 22 January. The next day they took the initiative and pushed some Germans back and took a number of prisoners who were handed over to the infantry. On 24 January, Merewood's tank was hit and the crew bailed out. Unfortunately Captain Patchett lost his way but he eventually found another tank. This was also hit, and he and the crew became prisoners-of-war. Trooper Merewood and his comrades eventually found their own tank and made the engine work again. On 25 January they fought their most serious battle.

Trooper Jack Merewood, 'To War with the Bays'

Things were going well. We had come across some vehicles and infantry a few hundred yards away, and were shelling and pouring machine gun fire into them. We really sorted them out and had their soldiers frantically running in every direction, but then German Panzer IV tanks turned up. (**Plate 6.**) Our tanks were no match for them: their armour was thicker and they had bigger guns with a much longer range than ours. We returned their fire but with our 37mm and two-pounder guns we couldn't reach them. We tried to hold our ground but it was an impossible task and as the light began to fade we were forced to withdraw.

We suffered our first casualties here. When we pulled back, our tank stopped beside Freddie Minks's Stuart. (**Plate 9.**) Freddie had been killed. . . he was a sickening sight. . . We wrapped him in a blanket, dug a grave and buried him. Captain Tatham-Warter read a short service over the grave. . . .

We kept moving until 4:00AM and then were up again at 6:30AM. Unfortunately our tank had developed a radiator leak, and it was decided that we couldn't continue fighting.

The repair was a difficult one, and Trooper Merewood had to take his tank back to workshops behind the line. He was therefore for the moment *hors de combat*. Meanwhile all the remaining men in 2nd Armoured Brigade, including the 9th Lancers, Colonel Draffen's party, and troops who had been LOB (left-out-of-battle), were ordered to make their way to Charruba and Mechili, which they all reached at the end of January.

During this active period of combat, the Germans demonstrated the effectiveness of their tactics, especially the close cooperation between their armour, infantry, anti-tank guns and dive bombers. In the course of their rapid advance, they managed to seize a number of British supply dumps. Enemy morale was high because they were surging forward, and the British supplies were a bonus to them. The most important of these dumps was at the airfield at Msus, in the bulge of Cyrenaica sixty miles inland from Benghazi, where the German booty included ninety-six tanks, thirty-eight guns, a dozen aircraft and 190 trucks. In taking Msus, which they did with great speed, they pushed the 1st Armoured Division into what has been rather unfairly described as a headlong retreat. In view of the number of short, sharp battles that had been fought, the Bays with five men killed and ten wounded suffered less than might have been expected. Although Dr. MacGill's first and foremost priority was tending the relatively few men who had to have medical attention, most of his time was spent at Regimental Headquarters, which was usually on the move, and where he remained on call day and night in anticipation of more casualties.

JSM Journal

We were static for a week before we went into action. I played Bridge with the Colonel and the young officers attached to HQ. They all came from wealthy families but money was no good in the desert, so we played for cigarettes. Then cigarettes became too precious so we played for matches! Each officer contributed ten shillings to the mess to buy whisky. The young officers took a very poor view of this because they did not like whisky, and the Colonel and I drank the lot! They grumbled to me a lot, but did not say a word to the

Colonel. I was playing Bridge in a small tent one night with the Colonel and two other officers, with a bottle of whisky between us. This was in the desert about twenty miles from Tobruk, when a corporal arrived with mail. Thirteen letters for me: the first we had received since sailing from Gourock on September 1941. The Colonel, who did not have any letters I believe, would not let me abandon the game to read my letters. He said 'Come on, Doc, you can read them afterwards.' So I had to sit up half the night reading them after we had gone to bed.

When we first saw Msus on our way to the front line, it was a collection of about 100 large tents and looked like quite a town. After the battle of Msus when we were retiring, we passed that way again and all the tents were gone. There was nothing but desert where Msus had been! (**Plate 34.**) One morning my scout car would not start and I was left behind. All the tanks went off and I was left with the Transport Officer, Captain Lindley, and two other trucks. They were working on my car and another all morning. Then we set off to the place where the tanks were making for. When we got there, there was no sign of the tanks, so we turned back and when it got dark stopped where we were. Soon we heard tanks coming and thought they might be Germans, so we up sticks and made a rapid retreat due east for two miles then bedded down again.

In the morning we set off north where we though Msus should be. Soon after we set off the near front wheel of Captain Lindley's truck fell off. He immediately said that the axle had gone, and started unloading all his gear off the truck onto his other one. In ten minutes all was transferred, and he jumped into the truck and left his standing there in the desert with one wheel off. About midday we were all running out of petrol when we came across a lorry full of tins of petrol which was firmly stuck in the sand and couldn't move. We filled up and made Msus before nightfall. On the way, we picked up two strange British soldiers who were lost and just wandering about aimlessly in the desert. We spent the night in Msus and found out where the Queen's Bays were and rejoined them next day. They had not gone to where they said they were going, but on the way spotted German tanks and went off west after them.

One day when the tanks were in action but stationary and exchanging fire with German tanks, we came across a brand new scout car, far better than our own but with a flat tire. The previous owner evidently did not know that you could drive up to ten miles with a flat without damage. (They were called 'run-flat' tires.) My driver hurriedly changed the wheel and transferred all our kit to the new scout car and left ours there. We were in the middle of the battle so luckily I was not wanted while he was changing the wheel. It has only dawned on me recently that when my driver and I found the scout car with the flat tire, we should not have left ours there but I could have driven one and my driver the other, because we knew that it could be driven for several miles with a flat. Why did I not think of this?

Later in the battle of Msus we had about twelve men – three tank crews – clinging to the outside of my scout car as their only means of transport after their tanks had been knocked out.

After the battle of Msus, the Queen's Bays had lost so many tanks that they were left out of battle. Enough tanks were soon assembled from the Bays and the 10th Hussars to form a composite squadron of sixteen. I was ordered to go with it as the Medical Officer. At the time I was at the Bays Headquarters and did not know where the composite squadron was, so I asked an officer I came across and he said 'they've gone that way', pointing south. So I set off in my scout car with my driver, and after a mile or two and seeing no signs of any tanks or anything, and as it was getting dark and pouring with rain, we bedded down for the night. At first light I got out my binoculars and went to the top of a small mound and searched the horizon. I could see some vehicles in the distance, so we went to them and asked if they knew where the composite squadron was. They directed us correctly this time and we were soon with the squadron.

At another time I was going from the tanks to the Main Dressing Station in the ambulance. We went by compass for five miles to where it was supposed to be, but it was just bare desert as far as the eye could see. So we turned round and retraced our tracks. Soon we could see their tents away to the left. When we got there and told them of our error in navigation, they said 'Oh! We moved here yesterday from where you were looking for us.' One day, when I was with the Bays and we were in action, I was sitting in my scout car with my driver 100 yards behind the Colonel's tank, waiting for orders. (He was in wireless contact with all the tanks and I was not.) The tanks were firing at the enemy but were stationary.

JSM and his driver, who was half his age, spent much time together and on one occasion, when there was intermittent shelling, they talked casually about the things the driver did not know. He said that what he did not know now he never would. This struck JSM as a sharp reminder that they could have been blown to pieces at any moment. (This happened a few months later to JSM's successor as Medical Officer to the Bays.)

At this time summer had not arrived, but the battles that began in May 1942 were fought on a battlefield that was very hot and very dry. The empty spaces in which soldiers lived and fought were more comfortable (or perhaps less uncomfortable!) than the battlefields of Europe or the Far East. The worst hardship was the shortage of water. One of the Medical Officer's unusual jobs was to test water from the many wells that were found in the desert. Another strange feature of the desert war was that, on occasion, petrol was used to wash clothes.

JSM Journal

Before we went into action, when we were in camp in
the desert about twenty miles from Tobruk, there was a
well near the camp with water which looked clear. The
Colonel told me to test it to see if it was drinkable. I had
never tested water before, but had a box in the medical
kit which said: 'Water Testing' on the lid. I did not
know what was inside and had never opened it. I did
not tell the Colonel of course. I found it contained some
small test tubes, about ten little bottles of chemicals,
a spirit lamp and a book of instructions. So there was
me one morning alone in a small tent doing tests that
should be done in a laboratory. There were tests for
metals such as lead and poisons such as arsenic. I don't
remember what else, but it took me about two hours
and at the finish I found the water did not contain any
poisons except 'animal matter', which meant it could be
contaminated and therefore undrinkable. The Germans
used to throw dead camels into the wells to make them
useless. So, in due course I reported to the Colonel
that the water was undrinkable but could be used for
washing purposes.

It was at this time also that, although we had two large
crates of medical equipment in the regiment, we were
not allowed to use it until we went into action. All
I had was a large bottle of Tincture of Iodine, and a
large bottle of Aspirin Powder. I had sick patients every
morning. There were 200 men I remember, and the
Iodine was used for cuts and scratches, and painted
on for sprains and muscle pain. I made up the Aspirin
Powder into ten-grain packets in different coloured
papers, and gave a white-paper powder for headache,
a pink-paper powder for backache and a blue-paper
powder for toothache etc. In the medical kit, which
we were not allowed to use until we were in action,
there was a bottle of brandy. Well, when we were at
Marlborough before we went abroad, someone pinched

it, so we had to fill an empty brandy bottle with tea so that it was there for inspection if anyone came to inspect the kit. We took the bottle of tea to the desert, and as soon as we were in action I threw it away and indented for a bottle of brandy from the quartermaster's stores. I am afraid that it was drunk by me and the other officers. Besides, brandy is the worst thing to give a wounded man. It would probably start the patient bleeding if one gave him enough of it.

In the desert we used to wash our shirts in high-octane petrol which was used by some of the tanks. You got a two-gallon tin of it, took the top off and dropped your shirt in for about ten seconds. The shirt came out spotlessly clean and was dry in the sun in ten minutes. The only thing was that the third time you washed your shirt in the petrol, the shirt disintegrated and disappeared entirely. It just dissolved away in the petrol!

Dr, MacGill's reminiscences emphasize repeatedly the strange war that the 8th Army was fighting: the loneliness of the desert and how easy it was for individuals and small groups to get lost; how often vehicles broke down and ran out of gasoline; the scattering of abandoned vehicles; the uncertainty of the weather; the discomfort of the soldiers' lives; and the long periods when nothing much was happening. The limited range of medical supplies available to a Regimental Medical Officer is, in retrospect, very surprising. This emphasizes the standard procedure that battle casualties had to be evacuated from Regimental Aid Posts with great speed, for surgery and other treatment at Field Ambulances and General Hospitals behind the lines. On 1 June 1942, JSM joined the 1st Light Field Ambulance as Second-in-Command and promoted Major.

Around Msus there was a good deal of tank action, but much of the gunfire was from stationary positions and tanks kept being knocked out. The status quo was being maintained. To the 2nd Armoured Brigade, which contained all the tanks in the 1st Armoured Division, there was no question of a rapid retreat pursued by a triumphant enemy. Nevertheless, Major General Messervy, the Divisional Commander, viewed a broader picture. The tank battles around Msus were small-unit actions, uncontrolled and unsupported. The division was not yet closely knit because much of the artillery and infantry was diverted into battle groups called 'Jock Columns'. The clashes in January 1942 demonstrated that the 2nd Armoured Brigade and the divisional Support Group, with whom they had trained in England, were fighting separate wars.

The 'Jock Columns' (named after the legendary gunner, Major General Jock Campbell VC, who was to lose his life later in 1942), were small mobile groups of artillery and infantry. Each held an RHA battery, an anti-tank troop, an anti-aircraft troop, and two infantry companies. Their job was to move constantly to reconnoitre and harass the enemy without getting held down. In doing this, the columns were not under the orders of the 2nd Armoured Brigade, to whom the horse artillery batteries were originally attached. Each battery was armed with eight 25-pounder field guns. (**Plate 19.**) Each of the regiments in 2nd Armoured Brigade worked with a separate battery. The gunners supporting the 2nd Armoured Brigade were 11 RHA (HAC). The Honourable Artillery Company (HAC) is the oldest regiment in the British army, in existence since 1537, and the senior unit in the Territorial Army. After two years of war, most of the officers were still pre-war members of the HAC, but the NCOs and other ranks were 'wartime only' conscripts. The regiment landed in Africa in early December 1941, well trained and fully equipped.

The three batteries of the regiment were allocated to three 'Jock Columns,' and began to operate in mid-January 1942. They had two weeks of very active contact with the enemy, but one problem they consistently encountered was soft sand that bogged down their vehicles. The columns were bruised. They suffered a number of casualties, lost some guns, and many of their vehicles were damaged and needed repair. But the main problem of the 'Jock Columns' was that, despite their aggressive nibbling at the enemy, they had no clear strategic function. At the end of January 1942 they reverted to the command of 2nd Armoured Brigade. The Queen's Bays welcomed back their gunner friends, 'A' Battery, under the command of Major John McDermid, who was later in the year wounded and captured by the Germans. (**Plate 21.**) The gunners' Forward Observation Officers (FOOs) were mounted in Stuart tanks driven by Bays drivers. (**Plate 20.**)

Messervy judged that the British force in Cyrenaica was no match for the Panzerarmee Afrika, which was driving forward with unknown numbers of experienced troops in superior tanks. He therefore gave the order to retire. The Queen's Bays, now in Mechili, pulled back to where they would participate in the prolonged and important battle of Gazala. This was to lead to Rommel's capture of Tobruk, which was to be a bitter blow to the 8th Army and also to the politicians and military chiefs in Britain.

The First Set-Piece Battle

A set-piece battle is one in which both sides occupy strong positions and both employ all arms to attack and defend, with the object of a decisive breakthrough. The battle of Gazala was the first set-piece battle of the North African campaign and the breakthrough was made by the Panzerarmee Afrika. Gazala was followed in October/November 1942 by El Alamein, a larger set-piece and one that was very tightly planned by Lieutenant General Montgomery. This was the most decisive battle of the campaign and led to the eventual defeat of the Axis forces in Africa.

In early February 1942, Major General Lumsden was fit enough to relieve Messervy and take back command of the 1st Armoured Division. (Lumsden was a member of the Honourable Artillery Company, having been an officer in one of the batteries during the First World War.) The division had drawn back and was occupying parts of the Gazala line, an interrupted chain of strong points, called boxes, that ran south from the Mediterranean coast. (**Map 6.**) Peace had surprisingly descended on the battlefield as the two sides reorganized, repaired their equipment and replenished their supplies. Rommel was as usual hatching plans to attack. The British troops' main task was to reinforce their defensive positions and in particular sow minefields. These minefields planted to cover the unoccupied ground between the boxes were constructed to channel invading forces into corridors where they could be attacked. As the fighting developed and as the minefields were partially breached, the boxes needed to be covered with much more artillery fire than had been originally planned.

The strength of the 8th Army was at the time about 120,000 men, approximately the same as the Panzerarmee Afrika. Although Rommel had in January taken the initiative and advanced rapidly for 400 miles, the British had retreated in good order to the Gazala line. Both sides prepared to resume the battle, but the process took a surprisingly long time. An important reason was that the attitude of Rommel's military superiors put a brake on his customary zeal for action. Although Rommel was now receiving unexpected quantities of supplies, the Italian Supreme Command in Rome, to whom Rommel reported, were reluctant to make further attempts to invade Egypt, in view of their earlier experiences there.

And the generals in the German High Command were far more focused on Russia than on North Africa, although they agreed to participate in a large increase in the Italian bombing of Malta. The high-level discussions in Italy and Germany about Rommel's plans all imposed delays to his timetable. In addition, the heavy bombing of Malta diverted airpower that could have been used by Rommel in the desert. Rommel was forced to rely on the existing strength of the Panzerarmee Afrika, although he still had the Italian divisions that were under his direct command.

The British work on the Gazala position needed effort, resources and time. During the period of more than three months during which the defensive positions on the Gazala line were being constructed, regimental commanders took the opportunity to send some of their men on short leaves to Cairo. Dr. MacGill, whose workload was fairly light when the tanks were not in action, was fortunate enough to be given a five-day break.

JSM Journal

> We had leave of five days every six months and my first
> leave became due when I was still with the Bays. I took
> it with the Padre and we went in his truck, as I could
> not very well go in a scout car. He said he would come
> to the races in Alexandria with me if I went to church
> with him. We arrived at the Alex racecourse looking like
> a couple of ragamuffins straight from the desert. Our

uniforms were ragged and dirty and we were ingrained with sand. An officer in a spick-and-span uniform said: 'You cannot go into the races looking like that.' I said: 'We have just arrived from the Western desert and my kit is in Cairo.' He said: 'I don't care, you cannot go in.' So I said: 'Come on, Padre, let's go.' When he heard us calling each other Padre and Doc he realized we were officers and said: 'It is alright you can go in.' And we went in and lost some money. Come Sunday, I went to church with the Padre. He was Church of England! (*JSM was of course a member of the Church of Scotland, which is Presbyterian.*) During the six months in the desert, our pay would accumulate and I would have about £60 in the bank at Alexandria, which I drew out and spent it all in the five days: mostly the hotel bill and buying presents for home. I had my photograph taken in Cairo and sent one to my wife and one to my mother. (**Plate 41.**) (*He was soon back with the Bays.*)

Gazala was an important block against any German advance, and the proximity to the port of Tobruk gave it additional importance. During February, March and April 1942, Auchinleck was also receiving reinforcements. However, the messages from Churchill and the CIGS in London continued and became increasingly insistent. In view of the disasters that were happening in the Far East, Churchill was desperate for a British victory anywhere. It did not help Auchinleck that he knew that the German tactics were superior to the British and that British armour was no match for the Panzer III and Panzer IV tanks. (**Plate 6.**) The 8th Army was actually in the process of being re-equipped with large numbers of the new American Grant tank (**Plate 11**), with its formidable 75mm gun, although even the Grant was not as good as the Panzer IV. The armour was less robust. And the 75mm gun was mounted in an unusual way: in the body of the tank and not in a rotating turret. This meant that the Grant had to fire head-on to the enemy, because of the limited scope for changing the elevation and traverse. Nevertheless although the Panzer IV was superior to the Grant, it was not vastly superior. The early Allied tanks were feeble in comparison. Auchinleck did not fully realize how good the Grants were but in any event they came as an unpleasant surprise to Rommel when battle was joined.

Auchinleck still saw reasons to be pessimistic because he believed that the 8th Army had low morale: a result of too many defeats. He sent a clever but unpopular staff officer to the front to take soundings and recommend ways of improving matters. His analysis was curtailed by pressure of time, but on his return to Cairo he recommended that Ritchie should be removed from command of the 8th Army. (This would happen before long.) Many senior British soldiers looked on the gloomy side and constantly studied intelligence reports. Both armies in the desert broke enemy codes, and in May 1942 Auchinleck was anticipating Rommel's attack and Rommel was anticipating Auchinleck's. On the night of 26/27 May Rommel struck first.

The right of the British line was anchored on the small port of Gazala on the Mediterranean coast. (**Map 6.**) Gazala is fifty miles west of Tobruk, where all the British supplies were landed by sea. Both places are overlooked by the main desert escarpment five to ten miles to the south. From Gazala the British line ran south, including a large dog leg and some small escarpments, until it reached the left of the line, the southern anchor at Bir Hacheim. Bir Hacheim is fifty miles south of Gazala as the crow flies. The British line was defended by a minefield that bent back north-east at Bir Hacheim. This was constructed to protect the British from an enveloping attack, and this extension of the minefield reached two locations that were to be important in the forthcoming battle. Fifteen miles north of Bir Hacheim there was a saucer of low hills, three miles in diameter, which was before long known as the Cauldron. (**Plate 38.**) This was a suitable description of a place in which brutal fighting would soon take place. Five miles north-east of the Cauldron was a defensive box built at a track-crossing marked by two oil drums and a banner, labelled with its map reference and the name Knightsbridge. (**Plate 37.**)

The best description of the battle line itself was made by someone who was there. He was Geoffrey Armstrong (**Plate 40**), a member of the Honourable Artillery Company, and now a Captain in 11 RHA. After the war he found his original tactical map and used this to describe the topography of the battle.

Captain Geoffrey Armstrong, 'The Sparks Fly Upward'

On the ground the only natural, identifiable landmarks were the escarpments, the birs (*wells, many in use from Roman times*), and an occasional Trig Point (*a number on the map indicating in metres the height of a prominent feature*). Tracks had become a mass of wheel marks, hundreds of yards wide and could be picked out only from the numbered forty-gallon drums. Of man-made buildings there were none save an Italian blockhouse in Knightsbridge. And the map picture is completed by tracing in the minefields and the defended areas, or boxes. The former ran continuously south from Gazala on the sea, to Bir Hacheim: our 'outpost' box. Here it turned sharply left-handed and ran back northwards to near the Knightsbridge crosstracks. The arrangement of the minefields and boxes and escarpments was artfully conceived to 'canalise' enemy intrusion and movement. It reduced his options and forced him to adopt a massive supply line, or to accept a very high risk. He did both and thereby almost lost the battle in the first few days.

Rommel's Master Stroke

Auchinleck had anticipated that the Panzerarmee Afrika would attack at the north of the Gazala line and feint in the south. But he was wrong. Auchinleck and Ritchie and the other senior commanders were caught by surprise. The actual attack came in the south, with a carefully planned feint by Italian troops in the north. While British attention was being distracted, Rommel enveloped Bir Hacheim in the south and started to advance on Tobruk. The weight of the attack came from large numbers of Panzer IV tanks, supported by Panzer IIIs and motorized infantry. The leading elements of the British 7th Armoured Division in the south could not at first believe what they were facing. This division was now commanded by Major General Messervy, who was captured but managed to escape by pretending to be a private soldier, a far less prominent individual than a general. The 7th Armoured Division was overrun and leading German elements, driving north, came within twenty miles of the minefields surrounding Tobruk.

However, the impetus of the German attack soon slowed. The invariably effective fire of the British 25-pounder guns rained destruction. And, to the shock of all the German soldiers who saw them, 167 newly-arrived Grant tanks started attacking the Panzers with success. Such a thing had never happened before. The British Desert Air Force was also active, and the minefields were initially effective in sealing possible gaps in the British line through which German attacks might have penetrated, but things soon deteriorated. The Bays retired to a new position in the centre of the British line, five miles east of Knightsbridge. The regiment now had one squadron of Grants and two of Crusaders. (**Plate 10.**) The Grants were stubby and tough; the Crusaders may have had more elegant lines but were less effective.

JSM Journal

> The tanks were ensconced behind a vast minefield. It was just a place in the desert about thirty miles from the port of Tobruk, so they had to call it something and it was christened Knightsbridge. A bulldozer came and dug great holes in the sand and the tanks were driven into these holes so that only the turrets were above ground and they were protected from shelling and air attack. The bulldozer dug a big hole for the officers' mess, about fourteen feet by ten feet, and over six feet deep. It was furnished with a table in the centre and benches along each side. A tent was stretched out over it, and there were steps down into it at one end. There was another dugout connected to it where the mess staff did the cooking etc.

> The light was provided by a battery under the table connected to a light bulb up above. One day I was sitting on the bench writing a letter home when I noticed the battery under the table. On it was written 'Oldham & Sons Ltd., Denton, Manchester.' It made me think of home because the surgery where I worked

for fifteen years before the war was not a quarter of a mile from Oldham's factory, where they made batteries of all sorts, and I used to go as factory doctor once a month to examine the men for lead poisoning.

One day 'B' squadron, to which the bulldozer was attached, had orders to go out through the minefield, and 'swan' out forward and attack any enemy they found. The bulldozer had to go too, or it would have been left all alone in the bare desert. It was all it could do to keep up with the tanks, and when the tanks went into action and the guns started firing, the bulldozer quickly dug itself a hole and went into it! One day when we were static behind the minefield, I had a game of chess with a young officer, I forget his name, who was reputed to be the champion player of the Queen's Bays officers. I managed to beat him but he went and got killed before we could have another game.

Trooper Merewood (mentioned earlier), who was also a keen observer, left a vivid account of one of the many minor engagements during the first days of the battle of Gazala. He was mounted in one of the new Grant tanks.

Trooper Jack Merewood, 'To War with The Bays'

We were fighting with the best tanks we had had so far and had confidence in them, but our confidence was soon shattered. Through my periscope I saw a spurt of sand from the ground in front of us. Within seconds the next shell hit us. It was certainly an Armour-Piercing/High Explosive (AP/HE) because it came straight through the front of the tank and exploded inside. I looked as Jim; he had taken the full blast of the shell in his face and was dead. I had blood on my face and arms but what was hurting most was my leg. It felt as if it had been hit by a sledgehammer. On looking at it I saw a hole in my thigh an inch or more across . . . (*He then bailed out. The Grant had a large crew. Six men were needed because of the two guns, one in the body of the tank and one in the turret. It was always difficult for all six men to get out in an emergency.)* . . . There were scout cars running about, and one driven by a very courageous Sergeant Harris picked me up and took me back several hundred yards. . . I was laid on the ground alongside some other men, none of whom I knew, and an MO (*Dr. MacGill*) gave me a shot of morphine to ease the pain. There were three ambulances there, and we were lifted into them on stretchers, perhaps six in each, the stretchers fitting in racks like bunk beds.

Captain Armstrong, now Battery Captain of 'A' Battery, 11 RHA, was constantly involved in this fighting. His description of one episode demonstrated clearly and dramatically the difference between the 8th Army's armoured tactics that were based on small-unit action, and Rommel's concept of using armour in strength. During the battle of Gazala, the 8th Army had five armoured brigades – fifteen regiments – in the field. If they had been concentrated, the outcome of the battle would almost certainly have been different.

Captain Geoffrey Armstrong, 'The Sparks Fly Upward'

Our Bays group remained at readiness and my own first job of the day was to go north to observe and report on the main concentration there. Taking my wireless truck to the lip of a desert escarpment and creeping forward on foot, I was rewarded with the most astonishing sight. Spread out like Epsom Downs on Derby Day was what looked like the entire German army. I counted at least 200 tanks and miles of MT – hundreds of vehicles – and wirelessed back a brief account of this staggering sight. What a target if there had only been something available to shoot them up, or bomb them. There didn't appear to be, and my own battery was out of range and was anyway committed to support the Bays in their imminent attack. After this exhilarating morning it was back to the battery.

The battle was degenerating into a series of small-unit actions often fought with great heroism, but not leading to any decisive breakthrough by either side. The 8th Army had a problem of leadership and lack of 'grip' at the highest levels. The man who could have made a difference was Auchinleck, who was 500 miles away in Cairo, and for the moment was loyal to the principle that subordinates should be left free to do their jobs, although he flew up from Cairo on a number of occasions to give support and advice. However the inexperienced 8th Army C-in-C Major General Ritchie, and the commanders of the corps and divisions who reported to him, ran the battle by committee. They spent much time in staff conferences rather than injecting 'binge' (one of Montgomery's favourite words) into the fighting troops. The generals were all too far behind the lines to detect and respond to events on a fast-moving battlefield. It was a style of leadership associated with the British army in the First World War.

The situation in Panzerarmee Afrika was about to change. Rommel saw the confusion and lack of clear direction on both sides, and he determined to seize the initiative and impose his will and tactical direction on the battlefield. The 8th Army was continuing to fight in 'penny packets' – in brigades or regiments or battalions – while Rommel was fighting in divisions. In his customary way he led from the front, and on a number of occasions he was in personal danger from enemy fire. On 30 May substantial numbers of Panzers had broken through the minefields from the west, and there was not enough artillery fire to stop them. (These Panzers were probably the mass of tanks that Captain Armstrong had spotted but had not been able to fire at with his own battery.) Rommel's plan was to concentrate his forces locally, and make separate attacks on important British positions and thus defeat the British in detail. First, he planned to attack from south and west and destroy the British armour in the centre of the battlefield. At the same time he would reinforce the formations surrounding the Bir Hacheim box in the south and crush it. Then with the whole of the battlefield more or less in his hands, Rommel would sweep north and seize Tobruk by shock attack.

The first part of Rommel's plan was set in train by an attack from the west. A powerful Panzer force got through the minefield and the British artillery was not strong enough to stop them. They assaulted a strong

British box to the west of the Cauldron, held by the 150th Infantry Brigade with many tanks. This brigade was part of the 50th Infantry Division. The Panzers were desperately short of supplies of all types, and Rommel's senior subordinates begged him for permission to withdraw. But he had other ideas and ordered them to attack. This prompted local counter-attacks, which were carried out with sacrificial bravery, but they were all beaten back by the German 88mm anti-tank guns. On 2 June the position held by 150th Infantry Brigade was overrun, with the loss of 3,000 prisoners and 124 guns. During all this action Rommel was up with the leading platoons.

Ritchie learned without much delay what was going on and was nonplussed. His lack of immediate action was one of his major mistakes in the Gazala battle. A sudden British riposte would have stopped Rommel's assault in its tracks. On 5 June, after to-and-fro fighting in which the 2nd Armoured Brigade was continuously engaged, Rommel and his Panzers moved into the Cauldron. Here the British made a daylight assault and lost fifty of the seventy tanks that had attacked. They had been perfect targets for the enemy's 88mm guns.

In the south, the Bir Hacheim position had been besieged by the German attackers since 26 May, while other German formations had been fighting their way north. Bir Hacheim was held with conspicuous fortitude by a brigade of the Free French. This brigade, led by General Koenig, had been formed by volunteers from (nominally Vichy) French forces in Africa and the Middle East and included members of the French Foreign Legion. Their powerful resistance at Bir Hacheim was trumpeted by General de Gaulle as the revival of the historic spirit of France. However, on 10 June the Bir Hacheim garrison was overcome by an enemy force that had been boosted to three times the size of the defenders. 2,400 of the 3,000 tough, bearded Frenchmen managed to fight their way out. From now on, the battle of Gazala was headed for a German victory.

On 14 June, the remaining two brigades of the 50th Infantry Division managed to break away under pressure and escaped to the south-west, *away* from the rest of the 8th Army. Rommel then moved his attention to the British infantry and armour in the Knightsbridge box. In a sandstorm, the Panzers and Stukas attacked from a number of directions while the German and Italian infantry advanced through the minefields. British armour and infantry held their own despite many casualties. The 201st Guards Brigade in particular was noticed by Rommel and the stoical guardsmen earned his respect for their tenacity. The battlefield was devastated, with the bodies of the fallen illuminated by fires from stricken tanks, and the Panzerarmee Afrika was forced to call a halt. This would have been an opportunity for the British generals to counter-attack with force and rescue any tanks that were repairable. But the opportunity was lost, and it was not long before the Knightsbridge box was completely in the hands of the enemy.

The 8th Army was not far from collapse as a result of the enemy pressure from the centre of the original Gazala line. There were only seventy tanks left. The Bays, who had fought a number of small-unit actions in the Cauldron and the Knightsbridge box, had lost four-fifths of their tanks and were down to two Grants and nine Crusaders. On 14 June Ritchie made a firm decision, and ordered the 8th Army to retreat to the Egyptian frontier. Many of the departing trucks rumbled through Tobruk, depressing the garrison who would shortly be attacked themselves. The way was now clear for Rommel's assault on Tobruk and two Panzer divisions swept up to the coast and assaulted Tobruk from the east. During the course of the Gazala battle, Auchinleck was still receiving messages from Churchill and the Chiefs-of-Staff in London. Although Auchinleck had at an early stage planned to leave Tobruk to its fate, Churchill would not hear of this and Auchinleck changed his mind. The assault on Tobruk took place on 20 June 1942. The attack from the east came as a considerable surprise to the defenders, who had prepared for an assault from the west and south. Many of the defenders were inexperienced South Africans, some being unarmed labourers. The attack was preceded by a huge aerial bombardment, the defences crumbled with surprising ease, and Rommel himself moved directly to the port. On 21 June it was all over. 35,000 defenders went 'into the bag'.

When the news of this loss arrived, Churchill was with Roosevelt in Washington DC. Churchill was horrified by the defeat: a second blow that had followed the loss of Singapore on 15 February 1942. However he kept his iron control and was immensely encouraged by Roosevelt, who expressed comradeship in a very practical way. Against the advice of his top American military advisers, he sent 300 of the new Sherman tanks to the 8th Army. These were to make a substantial contribution to the victory at El Alamein in October/November 1942.

During the 8th Army's precipitate retreat to Egypt, Ritchie made an ill-considered plan to stand and fight at Mersa Matruh. Auchinleck then, at last, decided to relieve Ritchie and take command himself. (Churchill had advised him to do this a month before.) He ordered the 8th Army to fall back on a more natural defensive position at El Alamein, where he conducted a skilful engagement that halted the Panzerarmee Afrika, which was by now having supply problems. In doing this, Auchinleck demonstrated the 'grip' of a practised tactician. He chose the spot where he would stand and fight: the same place where the decisive battle of El Alamein would be fought almost four months later. If Auchinleck had commanded the 8th Army earlier, the Gazala débâcle would probably not have taken place. But it would have been unsound to combine the jobs of Commander-in-Chief and 8th Army Commander, because the load would have been too great for one man. The tragedy for the 8th Army was that Ritchie was the wrong general for the job, as Cunningham had been in late 1941. On the other side of the hill, Rommel at the age of forty-nine became the youngest Field Marshal in the German army.

The fourth lap of the Benghazi Handicap had lasted for five months: from the end of January to the end of June 1942. From the beginning of the battle of Gazala to the end of the retreat to El Alamein, the Queen's Bays had lost seventeen percent of their strength: 100 casualties, of whom thirty-five men had lost their lives. These were painful losses although reinforcements arrived before the battle of El Alamein, in which the regiment played their full part. After 1 June, Dr MacGill was no longer in his battle station at the Regimental Headquarters of the Queen's Bays. Newly promoted to the rank of Major, he was Second-in-Command of the 1st Light Field Ambulance, where he was to contribute his professional skills during the fifth and final lap of the Benghazi Handicap. After this, he soldiered on for the remainder of the desert campaign until the 8th Army reached Tunisia.

31. Bays officers' mess

A separate officers' mess was always set up when the regiment was concentrated (as described in Chapter 3). The officers in the Bays maintained as high a standard of living as possible in the desert. Their rations were the same as those of the NCOs and men, but the officers bought extras with their own money. These were shipped to the battlefield by provision stores in Cairo.

Copyright MacGill Family.

32. Church service in the desert

Attendance at church services was voluntary. The men in this photograph belonged to the 1st Light Field Ambulance. Note the Jeep. These were becoming a welcome addition to 8th Army transport before the Battle of El Alamein.

Copyright MacGill Family.

148

33. Field Ambulance dressing station

This was a well-planned, strong, temporary structure built around a three-ton lorry with two lean-to tents on the sides. It was some miles behind the front line in the El Alamein sector. The patients were shipped there by ambulance, which had been loaded at the Regimental Aid Posts. The soldier with the wounded arm had been given further treatment than first aid, and triage by RAMC officers would probably have sent him down the line for more extensive care.

Copyright MacGill Family.

34. Msus: Hurricane planes taking off

Msus was a barren piece of desert used at a supply dump and airfield, and with a hundred large tents it looked like a town. The Bays passed through it on the way to battle, and passed back when they were retreating, at which time Msus had reverted to barren desert. (This is described in Chapter 6.) The photograph shows the empty desert, with a flight of Hurricane aeroplanes taking off. This fighter was not as effective as the German Messerschmitt (Plate 35). However, Hurricanes destroyed Stuka dive bombers (Plate 36) in large numbers. They also knocked out tanks, for which they were fitted with specially-designed 40mm ground attack cannons.

Copyright IWM, negative CM 2184.

35. Crashed Messerschmitt fighter plane

This aircraft was equal to the British Spitfire, but there were not many Spitfires in the desert. The German fighter ace Marseille won many air victories in the desert in his Messerschmitt, but he was eventually killed in action.

Copyright MacGill Family.

36. Crashed Stuka dive bomber

In France in 1940, the Stukas were an integral part of a Panzer division. They were formidable when used tactically, in support of troops on the ground, and this performance was repeated on a more limited scale in North Africa. However, when Stukas were used in the Battle of Britain as strategic bombers, they were shot out of the air in large numbers by Spitfires and Hurricanes.

Copyright MacGill Family.

37. Action photograph of Battle of Knightsbridge

This fuzzy but dramatic shot shows the destruction of Panzer III tanks that drove close to an HAC battery. The empty desert does not convey the viciousness of the battle. (Chapter 6.)

Copyright HAC.

38. Action photograph of fighting in the Cauldron

Another dramatic photograph of the fighting in the Cauldron, a few miles from Knightsbridge. Because the shot was taken from a trench, it gives some idea what it was like to be under fire on 5/6 June 1942. (Chapter 6.)

Copyright IWM, negative 13100.

39. Remnants of Italian tanks at Mersa Matruh

This small port in Egypt is between El Alamein and the Libya/Egypt frontier in the west. The 8th Army halted there after their retreat from the Gazala position in June 1942. After the Battle of El Alamein, the 8th Army passed through it on its triumphant advance. This photograph was probably taken at this later time. The desert was barren, as usual. The British tanks had much less trouble with Italian armour than with the Panzers, which always inflicted more damage than they received.

Copyright MacGill Family.

40. General Auchinleck and Major Armstrong, HAC

Following the Battle of Gazala, General Auchinleck devoted his time to nurturing his retreating troops and maintaining their cohesion. (Auchinleck had just taken personal command of the 8th Army.) In this photograph he is talking to Major Geoffrey Armstrong, then commanding A Battery, 11 RHA (HAC). The regiment had suffered considerable casualties and was being reorganized. This photograph shows that these officers, both under pressure, remained optimistic. Armstrong's cap was missing, and he had picked up a solar topee that he had found discarded on the ground.

Copyright HAC.

41. JSM on leave in Cairo

In the spring of 1942, before Rommel's attack on the Gazala position, Dr. MacGill managed to take five days' leave which he spent in Cairo. He cleaned up his uniform and had this studio photograph taken by an Egyptian photographer. Note the fly whisk, a flamboyant device that cleared away flies which were a constant irritation and a vehicle for spreading disease. The fly whisk was sometimes seen as a symbol of a British officer's commissioned rank.

Copyright MacGill Family.

42. JSM as Major and Second-in-Command of 1ˢᵗ Light Field Ambulance

On 1 June 1942, a time when Rommel's assault at the Battle of Gazala was in full spate, Dr. MacGill was promoted and joined the 1ˢᵗ Light Field Ambulance. Note how his service-dress cap had faded in the sun.

Copyright MacGill Family.

43. 1ˢᵗ Light Field Ambulance officers' conference before El Alamein

The 1ˢᵗ Light Field Ambulance had a strength of 150 all ranks, about ten percent of whom were officers, all medical practitioners except for the non-medical quartermaster. It also had forty-five vehicles. The Main Dressing Station was twenty miles east of El Alamein, with a Field Dressing Station further forward. Note the camouflage net on the truck, to conceal the Main Dressing Station from the air.

Copyright MacGill Family.

John Philip Jones

44. Lieutenant Generals Leese, Montgomery and Lumsden

Three general officers with different interpretations of uniform regulations. Lumsden was an elegant cavalry officer who, despite his distinguished record, was sacked by Montgomery in November 1942. Montgomery was impatient with what he considered the inadequate vigour of the pursuit of the retreating enemy by the *corps de chasse*, under Lumsden's command.

Copyright IWM, negative E 19095

45. JSM's damaged staff car at El Alamein

This car was hit by an artillery shell that fortunately did not go off. It was hot and was lifted out of the car's engine, which still worked!

Copyright MacGill Family.

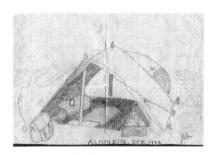

46. JSM's sketch of his tent at El Alamein

This drawing was sent in a letter that JSM wrote to his younger son Neil.

Copyright MacGill Family.

47. JSM's tent after it had been blown away

Another example of devastation caused by storms in an empty desert. (See Chapter 7.)

Copyright MacGill Family.

48. Survivors of 2 Rifle Brigade after El Alamein

One of the epics of the Battle of El Alamein was the action of 2 Rifle Brigade at *Snipe*, near *Kidney* Ridge, a small extension of the Miteiriya Ridge. Fifty-seven enemy tanks and self-propelled guns were destroyed by this battalion, whose Commanding Officer, Lieutenant Colonel Victor Turner, was awarded the Victoria Cross. This battalion was one of the infantry units in the 1ˢᵗ Armoured Division.

Copyright IWM, negative E 18717.

49. American ambulance with 1ˢᵗ Light Field Ambulance

This Chevrolet ambulance, named *Thomas F. Yawkey*, and its American crew represented one of the few parties of United States citizens who participated in the Battle of El Alamein. (See Chapter 7.) Another little-known group was a number of subalterns in the King's Royal Rifle Corps (KRRC, or 60ᵗʰ Rifles), who had been recruited from Ivy League universities. The KRRC, a prestigious regiment, was also known as the *Royal Americans*, because it had been recruited on American soil during the Revolutionary War.

Copyright MacGill Family.

50. Medical officer and orderlies in Advanced Dressing Station, 1ˢᵗ Light Field Ambulance

Eight orderlies and a medical officer (squatting on the right), in front of a 3-ton ambulance truck. This was parked above a shallow trench to protect the engine from bomb blast. Most of the men had steel helmets because they were in the battle zone. Note the absence of arms. The RAMC are non-fighting troops.

Copyright MacGill Family.

51. Victorious 8ᵗʰ Army troops with a smashed German anti-tank gun

The anti-tank gun is mounted on a German half-track, and the barrel of the gun, probably 57mm, still looks formidable. The soldiers are understandably triumphant.

Copyright MacGill Family.

52. German and Italian prisoners

'For you the war is over.' Most of the prisoners are German, but there is at least one Italian (on the left, in breeches).

Copyright MacGill Family.

54. JSM's camp chair

This still exists despite its fragility. The photograph shows the chair in a garden at Ascot, Berkshire, the home of JSM's son John.

Copyright MacGill Family.

53. 1st Light Field Ambulance at Tmimi

After the victory at El Alamein, the 1st Light Field Ambulance moved 250 miles to the west, to Tmimi. They remained there while most of the 8th Army was advancing west to Tripoli. The 1st Armoured Division was later called forward for the assault on the Mareth Line. (Plate 56.)

Copyright MacGill Family.

161

55. 1ˢᵗ Light Field Ambulance. Christmas dinner in the desert

The weather in December 1942 was still warm enough for men not to need greatcoats. In the customary way, the officers served the men their Christmas dinner. The soldiers ate from their mess tins, and their mugs were filled with modest quantities of beer.

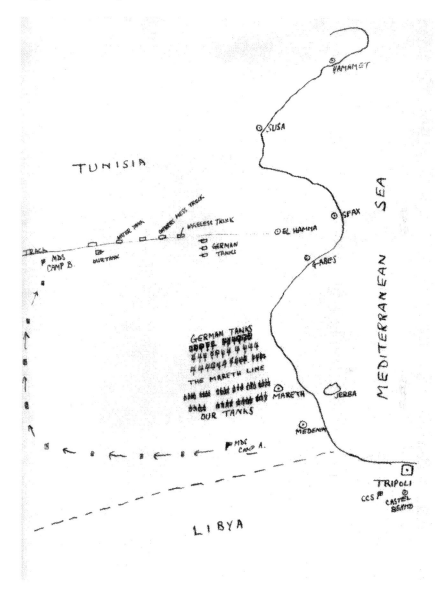

56. JSM's sketch map of the advance during the Battle of Mareth

This is a particularly interesting contemporary sketch map of the important action that defeated the Panzerarmee Afrika at Mareth, Tunisia. The 1ˢᵗ Armoured Division took a broad left-hand sweep and then moved east to envelop the enemy and capture El Hamma and Sfax (on the Mediterranean). During this assault, JSM came under heavy enemy fire and was pinned down until the enemy tanks were pushed back. (See Chapter 8.)

CHAPTER 7

'THE BRIGHT GLEAM HAS CAUGHT THE HELMETS OF OUR SOLDIERS AND WARMED AND CHEERED ALL OUR HEARTS'

This piece of Churchillian eloquence, delivered in November 1942, is surely the most memorable description of the impact of the great battle of El Alamein on the psyche of the British people. But before this victory, more than three months had passed since Auchinleck's defensive battle in the same place: the clash that halted the Panzerarmee Afrika. The battle of Gazala and the British retreat had been harsh experiences for the 8th Army. There was no shortage of doubts about the ability of the 8th Army to stop Rommel reorganizing and reinforcing his army and continuing his triumphal progress until he reached the Nile. Could the 8th Army be reinvigorated radically and grow strong enough – with powerful enough leadership – to win the first major British land victory of the war? The British army had after all suffered nothing but defeats during three years of bloody conflict. Summer in the North African desert lasts from April to October, an unrelentingly uncomfortable climate that was new to Dr. MacGill and the members of the 1st Armoured Division except those Regular soldiers who had served in the Middle East before the war. JSM's military career took him in a new direction just before the loss of Tobruk, when he was transferred from the Queen's Bays to the 1st Light Field Ambulance. This medical unit received wounded men from the Regimental Aid Posts and was attached to the 2nd Armoured Brigade, in which the Bays were serving. For him it was therefore 'au revoir' and not 'goodbye'.

El Alamein, Act One: the Block

The 8th Army was in position at El Alamein on 26 June 1942 and the Panzerarmee Afrika, full of optimism, faced them on 29 June. By this time, there was much disorder in the British rear. The British army and navy had partially evacuated Alexandria. The British Embassy in Cairo was publicly burning secret papers in large bonfires, prompting a wit to call the day Ash Wednesday. Many British civilians were evacuated, which caused huge inconvenience. The Egyptian population had little sympathy for the British, and Rommel's men would probably have been welcomed. Some elements in the Egyptian government and army were in fact making approaches to Rommel. Mussolini, the Joker in the Pack, flew to Libya and prepared to lead a victory parade in Cairo, riding a white horse.

By this time Dr. MacGill had been transferred to the 1st Light Field Ambulance. Before the British retreat, this unit was in the northern part of the battlefield, just outside the Tobruk perimeter. This was a potential danger spot, but was soon evacuated as the retreat began. Auchinleck called a halt when the army reached a prepared position well to the rear. The place chosen for the 8th Army to stop the enemy advance was not an ideal defensive position in view of the many square miles of the battlefield and the modest size of the British force, but the position was good enough. It was a broad neck of land connecting the Mediterranean in the north to the large Qattara depression in the south; this is a desert sea, 100 meters below sea level, with soft sand that is impassable for vehicles on wheels or tracks. The defensive line from north to south was forty miles long. It took its name from the small railway station of El Alamein, sixty miles west of Alexandria, the last stop on the single-track railway running along the coast from Alexandria to the Libyan frontier. The El Alamein position contains five low ridges that would play a part in the coming battles. The most important of these were Ruweisat (running west to east) and Alam el Halfa (running south-west to north-east). (**Map 7.**)

The length of the line meant that each mile from north to south was covered on average by 2,500 British soldiers, and these had to provide defence in depth, which meant keeping local reserves. As a consequence they were very stretched. Auchinleck's plan was to deploy his army in defensive boxes manned by infantry and guarded by minefields; strong artillery support on call; and armoured formations for immediate counter-attacks, although the shortage of resources meant that these were brigades and battle groups and not divisions. This was the old problem of 'penny packets.'

Rommel's attacks began on 1 July, with a diversionary move against El Alamein itself. This was immediately followed by a powerful right-flanking assault around the south of the El Alamein position. Both German attacks were halted, mainly by British artillery fire, some of which caught Rommel who was in his usual position with his forward troops. This was to be the pattern of all the engagements in the following days: the Germans making small gains, which were held or pushed back by British defensive fire and counter-attacks. In holding Ruweisat ridge, the Queen's Bays played an important part and during the battle the regiment suffered twenty casualties, of whom seven lost their lives. These included the very tall Lord Knebworth, newly-promoted major and squadron commander.

By 17 July the attackers, in particular the Italians, were not in good heart. This was made worse by the failing supplies because of the length of Rommel's administrative 'tail', which was between 750 and 1,400 miles from the ports where the supplies had landed. Auchinleck held on fiercely, although the casualties in the 8th Army forced him to break up some divisions and form small battle groups: a re-creation of the 'Jock Columns' that had not been a great success at the beginning of the battle of Gazala. The tough and independent Australians refused Auchinleck's instructions, and the divisional commander, Major General Morshead, threatened to appeal to the Australian government before Auchinleck changed his mind.

The fighting during July was a contest between Rommel and Auchinleck, two experienced commanders who had comparable 'grip' and tactical skills, and approximately equal resources. They had roughly the same numbers of men, but Rommel had better tanks and Auchinleck had superior artillery. This balance meant that one general's actions and impact on the battle tended to be cancelled out by the actions and impact of the other. All the time the resources of both were being whittled down. The two armies therefore soon confronted each other in conditions of comparable weakness, and the battle sputtered to a standstill. The battle had been an unambiguous demonstration of Auchinleck's generalship when for the first time he decided to take personal control of the action. The line held, which meant that El Alamein, Act One, had been a strategic – although not a tactical – victory for the British. The battle blocked the further advance of the Panzerarmee Afrika. British casualties during the battle totalled 13,000 men, on top of the 60,000 (*sic*) prisoners who had been taken in the battle of Gazala. Since January 1942, the British had also lost 2,000 tanks and armoured vehicles. The 8th Army was in desperate need of a large transfusion of men and weapons.

However, from now on the 8th Army would suffer no more defeats. After El Alamein, Act One, the British received a far richer flow of reinforcements and supplies than Rommel did. The American tanks, guns and motor vehicles, including the first Jeeps, made a major contribution to the improvement in British fortunes. An even more important reason for this improvement was the change in top command ordered by Churchill in August 1942. When El Alamein, Acts Two and Three, were being fought under the direct command of Lieutenant General Montgomery, Auchinleck was contemplating his future, which was to return to the east as Commander-in-Chief of the Indian army, the largest volunteer army in history. This mighty force would within two years be defeating in instalments the Japanese armies in south-east Asia, armies that until then had been unstoppable.

In Egypt in July to October 1942, while these great changes were taking place in the command, size and organization of the 8th Army, both sides of the battle line were continuing to endure the discomfort of summer in the North African desert, including rats, scorpions and snakes. Summer was particularly arduous for soldiers enclosed in tanks, which intensified the heat.

JSM Journal

> It did not rain at all from April to October. Warm sunshine and completely blue sky all day and every day, but I don't remember hearing anyone say 'Isn't it a lovely day?' It was just taken for granted, besides we had

more important things to talk about. It was very cold at night even in the summer. When in action and on the move, we went into close leaguer when it got dark. I would throw down my bed-roll on the sand beside the scout car, unroll it, and blow up the Li-Lo (*an inflatable mattress*), with three blankets over me and a waterproof ground sheet on top. In the early morning, this sheet collected dew that would otherwise wet the blankets. Three blankets was too hot really in the evening, but round about 3:00AM it got very cold. When we got up at first light, one put on battledress, scarf, greatcoat, hat and gloves. During the morning, one discarded them gradually till around noon one was in shirtsleeves; and as the afternoon progressed one put them on again. In the winter, that is October to April, there was only the odd short shower of rain. Usually on a still day you would feel a sudden puff of cold wind on your cheek and know it was going to rain. Then run for cover, because you knew that within one minute it would be a deluge lasting about half-an-hour, and then sunshine again and no rain for a few weeks. Of course if you were sleeping in a tank you did not need a waterproof sheet, but sleeping in the open it was essential also to cover up all the clothes you had taken off with waterproof sheets. Most of the time there was a very strong wind, and the only way to be comfortable was to turn the car sideways into the wind when you stopped, and drape a tarpaulin over it and down the left side (*the side away from the wind*). You would then sit behind the tarpaulin. (**Plate 15.**) Sometimes there was a terrific sandstorm lasting an hour or so.

Desert Battles and Wounded Soldiers

The 1st Light Field Ambulance, attached to the 2nd Armoured Brigade, was set up to handle all casualties – from fighting, accidents and sickness – who were brought in from each regiment's RAP. British and enemy casualties were treated in the same way. Captured German doctors sometimes lent a hand. The arriving patients came to the Advanced Dressing Station (ADS), and then passed on to the Main Dressing Station (MDS). (**Plates 33, 24.**) At these places they were given instant treatment, which often included surgery, and then passed back without delay to the rear. In the desert, the average distance from RAP to ADS was eight to twelve miles; from ADS to MDS it was twelve to fifteen miles. There was then a longer series of journeys to a chain of units behind the lines: a Rear MDS, a Casualty Clearing Station (CCS) and finally a General Hospital. The patients did not necessarily stop at all these places, but the establishments were set up in response to the flow of patients, which was much greater during battles than when there was less activity at the front. JSM's work was mainly at the 1st Light Field Ambulance's MDS.

The 1st Light Field Ambulance had a strength of 150 men, under the command of a lieutenant colonel in the RAMC. Dr. MacGill, was Second-in-Command. (**Plate 42.**) This meant that he had to learn new skills: in addition to his clinical work he was also engaged in administration, since the logistics of a field ambulance in the desert were often complicated. There was a constant need for a wide range of medical supplies which had to be kept in sterile conditions; also the need for vastly more water than the quantity given to the troops of all arms of the service: only four pints per man per day. The field ambulance also had a (non-medical) quartermaster, and at least six officers on strength who were all qualified doctors, mostly general practitioners. (**Plate 43.**) Motor transport was extremely important, especially in the desert when the wounded had to be transported for long distances. (**Plate 49** is a photograph of a Chevrolet ambulance donated by the Americans and driven by American volunteers who were not officially part of the British army.) The large numbers of NCOs and private soldiers in the Field Ambulance were grateful not to be wounded or sick and cheerfully carried out a variety of jobs. The most important was of course to be medical orderlies caring for patients. But there were drivers, and men who spent their lives carrying out soldiers' work: providing guards, fetching, carrying, lifting, sanitary and disinfecting jobs, and digging. (**Plate 50.**)

One important and surprising fact is that casualties from sickness outnumbered those from wounds. In June 1942 (JSM's first month with the 1ˢᵗ Light Field Ambulance), the numbers were 4,954 sick and 3,605 wounded in the 8ᵗʰ Army as a whole. A third of the sick had desert sores and fever of various types, a sharp indication of the rigours of desert living. Dr. MacGill had something special to contribute here. His specialist study in Edinburgh University leading to his post-graduate degree of MD had been in the field of tropical diseases.

Soldiers fighting in tanks, if they were unfortunate enough to become casualties, suffered every possible type of physical damage. They had more burns over their bodies than the infantry and artillery, and more wounds to the head. (**Figure 3.**) It is easy to understand why this should be so. Tanks often caught fire when they were hit, and a tank commander usually went into battle with his head out of the turret.

	Armour	**Infantry**	**Artillery**
Burns	10	1	4
Head Wounds	20	15	12

FIGURE 3
PERCENTAGE OF ALL WOUNDS

JSM Journal

On 2 June 1942 I was transferred from the Bays to the 1ˢᵗ Light Field Ambulance as Second-in-Command and promoted to the rank of Major. At that time we were in camp near El Adam, south of Tobruk. One night it was just getting dark when we were attacked by German tanks. We had to pack up and get out quick. We were in front of a minefield and had to steer a careful course in the dark alongside a row of telegraph posts. We were told that there was a clear passage alongside the posts. We had not gone far when I was called to a truck, and in it was a man with his leg practically blown off. I amputated it with a pair of stretcher-bearer's scissors. He had stepped on a mine. He was from Glasgow, so there is now a one-legged man in Glasgow who will remember me!

In the desert there were fantastic sunsets every night. They were beautiful. There is only one good thing in this Godforsaken land and that is the sunset. I suppose it was partly because there were no houses or trees to obstruct the going down of the sun, and no smoke or clouds to obscure it.

Bathing in the Mediterranean Sea could be tricky. I bathed quite a few times, but if you could not swim very well it was dangerous. The sand on the shore sloped down so steeply, like the roof of a house. Ten feet out from shore you were well out of your depth. It was easy enough to go in; it was the getting out that was difficult. You had to sort of climb up the sand and it was slipping away from under you. Several men were drowned. I remember one day I was thinking of going for a swim and heard that a man had been drowned that morning so that I did not go. I think it was particularly bad at certain places and that was probably one of them. On one occasion when we were in camp near Tobruk we went and bathed in the Med. We had to watch out for mines we were told were in the water, but we did not see any.

At this time we were static, but were set up as a Main Dressing Station. We used to sit in the sun on our folding chairs (**Plate 54,**) and watch enemy planes come over and bomb vehicles (not ours) we could see in the distance. We had a large Red Cross flag spread out on the ground in the centre of the camp, so they did not bomb us. We would see these planes in the distance swooping down and dropping their bombs, and hear the Boom! Boom! Boom! And then about twenty minutes later a convoy of ambulances would come rolling in and we had to deal with the wounded. One day however I was standing talking to the Regimental Sergeant Major and a plane came down. He said: 'It is one of ours', when we saw five bombs come tumbling out of it! We both lay down quickly and no one was hurt. We had the American ambulance drivers attached to us, and one day when an ambulance was full, I went to the driver and told him he could go. He said: 'The *sergeant* will tell me when to go'. I was only the major! The Americans camped by themselves and as I passed their tent they had a little American flag stuck in the sand. Later I went by and it was gone. I asked the man where it was, and he said: 'Oh, we lower it at sundown'. One night I put my bedroll in a slit trench dug before we arrived. I was awakened by a snake crawling away from under my pillow. I steered clear of disused slit trenches after that.

One evening we were camped south of Tobruk outside the perimeter. After the battle of Knighsbridge, Tobruk was surrounded by a ring of guns and tanks so no enemy could get into it. It was called the Tobruk perimeter, and inside it one was safe from enemy attack. Well, a squadron of armoured cars came swanning through our camp and one of them stopped and asked what we were doing there. We said: 'Stopping for the night'. He replied: 'Well, you are in no-man's land, and could be attacked by German tanks. We are now going inside the perimeter.' However, we stayed there the night and were not attacked by any tanks. Next day we had orders to go inside the perimeter, and in the afternoon my driver spent about three hours with a pickaxe, digging a slit trench for me to sleep in out of solid rock. After he had done it, at about 10:00PM, we had orders to move out of Tobruk and travelled all night and in the morning we were in Egypt. That was the night that I travelled in the ambulance with Lord Knebworth (*who had earlier been wounded and later died*).

We had a short stop of a few days at Fuka on the Mediterranean coast (*fifty-five miles west of El Alamein*). We were in camp right on the shore, and I had my bed roll just about ten feet from the water. When I woke in the morning, I pulled off my shirt (all I had on) and plunged into the sea. One night when we were there an ambulance ran over my bivvy tent in the dark and smashed my compass. Luckily I was playing Bridge in the Officers' Mess tent or I would probably have been killed. We were only there a few days unfortunately, but it was grand while it lasted. When we were at El Alamein, a few days before the battle started, I took a party of men to the coast, about ten miles, and we had a grand bathe in the sea. This time we were static as a Main Dressing Station at El Alamein and were bombed by enemy planes at night. We slept in slit trenches under bivvy tents. (**Plate 46.**) The nearest bomb dropped about twenty yards from my tent. Only one man was wounded, the Regimental Sergeant Major. He was very unpopular as usual, so a cheer went up as he went off in the ambulance!

El Alamein, Act Two: the Defence

Despite Auchinleck's skill and resolution in fighting the First Act of El Alamein, Churchill had already decided that there had to be change of command. As with all military appointments in the North African campaign, this was not a smooth process. Churchill confirmed the decision when he visited Cairo in August 1942 *en route* to Moscow for one of his difficult meetings with an uncooperative Stalin.

General Alexander, who had earned a considerable reputation in the disastrous campaigns in France in 1940 and Burma in 1942 – defeats for which he could not in any way be blamed – had already been selected for another job. This was command of the British army for Operation *Torch*, the invasion of North-West Africa in November 1942. However when Churchill and Brooke, the CIGS, took a hard look at the situation in Cairo, they decided that Alexander should be appointed immediately as Commander-in-Chief of the British armies in the Middle East. His first task would be to rejuvenate the 8th Army, which needed more effective senior commanders, more troops, better tanks, and intensive training at all levels. Alexander would impose a stronger 'grip' than his predecessor, and improve the morale of all ranks. Defeating the Panzerarmee Afrika was not just desirable, it was a matter of overwhelming urgency.

Alexander was a good choice, but a problem was later to emerge as his responsibilities grew. He was a talented strategist and had abundant charm which made him popular. He gave his subordinates wholehearted support. However, when he had American as well as British armies under his command, he was criticized for not imposing his will strongly enough on the conduct of his battles. This difficulty was to emerge in Sicily and Italy.

Meanwhile, the 8th Army needed a new commander. Churchill and Brooke realized that because of the problems that had confronted Auchinleck when he was forced to take over the 8th Army, there had to be a strong commander whose sole task would be to win the desert war. For command of the 8th Army Churchill, with Brooke's reluctant agreement, selected Lieutenant General Gott. He was highly experienced in the desert and was Auchinleck's best corps commander, although some people thought that he was tired and deserved a rest. Gott flew back to Cairo from the El Alamein position, but his ancient aircraft was forced to land for repairs because of a mechanical problem. The passengers got out and were machine-gunned by a marauding German aeroplane. Gott – like Lumsden in 1945 – was one of the few senior British officers to lose their lives in battle. Churchill agreed to Brooke's original candidate, and Lieutenant General Montgomery flew from England and was in Cairo forty-eight hours later.

Montgomery was a superbly equipped soldier. By the end of the war he had won all his battles with a single exception, the bold but hazardous Arnhem operation in September 1944. He was always conscious that the price of success in battle was paid for by men's lives. He made the hard decisions to pay this price, but he did everything he could to minimize it. He was a ferocious trainer of men, and he prepared his operations with punctilious care, which some people thought made him too slow. The lower ranks appreciated his care for their lives, and he was popular with the private soldiers, NCOs and junior officers. But Lieutenant Colonels and above were scared of him because he would sack them without appeal if he thought them incompetent or not physically fit.

In Europe in 1944, a number of officers were his superiors or equals in rank: the Americans Eisenhower, Bradley and Patton, and the British air chiefs Tedder and Coningham, and the head of the Royal Navy, Cunningham. These all disliked him intensely because they thought him dogmatic and slow. Brooke, his direct superior and patron, never wavered in his support. Churchill always tended to reserve judgment, and invariably in the end deferred to Brooke.

Montgomery took command of the 8th Army before the official date, and immediately imposed his 'grip.' He escaped from his headquarters as much as he could, and visited unit after unit and demonstrated his ability (in the view of an experienced artillery officer) to 'get under the skin' of officers and men in the ranks. In his curious black beret with two badges, he was seen everywhere, and as new divisions arrived they were left in no doubt that they had joined the 8th Army. He addressed soldiers *en masse* and also talked to them individually. On these occasions he learned about problems which he subsequently did something to solve: infrequent letters from home, shortage of cigarettes and NAAFI comforts, lack of spare clothing, and no leave when soldiers were out of the line. Most importantly – and an unprecedented innovation – before units went into battle, orders were moved down the chain of command and troops were told the strategic and tactical plans, and the precise jobs that they would have to perform.

Montgomery had not been long in Egypt before he had to prepare for battle. Rommel had been blocked during Act One of El Alamein. He was now going to renew his assault, and Montgomery was able to make preparations because he was receiving accurate *Sigint* from the incomparable Ultra intelligence, the work of the British code breakers.

During August, Rommel was suffering even more logistical problems than those that had always held him back. Malta had been reinforced in mid-August by a convoy that had taken terrible losses during the voyage. The embattled island therefore continued to impede the flow of supplies to the Panzerarmee Afrika, a situation made worse by the way in which British aircraft managed to target the supply ships sailing for Tripoli, Benghazi and Tobruk. (The local British commanders were unaware of the help that was being provided by *Sigint* from Bletchley Park.) Meanwhile, more men and vast quantities of supplies were reaching the 8ᵗʰ Army, and getting to the front along a much shorter line of communication than Rommel's extremely extended line.

With a worsening overall situation, and in particular a catastrophic shortage of gasoline, Rommel succumbed to pressure from his superiors in Germany and Italy, and decided on the date of 30 August to make a powerful thrust to reach the Nile, which was so temptingly close. At the back of Hitler's mind was the chimera that Rommel, advancing east, would link up with the German armies in the south of the Soviet Union: a grand strategic manoeuvre that would have blocked the British land route to India and even perhaps cause the British Empire to crumble.

The two most prominent features in the El Alamein position are (as mentioned) the two long low ridges: Ruweisat and Alam el Halfa. Ruweisat, stretching west to east, is fifteen miles south of the Mediterranean coast; Alam el Halfa is ten miles south-east of Ruweisat. (**Map 8.**) Rommel's plan was to make a right flanking armoured assault in the gap between the two ridges and from the south of Alam el Halfa. This showed good tactical judgment, and it is not surprising that Auchinleck and Montgomery – also excellent tacticians – believed that this would be Rommel's plan. In a battle between historians years later, Montgomery was criticized for supposedly adopting Auchinleck's defensive strategy. It is difficult to see how this matters, since both British generals were more-or-less right, and Montgomery was also guided by *Sigint* that revealed what Rommel would do.

Montgomery strongly reinforced the line from Ruweisat north to the coast. In anticipation of the enemy thrust, he concentrated 940 artillery pieces in static positions at the west end of Alam el Halfa ridge: 400 tanks, 300 anti-tank guns, and 240 field guns, all protected by a thick minefield. This fire power was set up to counter any advance from the west and south, and the units were ordered to stay where they were and not counter-attack. As an imaginative addition to the defences, Major General de Guingand, Montgomery's Chief-of-Staff, arranged for a false map of desert 'going' (i.e. suitability for motor transport) to fall into German hands, which had the result of guiding many German tanks into areas of thick sand.

The 8th Army tanks on the Alam el Halfa ridge were dug in hull-down defensive positions, with only their turrets in full operation. Tanks dug in so deeply can only re-emerge with difficulty, and the British crews' nerves were strained at the sight of the many advancing Panzers. Nevertheless, Montgomery's plan worked and his greater number of tanks tipped the balance. By the end of the three-day battle, Rommel had lost fifty tanks, an equal number of guns, and 400 lighter vehicles. The 8th Army had a far greater weight of gunfire from tanks and artillery, and after the ground was clear of periodic desert storms, the RAF pounded the enemy positions.

By 3 September, the German forces had retreated to their start line. Montgomery then authorized a minor counter-attack, but this was badly mishandled and did not succeed. However, the fact that Rommel's attack had been broken left no doubt that Act Two of the Battle of El Alamein was a defensive victory for the 8th Army. Comparing battle casualties with the size of the armies engaged, the 8th Army's loss of 1,750 men was a much smaller proportion than Rommel's loss of 2,900. Not surprisingly, the performance of the 8th Army did a great deal to boost the army's confidence in its leader.

The 8th Army now engaged in seven weeks of reinforcement, planning, training, and preparation for battle. These phases were necessary before Montgomery was comfortable enough to embark on the fifth and final (east to west) lap of the Benghazi Handicap. The British assault at El Alamein was to be one of the handful of turning points in the Allied progress to victory in the Second World War: Midway, El Alamein, Stalingrad, Normandy, and Hiroshima.

El Alamein, Act Three: the Victory

During the days before the Third Act of the battle, the 8th Army and the Panzerarmee Afrika were facing each other across the forty-mile El Alamein line, with Rommel's main position eight miles west of the forward units of the 8th Army. They were separated by a belt of half a million mines, 'the devil's gardens', the heaviest in two places: within a few miles of the Mediterranean coast and in front of the Ruweisat Ridge, fifteen miles to the south. It was obvious to both sides that it was impossible to outflank the opposing army, since between the sea and the Qattara depression both defensive lines were continuous. Surprise over the place and time of attack would be very difficult although not totally impossible. The position resembled that during the First World War when there were two long fortified lines that stretched from the North Sea to Switzerland. There, as at El Alamein, the sole possibility for an attacker was to force a penetration against an enemy who had strength in depth.

There were however a number of points of difference at El Alamein, and these would be exploited by Montgomery. First, the Panzerarmee Afrika did not have strategic as opposed to tactical reserves. In the First World War, the Germans were able to rush forward formidable reinforcements from rear areas at any signal of a British or French attack. This was normally made clear by *days* of preparatory artillery bombardment before the infantry assault. Second, Montgomery had larger numbers of men and vast supplies, notably of artillery and the 300 Sherman tanks that Roosevelt had promised Churchill at the time of the fall of Tobruk. The American president did not fully realize how valuable these tanks would be to the British. Montgomery planned to fight in corps and full-strength divisions, and not in brigades or battle groups. This was itself a major change from the hand-to-mouth fighting that had characterized British tactics in North Africa until then. The third difference was Montgomery's tactical plan, which was to open the battle with a night assault, beginning with a barrage of devastating weight by almost 1,000 guns. The infantry, who had been intensively trained, would move forward accompanied by engineers to clear paths through the minefields. The men of all ranks would be fully briefed about the battle plan and the specific jobs that they would have to carry out. This was also different from previous practice.

Both sides had approximately equal numbers of divisions, but Rommel's were all under-strength, a total of 108,000 troops. The British had the initiative, and Montgomery had greatly improved the morale of his men. The 8th Army had full-strength divisions with a total of 200,000 men overall, vast supplies, and superiority in artillery and air power. The Germans had their traditionally excellent tanks (although only 250 of them), and the incomparable 88mm anti-tank guns. The Axis soldiers were tough and resilient: certainly the Germans, although the

Italians were mostly not quite so reliable. The Panzerarmee Afrika also had Rommel's leadership, although they would lose him temporarily at the crucial beginning of the battle.

The 8th Army had a total of 939 tanks: the older Crusaders and Grants, and the 300 Shermans which were the best tanks in the British inventory and had arrived in time to be prepared for battle. The Shermans were reliable and comfortable for the crews, but they suffered from two serious defects. Their short 75mm gun was not as effective as that in the Panzer IV. The Shermans were also high off the ground and did not have enough armoured protection for their petrol tank and ammunition racks. This made them easy to catch fire, which was not good for the confidence of the crews. In the Normandy campaign, the soldiers called them 'Ronsons,' the name of the popular cigarette lighters. As explained in Chapter 4, the British armoured divisions were much better balanced than those that had fought in 1940 and 1941. The 1st Armoured Division now had three tank regiments and one of armoured cars; more than four lorried infantry battalions; six artillery regiments; five engineer field squadrons; plus the usual services.

The Panzerarmee Afrika had 548 tanks, although fewer than half were the two best German designs. The Panzer III was as good as any British vehicle, and the Panzer IV was significantly better. Following the normal German practice, the Panzerarmee Afrika armoured divisions were well balanced.

The Panzerarmee Afrika was deployed as follows :

- *Between the sea and Ruweisat Ridge.* One German and three Italian infantry divisions.

- *Between Ruweisat Ridge and the Qattara depression.* Three Italian infantry divisions and a German Reconnaisance Group (in the extreme south).

- *In reserve for tactical deployment during the battle.* Two German and two Italian armoured divisions, and one German and one Italian infantry division.

The German deployment was a typical illustration of Rommel's tactical doctrine. He was always light on his feet, and rushed forward reinforcements (normally accompanying them) to any places where extra armour and infantry were needed. Hence his large force of reserves, especially tanks.

The individual elements of the 8th Army were organized before the battle to the following plan (**Map 9**):

- *Between the sea and Ruweisat Ridge.* Lieutenant General Leese's XXX Corps, of five infantry divisions. These were Australian, New Zealand, South African, Indian, and the newly arrived 51st Highland Division that had been re-formed after their disaster in France in 1940.

- *Between Ruweisat Ridge and the Qattara depression.* Lieutenant General Horrocks's XIII Corps, the equivalent of three infantry divisions: two British divisions plus a Greek brigade and the Free French. He also had the 7th Armoured Division in reserve.

- *In reserve to exploit a breakthrough.* Lieutenant General Lumsden's X Corps of two armoured divisions, 1st Armoured Division and 10th Armoured Division in the north. These represented Montgomery's *corps de chasse*. Dr. MacGill, in the Light Field Ambulance, was with 2nd Armoured Brigade in the 1st Armoured Division.

Of Montgomery's three corps commanders, he had more confidence in Leese and Horrocks than in Lumsden. In fact he had originally offered Horrocks the command of X Corps, the *corps de chasse*, but Horrocks declined for a reason that many people would find difficult to understand. He had spent his earlier service in the Middlesex Regiment, the 'Die-hards,' a body of fighting soldiers, mainly Londoners, with a long and bloody history. But Horrocks feared that the aristocratic cavalry officers in the two armoured divisions would not respect someone from such a modest military background. Although such an attitude might be deplorable, it is a rather perverse manifestation of the regimental pride that is such a source of strength in the British army.

Montgomery also came from a relatively modest infantry regiment, the Royal Warwickshire Regiment. But he lacked Horrocks's sensitivity and was not troubled by the attitudes of his subordinates. Leese had been a Coldstream Guardsman, and Lumsden had been a 12th Lancer, and before that had served in the Royal Horse Artillery and the Honourable Artillery Company. (**Plate 44.**)

After Churchill had returned to London on 24 August 1942, he found himself in a major dispute with the Americans over the plans for Operation *Torch*, the planned invasion of North-West Africa. Churchill was anxious to move quickly, but this meant that he had to put pressure on Montgomery to attack the Panzerarmee Afrika without delay. Rommel had to be on the run before the Anglo-American landings, because the ultimate intention was to force Rommel's troops into a trap between the 8th Army coming from the east and the Anglo-American force advancing from the west. Alexander and Montgomery stood their ground. Montgomery was insistent that his troops would not be well enough trained, nor would his tactical plans be sufficiently well developed, for an early attack. The clinching argument was that the assault had to take place during the period of full moon. This dictated Montgomery's final plan, which was for an assault during the night of 23/24 October 1942. The battle developed in such a way that it was fought in two phases, with a gap in-between for re-grouping.

The initial British advance was launched by the foot soldiers. The engineers had to clear paths through the minefields to make way for the infantry, and after their advance, the *corps de chasse* would finish crumbling the enemy positions and then be turned loose to drive the Panzerarmee Afrika off the field. This was to be a stickier process than Montgomery had anticipated. The artillery barrage from almost 1,000 guns of all calibres lasted from 9:40 to 10:10PM on 23 October. Montgomery witnessed it and then went straight to bed. He had done his job when he had formulated and communicated his plan and made sure that its execution was in totally competent hands. Meanwhile the advancing troops had been concealed in slit trenches since nightfall.

A documentary film exists of the first minutes of the battle. First there are some moments of the blinding barrage. Then in the flickering light of searchlights and tracer ammunition, the soldiers can be seen rising from the ground, cold and stiff, and advancing steadily. The sappers are clearing the way and marking paths with tapes. The Highlanders are then moving forward with fixed bayonets. Most dramatic of all is a sound that can be heard above the noise of shells and small arms: the tribal skirl of the bagpipes played by the intrepid pipers marching among the leading groups of infantry. (Pipers had a particularly dangerous job because in daylight they were choice targets for sniper fire.) The advancing sappers and infantry had to leave behind many dead and wounded men who would be collected by the stretcher bearers who were coming immediately behind.

The enemy had been caught totally by surprise. Nevertheless they defended their positions in and behind the minefields with their customary stoicism. But their leader was absent. Exactly one month before the British assault, Rommel was forced by ill-health to fly to Germany for six weeks sick leave. He was suffering from the prolonged strain of battle and was exhausted, with digestive problems, and was subject to fainting fits. In his absence, the Panzerarmee Afrika was commanded by General Stumme. As soon as he learned that the 8th Army offensive had started, he contacted the German High Command and Hitler talked to Rommel and asked him to return. Stumme himself did not last long and on 24 October he succumbed to a fatal heart attack.

Montgomery's main thrust was in the north, made by Leese's XXX Corps. The infantry forced two broad paths through the minefield and the tanks followed through. However, the southern thrust towards Miteiriya Ridge was stopped in a devastating hail of artillery and small arms fire. Before dawn on 24 October this thrust had been halted, causing a vulnerable traffic jam as 200 tanks were held up in the narrow paths that had been cleared through the minefield. Twenty miles to the south, Horrocks's XIII Corps also encountered trouble on the Himeimat Ridge sector. As part of Rommel's master plan, Horrocks was to engage the enemy in a feint attack that had been preceded by the building of elaborate structures behind the lines for the enemy to discover from aerial reconnaissance. The enemy was to be persuaded that this is where the main attack would come. XIII Corps made a number of small attacks which did no more than tie down the enemy forces facing them:

their main objective, because the enemy was prevented from reinforcing his defences against the attack of XXX Corps.

Meanwhile, Montgomery was not happy with the situation in the north, and he met Lumsden and ordered him to continue to attack or be sacked. However, Lumsden had already taken steps to rescue the situation. The Shermans were beginning to succeed in long-range duels with enemy tanks and 88mm anti-tank guns. Because of the strong attacks from the RAF, many of these guns were used in their original role against aircraft. With their barrels pointing upwards, they made excellent targets for the fire of the Sherman tanks: a nice piece of serendipity.

By this time the battle had become a brutal killing match. Montgomery, ever sensitive to changes in the battlefield, moved the angle of attack from north-west to west. The centre of action now became a small depression at the end of the Miteiriya Ridge, called Kidney Ridge. The fighting continued with great intensity and even more confusion. The Panzerarmee Afrika was now suffering crippling losses, many from the British 6-pounder anti-tank guns in the hands of artillery regiments and infantry battalions. (**Plate 48.**) Lieutenant Colonel Victor Turner, the Commanding Officer of 2 Rifle Brigade (in the 1ˢᵗ Armoured Division) won the Victoria Cross when his battalion destroyed fifty-seven enemy tanks and self-propelled guns. He personally manned a 6-pounder when its crew was knocked out. Rommel was firmly in command, but he was hamstrung by shortages of material, notably petrol. Realising that the XIII Corps attack was a feint, he moved his reinforcements to the north, in the process using up all their fuel.

It was at this stage, on 27 October, that Montgomery was conscious of his losses as well as the partial success of the operation and decided to pause and re-group. He knew that the battle was reaching what would now be called a 'Tipping Point.' A further mighty shove and the door would open. The New Zealand Division (in Rommel's opinion the best infantry in the 8ᵗʰ Army) and X Corps were both temporarily withdrawn. This caused consternation in London because Churchill feared that Montgomery was throwing in the towel, but Brooke defended the 8ᵗʰ Army fiercely. Montgomery was now about to embark on the second phase of the battle. It was all-important that he should retain the initiative and make Rommel dance to his tune. From what he had learned from *Sigint*, Montgomery knew that Rommel had brought reinforcements north from the forces facing XIII Corps.

On 30 October, Montgomery wrote out his orders for the second phase of the battle, which he called Operation *Supercharge*. Rommel was expecting the assault to be in the extreme north of the battlefield. The Australians here had suffered terrible casualties but had inflicted enormous losses on the Panzerarmee Afrika. By now, Rommel had lost more than half his tanks. Ammunition was short, as was petrol. Against Rommel's expectations, Montgomery planned the attack much further south. Major General Freyberg, Commander of the New Zealand Division, would lead the spearhead, which would comprise an *ad hoc* formation of three British brigades, two infantry and one armor. The attack began at 1:00AM on 2 November.

Preceded by a creeping barrage from 360 guns, two infantry brigades moved relentlessly forward to the west from near Kidney Ridge. The frontage of attack was 4,000 yards. In a cold desert night German and Italian troops were soon surrendering in numbers. The infantry passed through the enemy front line at dawn and reached their objective beyond it: a position that they fortified with difficulty and would serve as a bridgehead for exploitation by 133 tanks of the 9th Armoured Brigade. The tanks moved through, but in the early light of dawn, they were picked off in large numbers by carefully sited anti-tank guns. Seventy-five tanks were knocked out, many in flames.

The 2nd Armoured Brigade now joined the battle, and the RAF continued pounding the enemy (and in Montgomery's view winning the battle for him). Rommel ordered a desperate counter-attack by the 21st Panzer Division, but by now the British had a four-to-one superiority in numbers of tanks. The first major crack was in two Italian divisions, which began to disintegrate. Rommel stared defeat in the face, and late on 2 November he ordered a general retreat. He planned to pull back the remnants of the Panzerarmee Afrika fifty miles to the rear, to a new defensive line at Fuka. The withdrawal began at 10:00PM, and he immediately informed Rome and Berlin of his decision.

The news had a shattering effect in Berlin. Hitler in his fury demanded that the Panzerarmee Afrika should stand fast and face victory or death. This meant that Rommel had to countermand his earlier order, although the retreat did begin on 4 November. The German and Italian troops put up a token resistance but this was quickly overcome. General von Thoma, Commander of the Afrikakorps and Rommel's senior subordinate, was left alone on the battlefield and was captured by a young officer of the 10th Hussars (in 2nd Armoured Brigade), Captain Grant Washington Singer, who was killed the next day. The enemy general was invited to dinner by Montgomery on 4 November. The British public did not approve of this, although Churchill was impressed, especially after he learned that von Thoma had sent a chivalrous letter of sympathy to Captain Singer's mother.

The Panzerarmee Afrika lost 20,000 men killed and wounded, plus 30,000 prisoners; also 450 tanks, 1,000 guns, and large numbers of vehicles (**Plates 51, 52.**) The church bells in Britain were rung, for the first time during the course of the war. The battle lasted for twelve days and the 8th Army had suffered 13,500 casualties: a terrible toll, but nevertheless less than one quarter of the British casualties during the *first day* of the Battle of the Somme, 1 July 1916. Before El Alamein, Montgomery had forecast the length of the battle to come, and the number of casualties that were unfortunately likely. Both his estimates were astonishingly accurate.

During the days of the bloody battle, Dr. MacGill and his comrades worked day and night. The 1st Light Field Ambulance was established about ten miles south of the Mediterranean and twenty miles behind the front line. It had to be out of danger of bombing from the air and artillery fire from the ground. JSM's place was in the Main Dressing Station, although he drove forward occasionally to the Advanced Dressing Station, half way towards the fighting. The casualties, mainly from the 2nd Armoured Brigade, were transported in ambulances, clearly marked with the Red Cross, to the ADS, and from there most would go to the MDS. While at the MDS, Dr. MacGill slept in a slit trench covered by a small tent (**Plate 46.**) On one occasion it was blown apart by a desert storm (**Plate 47.**)

Before the battle, there was nothing that the men of the 1st Light Field Ambulance could do except sharpen their preparations to be one hundred percent efficient when the firing began. The officers had a detailed pre-battle conference (**Plate 43**) and officers and men (**Plate 50**) approached the forthcoming battle keenly aware of the importance of their work.

JSM Journal

On the second day of the Battle of El Alamein I went up in my car to visit the ADS. We must have missed it because we passed a field gun firing away at something. (*The British 25-pounder had a reach of almost eight miles, so it must have been firing at extreme range.*) Soon after that, we decided to turn back. We turned around, and very soon a shell hit the bonnet of the car and penetrated under the bonnet (**Plate 45.**) The car stopped and I opened the bonnet and there was a shell, about eighteen inches long and four inches across, lying on the side of the engine. Another fellow and I lifted it out gently – it was quite hot – and placed it on the ground! The car would go so we drove away quickly. Soon after that I learned that the Medical Officer of the Queen's Bays had been killed. That was the young doctor who had taken my place when I left the Bays. I remember he once said to me that after the war he was going to stay on in the army as a medical officer. But he did not make it.

In the Battle of El Alamein, the 1st Armoured Division had a strength of 15,290 men. Of these, 264 were killed or died of wounds, and 1,003 were wounded and likely to live. 670 of the 1,003 were evacuated because their wounds called for radical surgery. The division had two light field ambulances, in one of which Dr. MacGill was serving. The number of wounded men gives an idea of the load he carried during the battle.

Mark Harrison, 'Medicine and Victory: British Military Medicine in the Second World War'

The surgeons at a Casualty Clearing Station during the battle of El Alamein . . . "their eyes dark with fatigue, cutting away sections of blood-soaked uniform, trimming, probing and sewing up the gaping flesh with calm and studious concentration."

After the battle was over and the casualties had been passed back down the line, the 1st Light Field Ambulance was free to join the tail of the 8th Army, and before long it moved forward with the rest of the 1st Armoured Division, to Tmimi. This is a patch of desert west of Tobruk and south-east of Derna, more than 250 miles beyond El Alamein. (**Plate 53.**)

CHAPTER 8
WEST TO TRIPOLI AND BEYOND

El Alamein was fought according to a firm plan but it turned into a soldiers' battle, as all of them do. The fighting took its toll on the 8th Army, which suffered significant losses and general exhaustion. The Panzerarmee Afrika was defeated but by no means annihilated, and during its long retreat Rommel was firmly in control. It took three months, until 23 January 1943, for the 8th Army to get to Tripoli, which had always been the objective but until now had never been reached. During November and December 1942, the Angle-American invasion of North-West Africa had established a firm footing, but the fighting had come to a virtual halt in the wintry mountainous terrain of Tunisia. With the withdrawal of the Panzerarmee Afrika from Libya and now holding a firm line in southern Tunisia, Rommel returned to his normal aggressiveness and turned around to inflict a sharp defeat on the American II Corps at the Kasserine Pass. The 8th Army soon retained the initiative and made a difficult but successful assault on the Mareth Line. The 1st Armoured Division, in which Dr. MacGill was serving, did not play much part in the three-month advance to Tripoli, but it took the lead in the final and decisive phase of the Battle of Mareth. In mid-May 1943, as the result of a massive battle the Axis forces had been expelled from Africa, leaving behind more prisoners than had been taken in Stalingrad,

The Long Supply Line

Although the battle of El Alamein had been a great victory, it was not followed by a rapid advance to push a beaten enemy back along the North African coast. The further the 8th Army moved forward from El

Alamein, the greater became its logistical difficulties. There was a great strain on the supply line, and the army's Quartermaster General, Major General Robertson, performed magnificently in bringing forward by road the vast amounts of petrol, oil and lubricants needed by the masses of vehicles, in addition to the ammunition, food and water and comforts that had to be constantly supplied to an advancing army. (Robertson's father had done the same job with the BEF in France and Belgium in 1914, and had made a reputation for his drive and efficiency as he carried out his tasks on the move. He was the celebrated 'Wully' Robertson, the only man who had ever started life as a Regular private soldier and ended as a Field Marshal.)

Rommel was in the opposite situation. The further he retreated, the simpler his supply problem became, as the Panzerarmee Afrika approached the ports of Tobruk and then Tripoli. During the retreat Rommel kept a tight control of his army. Five divisions, four of them German, were intact although badly under-strength, and he soon received reinforcements of four divisions: two Italian and later two armoured. Rommel's army had to fall back along the single metalled road following the North African coast, and his men planted minefields including booby traps on the verges which impeded his pursuers although, during the early days of the pursuit, two flanking attacks netted 1,500 Italian prisoners. On 13 November British forward units got to Tobruk, and on 20 November the 1st Armoured Division, traveling on tank transporters, arrived at Tmimi, 250 miles beyond El Alamein. They were soon joined by the 1st Light Field Ambulance. Montgomery had by now been knighted and promoted full general (what is now called four-star rank).

The 8th Army had been badly bruised at El Alamein, with a loss of eight percent of its men. However, although much armour had been knocked out, a good deal had been recovered. Montgomery fielded 600 tanks, but he became increasingly disappointed in the energy displayed by his *corps de chasse*. Not surprisingly, Lieutenant General Lumsden was sacked three weeks after the end of the battle. A serious problem for the armour was the wet weather that signaled the beginning of autumn. South of the coast road there was nothing but desert and the tanks were immobilized in the mud as they constantly tried to outflank the retreating enemy.

It was all a laborious slog, and although there was no serious fighting except for local engagements, it was three months after the beginning of the battle of El Alamein that British troops began to move into Tripoli. The fifth lap of the Benghazi Handicap had been won and the 8th Army had advanced beyond. (**Map 10.**) But there was to be stiff fighting ahead, in particular the difficult assault on the Mareth Line.

Between 24 October and 28 October, the 1st Armoured Division had borne much of the fighting. During the first four days of the breakout, the division led the way, but the process was interrupted by enemy rearguard actions, lack of petrol, and the beginning of the rainy season. Montgomery now decided that the pursuit would be led by two formations, the 7th Armoured Division and the New Zealand Division with some armoured reinforcement. The 51st Highland Division would later join them. The tail of the retreating Panzerarmee Afrika was in the competent hands of the German 90th Light Division, reinforced by some Italian units. The 8th Army crossed into Libya on 11 November, and Benghazi was reached on 20 November. During this advance, Montgomery continuously called on the fire power of the Desert Air Force. This was a precursor of the Tactical Air Forces that operated so effectively in support of the armies in North-West Europe in 1944 and 1945.

The 1st Armoured Division, which would be needed at a later stage, stayed behind to receive new tanks, and it then proceeded slowly towards Tobruk. On 20 November, as mentioned, the division arrived in Tmimi. They were all to stay in Tmimi for three-and-a-half months, and they soon adorned the camp with improvised buildings that offered more protection against the weather than their tents. The time spent there was relatively tranquil, with continuous training.

JSM Journal

> After El Alamein we advanced as far as Tmimi, where we stopped. First the tanks were sent on forward, and then practically all the other vehicles. We were camped out in the desert about thirty miles from Tobruk, with no means of transport at all except the odd car or truck. For three months we did nothing, and we were

there over Christmas 1942 and the New Year 1943. Every night the officers, nine of us, played Bridge (it was rather extraordinary that all nine of us played the game), and drank whisky in a small tent. We played two tables, and one of us had to sit out each night in turn. I used to drink about half a bottle of whisky a night, and wondered if I would end up a confirmed drunk. I did not.

Captain Baker was a young Jewish medical officer who developed hepatitis while we were at Tmimi. We kept him in an ambulance for a few days. One day I was in the ambulance talking to him and he wanted to go to the toilet. The latrine was about 300 yards away and he could not make it, so I drove the ambulance to the latrine and drove him back afterwards. He was very grateful and seemed to think that it was a wonderful thing for a senior officer to do. (I was a Major.) Before he was taken ill when we were advancing after El Alamein, a three-ton truck got stuck in the soft sand, so the Colonel went on with the rest of the unit and left Captain Baker and me to look after the truck. We got the truck out, and when it got dark I had a long chat with him in the cab of the truck all evening. Next day we got on the blower, and Brigade told us where the MDS was. Captain Baker was later evacuated to hospital in Cairo, where he died.

My most treasured possession in the desert was my collar stud, because with it I could wear a collar and tie. When you had lost your collar stud the only thing to do was to wear a scarf. That is why so many officers in the desert wore scarves. I had one pillow, and when it got dirty and smelly I had a little bottle of Californian Poppy perfume which I sprinkled on it so that it smelt nice. When we had a concert and two of the men dressed up as girls and did a female impersonating act, I gave them what was left of the perfume to make it more realistic. They came down amongst the audience and sat on chaps' knees and wafted the perfume about. Their pals said that it reminded them of home.

I had a rat in my tent once and killed it with a trap. (**Plate 16.**) A petrol tin was buried in the sand up to the top and half full of shaving water. A flat piece of wood juts out half way across the tin, and is hinged at the edge of the tin. Cheese is fixed on the end of the wood. Rat walks along wood to cheese, and falls in water and is drowned.

We had tinned food all the time – corned beef, butter, milk, cheese, meat & veg., bacon, sausages, tea and coffee – all in tins. The only things not in tins were sugar and biscuits. We had no bread, only very hard oatmeal biscuits, like dog biscuits. When I bit the biscuit it was touch and go whether the biscuit or my denture broke first! I don't know what I would have done if my denture broke because the Dental Officer had no facilities for mending it. With eating all-tinned food I got a stomach ailment which lasted about two weeks. I had fairly frequent baths, which consisted of standing naked in the open (and occasionally in a primitive bathtub), and sponging down with about a pint of water in a petrol tin. One did not have to worry about the people round about. One chap said to me 'you always seem to be having a bath.' I suppose I did have one more often than most people, about twice a week on average. I had a bath at every opportunity when things were quiet and there was no battle pending. I was once standing in the middle of my bath when firing started – and hurried up I can tell you! (**Plate 17.**)

All the eighteen months I was in the desert, I was fitter than I have ever been before or since. I had a terrific appetite and felt really well, and I smoked a lot, pipe and cigarettes. I remember the Quartermaster was a devil, he would always accept a cigarette if you offered him one but never offered any of his own. Although we had little or no exercise, I suppose being so fit was due to being in the open air all the time: night and day, plenty of fresh air. We got very brown. The only exercise we had was walking from the car to the officers' mess, about 100 yards. We went everywhere in the car. The Padre used to run a mile or so over the desert and back. When asked why he did it, he said: 'It is so nice when you stop!'

I had only skin diseases during my time in the desert, five of them at one time or another. There was Athlete's Foot and Dhobi Itch. One was fighting both of these all the time as they were aggravated by the heat and sweating. Then there was Eczema on my wrist, with my wristwatch irritating the skin and also sweating. Another complaint was from eating bad food, and Impetigo once for about two weeks. When I was on five days leave in Cairo, I went to the open air swimming pool for officers only. There were a lot of officers stationed at the base in Cairo who spent a lot of time sunbathing every day and so were brown all over. Then there were a few, like me, who were only brown on the face, neck, forearms and knees; otherwise white. This told everyone that we were Desert Rats, and had had no time for sunbathing, but only got brown with all our clothes on, fighting the war. I was rather proud of that! Of course after I was promoted to Major, I wore long trousers instead of shorts and my knees gradually became white again.

My next leave I went with the Colonel. He wanted to have breakfast in bed. I wanted to go to the pictures. We went to the pictures, but I don't think he got his breakfast in bed. My third leave to Alexandria was with the Quartermaster, Transport Officer, and my driver.

At Christmas 1942, Stobo (Captain Pritchard), one of the young medical officers, travelled 32 miles before he found a small tree, about eight feet high, for our Christmas tree. Two ENSA girls came up from the base to entertain us. (*ENSA, or Entertainments National Service Association, was an organization of actors, musicians and entertainers, including many of the most important figures on the London stage, who devoted their time visiting the troops in Britain and abroad.*) One girl sang songs and the other did card tricks. We had quizzes and panel games and also a male voice choir.

(*There was also a traditional army Christmas dinner, with the officers serving the men.*) (**Plate 55.**)

On ten separate occasions, when no Padre was available, I had to conduct a burial service over men who had been killed. One was a young officer who cadged a lift back when the Padre was on leave. He was very young and knew everything, argued all the time. He stepped on a land mine. When I was in the United States, I lectured to 100 Padres at one of the camps I visited.

Rommel's Dilemma

The Anglo-American invasion of North-West Africa began on 8 November 1942, with American troops landing in Morocco and Algeria. When the Allies got to Tunisia they faced strong German defences, including many troops who arrived as reinforcements from across the Mediterranean. The Axis force was commanded by General von Arnim, a leader with a formidable reputation who had been transferred from the Russian front. By mid-December the Allied and Axis armies were deadlocked in the mountains of northern Tunisia in miserable winter weather. The Allied Supreme Commander, Lieutenant General Eisenhower, was inexperienced and in early 1943 General Alexander was moved from Cairo to the west and appointed Eisenhower's deputy and head of all Allied ground forces in North Africa. (This added a new responsibility because he also remained Montgomery's chief. Montgomery was now moving geographically closer to Eisenhower's command.) The reason for Alexander's appointment was to bring battle experience and new energy to the battlefield. The head of the mainly British 1ˢᵗ Army was Lieutenant General Anderson, whom Alexander described as a 'good plain cook.' He applied himself seriously to his job, but this was difficult because his command was improvised. In addition to the British it included American and French components. But Anderson lacked Montgomery's 'grip' and relentless drive.

By the end of November, Rommel was conducting his carefully controlled retreat along the North African coast, but he was psychologically under pressure and seemed to be losing his nerve. The 8th Army he was facing had much greater manpower. And although the Sherman tank was not as good as the most advanced model of the German Panzer IV and the 6-pounder anti-tank gun was inferior to the German 88mm, the numbers of Shermans and 6-pounders were overwhelming.

Rommel, a bold tactical opportunist, was also a realist and he was happier attacking than defending. But the original concept of a German-Italian advance to the Nile with the aim of linking with German armies advancing south and west from Russia was no longer remotely possible. Even worse, there was the probable and unpleasant chance that he would be crushed between Allied armies advancing from east and west. Rommel became increasingly convinced that he should cut his losses and withdraw from Africa to the European mainland. His still powerful force would soon be needed to defend the Greater Reich from an Allied invasion that was certain to come as soon as the Americans and British had been massively reinforced and radically regrouped.

Rommel's proposal was strongly rejected by the Italian Supreme Command in Rome and by Kesselring, commander of the Mediterranean theatre and Rommel's direct superior. Rommel would not accept their refusals. He flew uninvited to visit Hitler at his headquarters in East Prussia, where Hitler was even more hostile. By this time Hitler was fearful of imminent disaster at Stalingrad, and he responded to all suggestions that troops should retreat with an unvarying order to continue fighting to the last round and the last man. Meanwhile the Panzerarmee Afrika continued to pull back before Montgomery's men. Although Rommel had reason to be encouraged by the arrival of reinforcements, including two armoured divisions and some Luftwaffe fighter squadrons, he took no steps to try and block the 8th Army's advance. There were two suitable defensive positions on the road to Tripoli, but Rommel ignored them.

On 23 January 1943, three months to the day from the artillery bombardment that signalled the opening of the Battle of El Alamein, advanced units of the 8th Army entered Tripoli. The harbour had been destroyed – or so the defenders thought – but the 8th Army engineers went immediately to work; within twelve days supply ships were landing. Tripoli, the handsome capital of the Italian colony of Libya, had always been the 8th Army's ultimate objective, but it had until now always been out of reach. With the capture of Tripoli, the Desert Campaign had indeed come to an end. Montgomery used this decisive moment to arrange, on 3 February, a triumphant military parade on a wide boulevard in the centre of the city. The most impressive part of it was the first moments, which were dominated by a large contingent of the 51st Highland Division. The soldiers found time to polish boots and buttons and scrub webbing equipment until it was white. And although they began to resemble parade-ground soldiers again, they had in fact played a major part in the Battle of El Alamein and had then advanced against a highly experienced enemy across 1,200 miles of North African desert.

The parade was led by the massed pipes and drums of the division: a hundred musicians marching six abreast. They were the survivors of the pipers who had stiffened the sinews of the Highland infantry when they were crossing the minefields during the first night of the Battle of El Alamein. Before they had left Britain, all the Highlanders had been forbidden to take their kilts on active service. Not surprisingly this order was not taken seriously. The hundred men in the pipes and drums were all now wearing their kilts, each with its regulation Regimental tartan. The Pipe Major made the dramatic gesture of throwing his staff high in the air and (miraculously) catching it, an instant before his dramatic word of command rang out. All the men swung forward, playing the tribal music of the Highlands that pierces the viscera of Scotsmen: music that goes 'straight to the gut.' As the pipes and drums advanced, they were followed by the bronzed and triumphant battalions. Churchill was in the reviewing stand taking the salute, with tears coursing down his cheeks. Brooke, the CIGS, was also there and confessed that he was also choked with emotion. Perhaps they both realized that the Desert Campaign was the last triumph of the soldiers of the British Empire. From now on there would be more victories, but they would be Allied ones, with the Americans taking an increasing part in the action.

Rommel Returns to the Attack

The geography of Tunisia has two important features, the Western and Eastern Dorsals, two modest mountain ranges running north-east to south-west, not quite parallel to each other. About 100 miles down the Western Dorsal, the Kasserine Pass divides the range. In February 1943 it was occupied by the American II Corps. The men were inexperienced and isolated from other formations. There was little military action; most of the fighting was taking place in the north.

The Panzerarmee Afrika had crossed from Libya to Tunisia shortly after the British had captured Tripoli. Rommel's force was at least temporarily safe behind a defensive line: a range of concrete bunkers at Mareth which had been built many years earlier by the French army to defend against a possible invasion from the Italian colony of Libya. Rommel, with his customary opportunism, now saw a chance to inflict damage on the Americans at Kasserine, which he saw was a tactically important position and where the Americans were vulnerable. Tunisia is not good tank country because of the mountains, but Rommel had seventy excellent tanks which he used to good effect.

Von Arnim now made diversionary attacks in the north on the Western Dorsal. While this was happening, Rommel's force on 14 February swept round from the south-west with the aim of turning to assault the American positions at Kasserine, coinciding with attacks from the north-east. The 30,000 American defenders were struck by panic and lost cohesion. The next day a counter-attack failed and it was some time before American resistance began to stiffen. At this stage Rommel planned to extend his offensive by crossing the Algerian frontier from the east and moving north to attack the main body of Anglo-American forces. This showed over-confidence and the Supreme Command in Rome would have none of it.

The fighting in the Kasserine region continued for some days and Rommel's men entered and advanced beyond the Pass on 20 February. But before long the Allied front was stabilized by the arrival of a number of American and British units from the north. On 22 February Rommel's force withdrew, with some degree of satisfaction. They had caused 6,000 American casualties (twenty percent of the total strength of II Corps); half of these became prisoners. The Americans also lost 183 tanks, 200 guns and 604 other vehicles. The Panzerarmee Afrika were delighted to receive such booty, but they were at the same time astounded by the quantity and quality of the equipment that the American army brought to battle. This would be a bad omen for the Axis forces in the future. Not surprisingly, the American commander at Kasserine was soon sacked. Two new American major generals came on the scene, Bradley and Patton, and the performance of the American army quickly improved.

One of the results of Alexander's appointment to command all the Anglo-American ground forces was his order to Montgomery to move as quickly as possible into Tunisia. The Mareth Line had to be taken before the 8th Army could move north along the coastal plain to cooperate in the final assault on the Axis forces. 7th Armoured Division and 51st Highland Division were soon on their way. After Kasserine, Rommel turned his attention immediately to the 8th Army. His tank force had been built up to 160 excellent machines, and he was determined to strike before Montgomery struck him.

From the Tunisian/Libyan frontier, the fortified village of Medenine is 100 miles into Tunisia, and the Mareth Line is twenty miles further north-west. Mareth is a strong position, composed of concrete fortifications stretching for more than twenty miles between the Mediterranean and the Matmata Hills. The 8th Army soon got to Medenine, where Montgomery made careful plans to receive an assault by the Panzerarmee Afrika. Battering through the Mareth Line would wait until Rommel had shot his bolt at Medenine. However, it did not quite work out that way.

The Italian General Messe, the strongest of Rommel's subordinates, was now in command of the Panzerarmee Afrika. In cooperation with armour from von Arnim in the north, Messe planned to attack at eight points on the seventy-mile front at Medenine. The assault began early on 6 March 1943. The 8th Army was well prepared, with 600 anti-tank guns and 400 tanks, with pivots held by infantry with powerful artillery on call. The 51st Highland Division, the New Zealanders and two brigades of British infantry were well dug in with anti-tank guns that were carefully sited. By now, 8th Army tactics had changed. After

El Alamein, there was a reversal of roles. The anti-tank guns were not there to protect the infantry; the infantry were there to guard the anti-tank guns. As the Panzers approached to within 400 yards, they came within effective fire. By the end of the day, the Panzerarmee Afrika had lost fifty-two tanks and with many damaged. The 8th Army had suffered 130 casualties but lost no armour.

After the Axis force limped back to the Mareth Line, Rommel tried in vain to persuade his superiors to allow him to retreat 200 miles to the north to prepare for what he thought would be the decisive battle of the Tunisian Campaign. On 9 March Rommel left Africa for good. He had suffered problems with his health for many months and badly needed to spend sick leave in Germany. In any event there were plans for his future. He was to play a major part in the defence of the Greater Reich: initially in Italy, then in 1944 preparing the Atlantic Wall in north-west Europe for a probable Anglo-American invasion. Meanwhile the Panzerarmee Afrika, under Messe's command, fell back on the narrow and well-fortified Mareth Line. He did not have much time to prepare for Montgomery's attack, in which the 1st Armoured Division would play a major part.

JSM Journal

> When the Field Ambulance advanced from Tmimi to Mareth, about 400 miles, I was in charge of the advance party, consisting of me, my car and driver, and a 15-hundredweight truck carrying four men. We set off at first light – 05:00AM – each morning for six days, doing sixty to seventy miles a day, and joined up with the advance parties of all the other units in the division. When we got to our destination – we were going along the coast road by the way – we were allotted an area of desert for our camp. The thing was that the Jerries used to lay mines *along the side of the road*, so that any truck going off the road was liable to be blown up. Our job was to find a place where there were some tracks in the sand where trucks had turned off before, so that we knew that it was safe for ours to leave the road and fan out into the desert. We did the 400 miles to Mareth

without mishap. Every day, the main body of the unit used to arrive in the afternoon.

As the 8th Army moved towards the Mareth position, the first obstacle they would meet was a small wadi called Zeus, a natural stream that was difficult for armour to cross, although in the event they managed to do so. There was then a minefield leading up to a much more difficult obstacle, the Wadi Zigzaou, which at places was 200 feet wide and twenty feet deep, with its sides made steeper by military engineers, who also constructed an anti-tank trap. Finally, there was the twenty-mile Mareth Line constructed of concrete bunkers. At all these obstacles there was carefully-placed infantry supported by anti-tank guns to plug any gaps in the fortifications. In an attempt to prepare forward positions four days before the main attack, two battalions of Foot Guards had lost 512 out of a total strength of 1,400 men. There was going to be trouble ahead.

Montgomery's plan was, as at El Alamein, a massive artillery bombardment followed by an infantry assault. This would be the job of the 50th Division, attacking first. The 51st Highland Division was to follow, and the 4th Indian Division was in reserve. The 7th and 1st Armoured Divisions would exploit a breakthrough. An important part of the plan was that there would be a substantial left hook in addition to the direct frontal attack. The left hook, comprising the New Zealand Division; a Free French brigade of Colonial troops (commanded by a leader who would become famous, General Le Clerc, who had taken his troops north across the Sahara Desert to join the 8th Army); an armoured brigade; and strong artillery. This force was to sweep to the west, then move into the Tebaga Pass through the Matmata Hills and make a double encirclement of the enemy positions, at Mareth and further north. This left-flanking attack, made by troops in 6,000 vehicles, began to move forward on 11 March, and took an unexplored desert route that might very well have been impassable for heavy transport. They reached the Tebaga Pass on 20 March, where the column unaccountably stopped.

Meanwhile the direct infantry assault on the Wadi Zigzaou faltered. Some of the infantry had carried scaling ladders (as their predecessors had done during the Peninsular War), but they only managed to penetrate the wadi in a few places. A small number of obsolete Valentine tanks with light guns managed to get through, but they were of little help to the outnumbered infantry who were engaged in bitter close-quarter fighting. The 50th Division was eventually forced to withdraw to its original start line south of Wadi Zigzaou. It was the worst setback for the 8th Army during the whole campaign. After a (highly unusual) loss of self-confidence from which he quickly recovered, Montgomery decided to change the axis of attack to reinforce the promising left-hand sweep. Not surprisingly, the inexperienced and unsuccessful commander of the 50th Division was sacked.

Montgomery now moved Lieutenant General Horrocks, one of his star corps commanders, to Tebaga to lead a strengthened force, including the two armoured divisions. Horrocks made the difficult journey to arrive in Tebaga in a third of the time it had taken the original force that had been carried in tanks and trucks. The Desert Air Force, commanded by Air Vice Marshal Broadhurst, was already making its presence felt with practised skill in low-flying strafing. Messe now realized his danger and he therefore moved his under-strength Panzer formations to the Tebaga Gap. Horrocks would have to fight his way through. He launched his assault late on 26 March, his last tanks having arrived on their tank transporters only thirty minutes before H-hour. They were attacking west to east, so they were silhouetted by the setting sun and were clearly visible to the defenders. The armoured attack, with many tanks carrying infantry on top, was virtually unstoppable. Horrocks's force was soon through the Tebaga Gap, taking 2,500 prisoners. However, the majority of Messe's infantry escaped to continue the fight in Tunisia, although as at El Alamein they left behind the majority of their heavy equipment.

JSM Journal

After the Battle of El Alamein, during which a shell struck my car but fortunately did not go off, the Germans retreated. It was not until we arrived at Mareth three months later – 1,300 miles west of El Alamein and 100 miles west of Tripoli – that we contacted them again and they made a stand. (**Map 10.**)

The Mareth Line ran east to west from the village of Mareth, and the tank battle lasted for several days without either side moving. I was at the Main Dressing Station at Camp A (*near the original start line for the assault.*) Casualties were attended to, and sent back to the Casualty Clearing Station near Tripoli. Some of them were then flown from Castel Benito (the airport of Tripoli) to Alexandria, and some were sent by hospital ship. Sometimes we were working all night attending to wounded men. Later I travelled as a passenger in a hospital ship from Tripoli to Alexandria with 300 wounded men and about forty doctors and nurses. We sailed at night, and the whole ship was lit up like the Crystal Palace. It was floodlit from stem to stern and could be seen for miles. Its safety depended entirely on the Red Cross.

After the Battle of Mareth had been a stalemate for several days, the 1ˢᵗ Armoured Division was ordered to make a detour westwards over the desert to get round the German lines. No one knew if it was possible to cross that area of desert with heavy vehicles, as it had never been tried before. We were to go by night, after the tanks had gone, and a patrol of sappers went in daylight placing lights at one hundred yard intervals on the route we had to take. These lights were a petrol tin with one side cut out and a hurricane lamp inside, so that the light could only be seen from the side nearest to us. The Colonel had gone to Brigade Headquarters, so I was in command of the (over-strength) Field Ambulance (200 men and 45 vehicles) and I had to guide them in the dark by these lights. (**Plate 56.**)

I was leading in my car, standing up in the passenger seat by the driver, with my upper half through the sunshine roof. We travelled all night, and although my sight in the dark is very bad I managed somehow. In the morning we arrived at Camp B, near where the track to El Hamma turned east. We were there all day and the Colonel was still at Brigade. He was very good that way, and when at Brigade he was in touch with what was going on, and could radio messages to me, telling me what to do and where to go. Unlike that Colonel in France who sat on his bottom at the MDS all day and was surrounded by Germans and the whole unit captured before he knew what had hit him.

During the next night at Camp B, I got a message from the Colonel to advance up the El Hamma track towards the coast at first light (05:00AM). So we started off. My car would not start, which was not unusual after the shell had hit it at El Alamein, so I was leading the column in the wireless truck that normally followed my car, and behind the wireless truck came the officers' mess truck and the others at 100 yard intervals.

The battle was about to begin, with the 1ˢᵗ Armoured Division taking a leading role. Two units whom JSM knew would lead the charge. They were the Queen's Bays and the 9ᵗʰ Lancers.

Trooper Jack Merewood, 'To War with The Bays'

As dawn broke we found ourselves moving across a wide grassy plain. Our squadron was leading, two troops in front and two behind. We ran into opposition, but nothing too serious and we overcame these pockets of resistance without much trouble, with no losses of tanks or men. We could see El Hamma ahead now. Between us and the village were trees and dense undergrowth. We trundled slowly and cautiously forward, our troop and No. 3 Troop in the lead. One of their tanks, commanded by Corporal Jim Nolan, was to our left and slightly ahead, I could see it through my periscope. Then the quiet was suddenly shattered by a terrific bang. Anti-tank guns hidden in the trees ahead opened fire. I saw Jim's tank hit and it immediately burst into flames. He and his turret crew bailed out, all three of them on fire. They ran about screaming . . . and all died. The other two crew members never got out of the tank.

Then we were hit too. I found myself covered with blood, but it wasn't mine, it was Nobby's. He'd been hit on the head and he dropped straight down into the turret behind me. Our wireless operator lay on his back on the floor in a state of terror, beating the floor with his fists and his heels. Colin, our driver, shouted over the intercom: 'My periscope's shattered, I can't see where I'm going.'

Without stopping to think, I jumped up, took Nobby's seat and, half out of the tank, saw we were still heading straight for the trees. Shells were flying everywhere. Any minute I expected we'd be hit again.

'Jink, Colin, jink,' I shouted.

Colin zigzagged but we were still going forward. I yelled at him: 'Pull on your right stick as hard as you can.'

He did as I said, and we made a compete U-turn.

'Put your foot down. Let her go.'

Colin kept his head, did as I directed and we kept going until it was safe to stop. We were all very shaken. Nobby had a bad cut on the head. We saw a Red Cross vehicle not far away and handed him over to the people there, then turned to assess the damage to the tank.

This small but heated action was typical of what was going on on the battlefield. The Red Cross vehicle was of course one of the ones under JSM's command.

JSM Journal

We passed one of our tanks on the right, and had not gone much further when the officers' mess truck shot past us on the left and stopped in front of us, and the men all jumped down, ran to the left of the track and lay down. I was just going to say: 'What the blazes!' when we were under machine gun fire, and my driver and I jumped down and lay down by the track, where fortunately there was a slight depression in the sand where we were under cover.

Then I saw three German tanks in a row, not fifty yards off. They were firing their big guns straight ahead, not at us, but at our tanks which we had passed, and which were to the right of the track. But they were machine gunning us as well, and as we lay there bullets were flying over our heads. Remember we had no weapons of any sort. Well, they must have been tracer bullets because very soon the officers' mess truck (which had very big Red Cross signs painted on each side) was in flames, and also the wireless truck, and very soon both were completely burnt out. The officers' mess truck had in it forty bottles of whisky and forty bottles of gin, and a little dog someone had picked up somewhere.

The German tanks kept on firing and advancing slowly, and we just lay there and watched. After an hour or so the German tanks retired, the shooting stopped, and we could get up and run back down the track to the rest of the column. The water tank had been hit, but the others were all right and headed back to Camp B where we had started from. I did not know until afterwards that the reason why the officers' mess truck shot past and stopped in front of us was to halt the column and prevent us from going any further. This was because the two men on the front of the officers' mess truck, which was a three-ton lorry, were high up and could see the German tanks long before we could. The wireless truck was only a fifteen-hundredweight, and we were low down in it. I only saw the tanks when I was lying down in the sand. When the machine guns started I did not wait to see where the fire was coming from.

When they had gone, there was a wounded Italian prisoner and a Jeep, plus me, and two mechanics trying to fix the water tank. As they could not drive the Jeep I took the Italian in it to the MDS. I have never driven a Jeep before or since. As we were driving along the track, a shell landed about ten yards behind me and the Jeep shot up in the air about three feet, but we did not stop. I remember thinking of letting off fireworks at home on Guy Fawkes Night, because the smell was exactly the same: exploding gun powder. I dropped the Italian at the surgical tent and went to look for the officers' mess truck, but there wasn't one.

A funny thing happened at Camp B. All trucks were parked 100 yards apart, and the Padre's truck, with him sleeping on the ground beside it, was way out by itself. When we moved off at 05:00AM, no one wakened him and he was left behind. When he woke up we had all gone and he was all alone. But he put up a prayer, and we all came back again!

Later that day the Colonel arrived from Brigade, having been unable to get us on the radio, and we heard all about it. He had not expected us to walk right into the middle of a tank battle, as they had expected our tanks to have advanced to El Hamma before we got there. The mechanics managed to fix the water tank. The tank itself was not hit, so we did not lose any water. We later advanced without incident up the El Hamma track, past the burnt out wireless truck and officers' mess truck, on to El Hamma. It was in that area that I first saw Arabs with their legs blown off from stepping on a mine. They were attended to at the MDS.

When we got to El Hamma we turned north and continued to advance to Susa. There we had orders to do another deviation west, a 'left hook' as Montgomery called it, round the enemy so as to meet up with the 1st American Armored Division who were moving into

Tunisia from the west. The Colonel must have been with us because I was not leading the column, but only had to follow his car. The only thing I remember about that journey was that we drove all night, and I slept on the back seat of the car. In the morning I told my driver to get into the back seat and go to sleep, which he promptly did, and I took the wheel and drove all day until we arrived at our camp site late in the afternoon.

We were now in Tunisia, and being so used to the desert we chose a camp site and put up our tents in a large flat area of sandy ground with no trees, so that we could be seen for miles around. We had a surgical team with us, who had a large tent in which they could put up six hospital beds and an operating table and were doing major surgery. Unfortunately the tent had no Red Cross on it. We were surrounded by hills, and in these hills was a big gun. Next day we knew about it when shells started dropping around the tent and we all had to take cover. It shelled us all afternoon and one of the surgical team was killed. We had to wait until it got dark, and the shells stopped coming, and we all packed up and made camp in a wood of big trees about a mile away, where the gun could not see us and did not bother us again.

I presume that we did join up with the 1st American Armored Division, but I never saw any of them, although when I left North Africa all the Germans and Italians had been driven out of the country.

The Battle of Mareth was a high point in JSM's military career. The German and Italian armies were expelled from North Africa in the middle of May 1943, leaving a huge number of prisoners. The decision had been made at the highest level, at the Casablanca Conference in January 1943, that Sicily and then Italy would be invaded. After Africa had been cleared, Eisenhower and his generals faced the complex task of planning the Sicily operation.

Dr. MacGill was not bound for Sicily. He was in fact not to see any more fighting. Out of the blue a new and exciting opportunity opened for him. He was to fly to the United States to impart some of his 'hands-on' knowledge to medical officers of the United States army.

CHAPTER 9

A TRANSATLANTIC ADVENTURE

*After the successful conclusion of the campaign in North Africa, the 1ˢᵗ
Armoured Division spent some months on garrison duty and re-equipping
and training for the Italian campaign. During the spring of 1944, some
months after the landings in Italy, the campaign was facing considerable
difficulties. However, Dr. MacGill was no longer with the Division. At
the end of May 1943, he was quite unexpectedly ordered to travel to North
America to deliver a series of lectures to 'medics': medical officers and other
ranks in the American and Canadian armies. His job was to give practical
advice on the best methods of treating soldiers who had been wounded in
tanks: battlefield experience that would be extremely helpful to the as-yet
uncommitted American and Canadian armoured divisions. In the event,
the lectures were given to the majority of the medical officers posted to
the North American armoured divisions that would fight in North-West
Europe after D-Day. JSM flew to America via the 'short' Atlantic crossing,
from West Africa to Brazil. He then flew north over British Guiana (now
Guyana), where he had been born. He finally reached Washington DC,
which was to be the base of his lecture tour. He traveled to many parts of the
United States and Canada and gave a total of thirty-nine lectures. By this
time, Dr. MacGill had been negotiating with his military superiors about
a possible release from the army, to rebuild his medical practice in Denton,
near Manchester. This had become inadequately staffed with the call-up
of his only partner, Dr. Robertson, thus depriving its many working-class
patients of full medical attention. The army agreed, and he returned to his
private practice on his return to Britain across the Atlantic.*

John Philip Jones

Sharing Battlefield Experience

The final, unstoppable, assault on Tunis was launched on 22 April 1943. It was a concentric attack: from the west by the Anglo-American-French 1st Army, and from the south by the 8th Army. The 1st Armoured Division had joined the 1st Army and fought in the last phase of the attack. On 12 May it was all over, and the Allied forces had mopped up vast numbers of German and Italian prisoners, more than at Stalingrad earlier in the year. They included the enemy commander, General von Arnim.

Some time after the victory in Tunisia, three prominent 8th Army divisions would be shipped home to Britain to prepare for the invasion of France on 6 June 1944. These divisions' experience was judged important although their performance in North-West Europe was disappointing during their early battles. Most of the other divisions in the 1st and 8th Armies were earmarked for the invasion of Sicily, scheduled for July 1943. But the 1st Armoured Division remained in North Africa in comfortable conditions, and spent almost a year in training, re-equipping and routine garrison work, with doses of rest-and-recreation. They were to be sent as reinforcements during the Italian campaign, and they moved there in May 1944 and were to fight many tough battles. However, Dr. MacGill was no longer with the 1st Light Field Ambulance. He had gone to the United States on a special mission: to deliver lectures to medical officers in the American army, based on his expertise in treating wounded tank crews.

Before the war, the American army was smaller than that of any other major power. However, the United States was clearly facing the possibility of going to war, and preparation became a high priority. This included selective conscription, despite its unpopularity. But the Americans moved fast. It was the remarkable achievement of General George Marshall, Chief-of-Staff of the United States Army (which at the time included the American Army Air Corps), that by the end of the war there were eight million in army uniform, including many women in non-combatant roles. In addition to the fighting and supporting troops, the United States – 'the Arsenal of Democracy' – supplied the Allies with massive military supplies under Lend-Lease.

A force of such size demanded a large number of medical officers: at least one per infantry battalion and similarly sized units of other arms, in addition to fully-staffed Casualty Clearing Stations, Field Ambulances, and Military Hospitals. Young doctors often reported for duty as newly-qualified MDs, and their service with the troops counted as their period of Residency in internal medicine and surgery. Their jobs with the troops called for large numbers of medical inspections, treatment of routine ailments, and (when in action) first aid and triage. This meant identifying injuries and transferring patients to Casualty Clearing Stations.

Since Dr. MacGill was a mature and experienced military doctor, he had much to tell American colleagues about the challenges they would shortly be facing. In the North-West Europe campaign the American army was eventually a force of more than 1,500,000 soldiers plus two air forces. In addition there were large American forces in the Mediterranean and the Pacific, and on training duties in the United States.

JSM Journal

It was 20 May 1943. Tunis had fallen and all the German and Italian troops who were not prisoners had left North Africa. We were in camp outside El Hamamet near Tunis, resting. All was quiet. No sounds of gun fire. I was sitting basking in the sun, minding my own business, when up comes a messenger with a telegram for me: 'Major MacGill to proceed forthwith and report to British Army Staff Headquarters, Washington DC, to give a lecture tour to the American Army Medical Corps on "The Evacuation of Casualties from Tanks."'

It was a bolt from the blue. No one was more surprised than me. I can truthfully say that it changed my whole way of life as from that moment. During the whole eighteen months in the desert, I was never without a book to read, usually a light novel, with which I passed my spare time. I once read 'The Yearling'. I remember that before I had finished it there were at least ten names on the fly-leaf of men who had asked for it after me.

211

Another book I read was 'The Long Alert', and many more.

But from the day the telegram came, all that was changed. From that day until four months later, when I had given my thirty-ninth and last lecture, I never looked at another book or newspaper. All my waking hours, from getting up in the morning to going to bed at night, were taken up with reading up all the information I could get about evacuation of casualties. I pumped everyone I met for all they knew about this, and found out all I could about a Casualty Clearing Station, air evacuation, sea evacuation, hospital accommodation etc. etc. Of course I knew all about getting men out of tanks and Advanced and Main Dressing Stations, but I had no experience of what happened to them after that. And after the man was out of a tank and in an ambulance, he was the same as any other casualty from then on. So I got all the articles, notes and information, and spent my time swotting it all up. I could then lecture for one and a half hours on it without notes when I got to Washington.

Having read the telegram I packed all my belongings, said goodbye to the Colonel, who thanked me for all I had done during my many months of active service, and set off in my car to Sfax, the nearest airfield. There I contacted a medical unit and spent the night with them. It was an eye-opener to me because their Colonel was a right martinet, and treated all the officers like schoolboys. He was dreadful. There was permanent tension in the mess. He had no sense of humour. I suspect he had an inferiority complex, and thought the other officers would laugh at him and did not obey him. Not at all like our Colonel, who treated everyone as a friend and was loved by all. I am glad I was not in that unit. After a night there I proceeded to the airfield where I dumped my kit and told my driver to get back to my old unit quickly.

I contacted the sergeant who appeared to be in charge of the airfield, and said I wanted to get to Alexandria. He said that it might be two to three weeks before I could get a plane to take me. I wandered across to where an American crew of two were loading an American plane with two aeroplane engines, and told them I was going to the USA, and wanted to get to Tripoli. They were eager to help, said 'Hop in. We are going there if we can get this crate off the ground with these heavy engines!' So I got all my gear, and I was sitting on one of the engines and we took off about twenty minutes after I had arrived at the airport. We were in Tripoli in about fifteen minutes, and I contacted the MO there, who shared his tent with me. He telephoned the port and got me on a hospital ship the next day to Alexandria. So I travelled as a passenger and there were 300 wounded on board, and forty doctors and nurses. We sailed all night to Alex, and did in one night the distance it took me eighteen months to do in the desert going the other way. The ship was floodlit and we sailed all night, lit like the Crystal Palace, and depending for safety entirely on our big Red Cross.

We got to Alex in the morning and I got a train to Cairo. There I was told I would have to have a Yellow Fever inoculation, and have to stay there for three weeks for it to take effect. So I was in a transit camp outside Cairo for three weeks. Monty visited the camp and I saw him, but only in the distance. Then I was waiting for a plane to take me on to the USA, and I found this waiting period a Godsend as I spent *all day every day* learning up all the mass of information I had collected about the evacuation of casualties. I had a whole book full of notes to learn off by heart so that I could give lectures without referring to my papers. I had no transport from the transit camp so there was no temptation to go into Cairo, about ten miles away, although some of the younger officers went in by taxi. It was rather like the last six months before my medical finals: I sat in my bedroom swotting, from immediately after breakfast until about 1:00AM next morning, smoking my pipe. It was a small room and soon full of smoke, and I only came out for lunch, tea and supper.

After the three weeks was up, so as to get things moving and having waited for a plane for a few days, I sent some of my clothes to the wash. Sure enough within the hour I got orders to report to the airfield at once. So my clothes are still at the transit camp. It was not easy to get to the airfield, which was about five miles away because there was no transport at all. I applied at the office and they just said 'Sorry, we cannot help.' I went to the gate for a taxi and of course there were none there. So I was telling this to one of the other officers, who said 'Look, I have a car and I will run you there.' So I hopped in and got there in no time at all.

A Bird's Eye View of British Guiana

Dr. MacGill was to fly to the United States by the southerly route. This took him south and west to West Africa. From here he took the relatively short crossing of the Atlantic to Brazil. He then flew to the north-west and north and after various different flights reached Washington DC.

JSM Journal

The plane held about twenty men and I found they were all American airmen except me. They were all ferry pilots, flying planes from the USA to the Middle East, and were flying back as passengers. We flew south to Khartoum, where we landed, and *was it hot!* As soon as they opened the door on the plane it hit you: like walking into an oven. We were driven to a camp nearby, where we spent the night. We slept in a chalet, and it was so hot that we pulled our beds out onto the lawn outside and slept in the open, naked. At 5:00AM we were wakened and driven to the airfield, but the plane was not ready to take off so we were driven back again and had breakfast and took off about 7:00AM. We landed to refuel at Kano and then on to Accra, where we spent the next night. There I was in an RAF officers' mess and dined with British officers. They all seemed very snobbish and stand-offish, in comparison with the Americans who are all so very friendly.

Next morning we were off again at the crack of dawn and landed on Ascension Island for lunch, and off again, arriving at Natal in Brazil at 7:00PM. We said: 'Just in time for dinner!' But they said it is only 4:00PM here, so we had to wait three hours for dinner. The next day was to be the longest flight I ever did in one day: 4,000 miles. We were off early and landed at Belem to refuel, then Georgetown for lunch, and then on to Miami, Florida. When we landed in Belem in Brazil, they were talking about a plane that took off from there going north, the same route as us, and crashed in the jungle twelve miles from Belem. It took three weeks for them to cut a path through the virgin jungle to get to the plane. All were dead of course.

Flying over Brazil, it was just trees all the way. I think that the man who wrote the song 'Trees' must have been flying over Brazil. When we got to British Guiana, we flew right over New Amsterdam where I was born, and I saw my father's church, where he was minister, and the manse we lived in. We only spent one and a half hours in Georgetown, so I could not even go into the town, but just had lunch at the airfield and then off. I remember the airfield at Georgetown was cut out of solid bush, and as we landed it just looked like a tennis court amongst the trees. I thought we would never land there safely, but we did. When we got to Miami, we took a bus into the town. So we came into the centre of Miami, and I was dropped off at a hotel, where they would pick me up at 9:00AM the next morning to take me back to the military airport. I went into the hotel and booked a room at the reception desk, and I asked where I could get a whisky and soda. The man said: 'You cannot, but I can sell you a bottle of whisky – bourbon.' So I bought a bottle and had a drink in my room in the tooth mug. I took that bottle on my travels to Washington, New York, Fort Worth (Texas), Los Angeles, San Francisco, and at Sacramento, where I spent a night in a private house and left the bottle half empty as I did not want it any more.

In the morning in the hotel in Miami, I went and asked the man at reception where the dining room was. He said: 'There is no dining room.' So I had to go out to the nearest drug store (chemist) to get some breakfast. At 9:00AM the bus arrived and drove me back to the military airport. I immediately contacted the American Army Air Force sergeant who was in charge of passengers. He had a sort of little office in the corner of a big shed, or hangar. I told him who I was, showed him my orders, and said I wanted to get on a flight to Washington DC. He was very skeptical and offhand and uncooperative. He said he did not know when he could get me on a plane, and obviously was very suspicious of me. I don't think he had even seen a British uniform before and thought I was a spy or something. Shortly after, I was talking to one of the officers who had been on the plane with me the day before from Accra. We were laughing and joking together and obviously on very good terms. Then I noticed the sergeant was watching us. Soon after this, I went to the sergeant again to ask about places, and he was very different altogether and most helpful. He got me on a plane within an hour.

So I arrived in Washington DC and booked in at the Roger Smith Hotel. Next morning at breakfast the only thing on the menu that seemed my style was 'wheatcakes', which sounded like porridge. When it came it was four drop scones one on top of the other, surrounded by sausages. Also a jug of brown liquid. The waiter saw me looking at it and said: 'Don't you want molasses on your wheatcakes?' The brown liquid was maple syrup. Now I like drop scones for tea, but not with sausages!

That morning I went round to the British Army Staff (BAS) office, and who should I find behind the desk but Michael Halstead, who was an officer in the Queen's Bays with me in the desert, and who had been badly wounded – lost an eye – and there he was. But he was as surprised to see me as they all were, and had had no information that I was coming. They said: 'Who are you and what are you doing here?' So I had to show them my orders, and then someone said: 'But there is a medical officer on his way out from England to do the lecture tour.' So luckily I got there first, so he had to be told to go home again. Michael and I were friends and he got busy and arranged my tour, which took a week. So meantime I went off to New York and enjoyed myself for a week.

I was going to visit all the medical units in the Armoured Divisions in camps all over the country. So when I arrived at the nearest town to the camp, I phoned up and spoke to the Divisional Surgeon (equivalent to the British Assistant Director of Medical Services, or ADMS), and he arranged my accommodation and lectures. They were very pleased to have me and I don't think they had ever had a British medical officer visit them before, and treated me like a being from another planet. It was the first time anyone had taken any interest in the 'medics', as they call them.

Travels Across the United States

During Dr. MacGill's two months of lecturing in the United States, he often stayed at private houses on his journeys. He addressed thirty-nine audiences, mainly of medical officers who were posted to armoured divisions. Such formations fought predominantly in the campaign in North-West Europe, from June 1944 to May 1945. There was less use of tanks in the Italian campaign because of the mountainous terrain. And in the Pacific, the land campaign was mainly island-hopping by the United States Marine Corps and some army infantry divisions. The number of medical officers who attended JSM's lectures was very high: probably the majority of medical officers in the American and Canadian tank formations who fought in North-West Europe. The hard-won experience of the 8th Army was now being offered to the Allies. This was some recompense for the generosity of Lend-Lease which had provided over the years so much American equipment and endless supplies to Britain.

JSM Journal

My first tour was to Fort Knox, Kentucky (where all the gold is). I had four days there, and then back to Washington. The second tour was to Camp Chaffie, in Little Rock, Arkansas. I was another four days there. One morning I sat down to breakfast with three Generals – I was only a Major. Back in Washington I was staying with the Stone family. I bought a map of the world for about three dollars, and I took it to the BAS office and left it on a desk to pick up later. I then found that it had disappeared, and discovered that one of the female army clerks had taken it in the belief that it had been issued from HQ, and had pinned it up in the General's office. I apologized for taking it away from the General. Also one day I went into a sweet shop and ordered a pound box of chocolates to be sent home each month for six months, and paid for them all. They all arrived safely and were still coming for three months after I had arrived home. I had ordered the same in Cairo when I was there, and *none* arrived. The Egyptians take your money and conveniently forget to send the goods.

My third tour was to Jackson, Louisiana, then to Houston, Texas. And on to Fort Worth near Dallas. Then back to Washington by air. A few days later I flew out to Los Angeles, via Dallas and El Paso. That flight was twenty-one hours. At Los Angeles I met Mrs. Stone's mother and spent a day with her visiting shops in LA. Then I went on to the desert and had a few days in the great heat, and flew one hundred miles in a small two-seater artillery spotter plane to Barstow. There was just room for the pilot and me and my suitcase in the back. Then by train to San Francisco, where I spent a night in a double bed with an American sailor who snored all night! From there on to another camp at Maryville. At one camp they got 100 padres together, and I gave an hour's talk to them on 'The Padre's job in combat.' When I said it was to bury the dead, they laughed and laughed!

From the camp at Maryville, the Colonel took me to stay the night at his home in Sacramento. It was there I dumped the remains of my bottle of Bourbon. They took me to a dance that night and found me a lady partner. During the dance, an announcer said: 'We have a British officer from the 8th Army in the North African desert with us, and I will play "I've got sixpence" in his honour.' I did not at first see the connection. Next morning I was in a men's clothes shop, and there was my lady partner behind the pay desk.

I was off by plane to Washington that afternoon, but the first stop was Reno, where all the women got off! (*Reno was the divorce capital.*) Next I went to Canada – Montreal, Ottawa and Toronto – doing one pair of lectures at each. I gave one lecture for the officers, giving technical details of evacuation of casualties, and one for the men which was more chatty and all about our funny experiences in the desert.

During my total tour I gave thirty-nine lectures in all, and sometimes it was in a hall or cinema to anything up to 600 men, with me on the stage with a microphone round my neck. One general after my lecture said: 'Thank you, and I have never before seen a man with his shirt hanging out and looking so smart.' I was wearing a bush shirt. One man said to me: 'It isn't what you say that is interesting, but how you say it. It is fascinating to hear a different voice to what one hears every day.'

My next and last tour was to Harrisburg, Pennsylvania, where I visited the Training Center for all medical officers. I remember starting my lecture with: 'I will start off by assuming that you don't know anything, and we will go from there,' which got a laugh. Then I met a British army doctor who must have been about sixty. He had won the VC in World War One. He took me to play golf with him one day, the only game of golf I played the whole four years I was in the army. The next three weeks I was waiting for a boat home. I was in Washington and staying at the house of the McGee family. Most days I took out their son Hugh, a boy of about ten. I visited the Walter Reed Hospital every morning, and I tacked myself on to one of their doctors to try and get back some medical knowledge. I thought that when I returned to the practice I would have forgotten all the medicine I ever knew. It was such a long time since I had treated any patient except wounded men.

A Farewell to Arms

For some time Dr. MacGill had been anxious about the condition of his medical practice in Denton, near Manchester. It drew its long list of patients from the working class, and the majority of the families were 'Panel' patients, who received routine medical care at very low cost. JSM had been in the army for the whole course of the war, and his practice had experienced difficulties, which meant that medical attention for hundreds of families was becoming progressively less adequate. As explained in Chapter 1, his partner, Dr. Robertson, had been called up, and JSM's wife Dorothy, who was not a doctor, kept the practice going with the help of Irish locum doctors who were not conscripted into the British armed forces. She also had a busy personal life, with two growing sons and no car because she had no petrol ration.

JSM began to negotiate a possible release from the army, to return to his long list of patients. By August 1943 he would have served for four years in uniform: a period during which he had been fully occupied, carrying out highly responsible work. He had been on active service in France for a short time in 1940, then a year and a half in North Africa, and at the end carried out the important although enjoyable lecture tour in North America. He was forty-two years of age. His discussions with his military superiors were eventually successful, and it was planned that he would return to Denton on his arrival back in Britain from America.

JSM Journal

> After about three weeks, I got a place on the *Queen Elizabeth* out of New York, and came home with 17,000 American troops and 100 American nurses. I was in a cabin normally for two, but there were six of us in it. The officers and nurses had a big saloon, where we spent the day and only left it to go down to the dining room and out on the deck for boat drill. Boat drill was five minutes on deck every morning, and then back into the saloon. That was the only time we saw the sea, as the saloon windows were blacked out and the lights were on all day. We had two meals a day, breakfast and dinner, and there were six sittings for each. The ship sailed quite alone and relied on her speed to beat the U-boats.

> We arrived at Gourock, Scotland, and were told to stay in our cabins until the Customs people came around. After waiting until the next morning, I decided to go ashore, so I got all my traps together and went on the next small boat. I never did see those Customs men. We landed right by the railway station, and all the

thousands of American troops were being herded into special trains and taken off, I don't know where. So I had to get me a porter and find out when the next train to Glasgow was, and get a ticket and travel alone. I had lunch in Glasgow and then a train to Manchester. I arrived in Manchester on my birthday (*his forty-third*) and telephoned home that I would be there in half-an-hour. I got a taxi which I shared with a young couple and arrived about 11:00PM. I had been away for two years and one month.

There were two funny things happened when I was staying in Washington with the Stones. One day I saw a toast rack on the sideboard with letters stuck in it. I said: 'I see you have a toast rack there with letters in.' They said it was a letter rack. I said it is a toast rack. They said: 'What is a toast rack?' They had never heard of them. Of course I don't think Americans ever have cold toast, always hot buttered. The other funny thing was that one day, after I had been there *three weeks*, Mrs. Stone said: 'Major MacGill, are you married?' I said yes. She said: 'Have you any children?' I said yes, two. 'Have you a photo of them?' I said yes, I think so, and showed them the one taken at Marlborough of the four of us. Then Mrs. Stone said: 'You British are funny. If you had been an American you would have shown me that within half-an-hour of arriving.'

On my return from America, there were two things that struck me about England. The first was the narrowness of the streets. There are no narrow streets in America like we have here. Second, walking in a crowded street, I would stop and survey the people, all hurrying about their own business and without another thought in their heads. No one thinking of America, or that there is such a country. Crowds in the USA all seem to be saying: 'We are Americans – God's own country,' all the time.

These two thoughts show that JSM has already re-entered his civilian world, and they provide an interesting *finis* to the long and interesting story of his war. From some points of view it is regrettable that he did not stay in uniform until the Autumn of 1945, serving devotedly in a Field Ambulance. It is likely that he would have become a Lieutenant Colonel and Commanding Officer of such a unit. However, he had already made a contribution to victory, and he deserved the reward of his return to his practice, which before long was in a flourishing state. In 1948, medicine in Britain was transformed by the new National Health Service (NHS), which began the process of funding medical service out of taxation, with physicians being paid by salary depending on the number of patients. This replaced the old 'Panel' system, although JSM was not too sure that the NHS was any better.

Dr. MacGill was a conscientious and prudent physician. During the early 1960s, Thalidomide, a drug to treat morning sickness in pregnancy, was found to cause physical deformities in unborn babies. Without any knowledge of the disastrous outcome of the drug, JSM would not take a chance. He refused to prescribe Thalidomide because he was unhappy about the extent of the clinical trials. And it was never accepted for that reason by the American medical profession.

John Sylvanus MacGill, who had been born in 1900, retired at the age of seventy, when he forgot the name of one of his 2,500 patients. He died when he was eighty-eight. His obituary referred to him as 'Dr. John,' the name that his patients had called him during his early years in general practice.

BIBLIOGRAPHY

The most valuable first-hand sources are indicated with an asterisk (*)

*Alanbrooke, Field Marshal Lord, *War Diaries, 1939-1945* (London: Weidenfeld & Nicolson, 2001).

*Alexander of Tunis, Field Marshal Earl, and North, John *The Alexander Memoirs, 1940-1945* (London: Cassell, 1962).

*Armstrong, Geoffrey, *The Sparks Fly Upward* (East Wittering, West Sussex: Gooday Publishers, 1991).

Barber, Laurie, and Tonkin-Covell, John, *Freyberg. Churchill's Salamander* (London: Hutchinson, 1989).

Barnett, Correlli, *The Desert Generals, 2ⁿᵈ and Enlarged Edition* (Bloomington, IN: Indiana University Press, 1982).

Bayerlein, Generalleutnant Fritz (Spayd, P.A. & Dittmar-Bayerlein, Fritz, eds.), *The Private Afrikakorps Photograph Collection of Rommel's Chief-of-Staff* (Atglen, PA: Schiffer, 2004).

Baynes, John, *The Forgotten Victor. General Sir Richard O'Connor* (London: Brassey's, 1989).

*Beddington, Major General W.R., *A History of the Queen's Bays (the 2ⁿᵈ Dragoon Guards), 1929-1945* (Winchester, UK: Warren – The Wykeham Press, 1954).

Bennett, Ralph, *Ultra and Mediterranean Strategy: The Never-Before-Told Story of How Ultra First Proved Itself in Battle, Turning Defeat Into Victory* (New York: William Morrow, 1989).

Bishop, Chris, *The Military Atlas of World War II* (London: Amber Books – Igloo, 2005).

Blair, Dr. John S.G., *In Arduis Fidelis, Centenary History of the Royal Army Medical Corps* (Edinburgh: Lynx Publishing, 2001).

Blaxland, Gregory, *Destination Dunkirk. The Story of Gort's Army* (London: William Kimber, 1973).

*Bright, Joan (ed.), *The Ninth Queen's Royal Lancers, 1936-1945* (Aldershot, Hampshire: Gale & Polden, 1951).

*British Army War Diaries (Kew, Surrey: National Archives):
Second World War, 11th Regiment, Royal Horse Artillery (Honourable Artillery Company), WO166/1461; WO169/1430; WO169/4560.

Citino, Robert M., *The Path to Blitzkrieg. Doctrine and Training in the German Army, 1920-1939* (Mechanicsburg, PA: Stackpole Books, 2008).

*Clarke, Dudley, *The 11th at War* (London: Michael Joseph, 1952).

Clarke, Sir Rupert, *With Alex at War – From the Irrawaddy to the Po, 1941-1945* (Barnsley, South Yorkshire: Leo Cooper, 2000).

Colville, J.R., *Man of Valour. The Life of Field Marshal the Viscount Gort* (London: Collins, 1972).

Connell, John, *Auchinleck* (London: Cassell, 1959).

Connell, John, and Roberts, Brigadier Michael (ed.), *Wavell, Supreme Commander, 1941-1943* (London: Collins, 1969).

Corrigan, Gordon, *The Second World War. A Military History* (New York: St. Martin's Press, 2011).

*Crew, F.A.E., *The Army Medical Services, Medical History of the Second World War, Campaigns, Volume II* (London: Her Majesty's Stationery Office, 1957).

Crimp, R.L., and Bowlby, Alex (ed.), *The Diary of a Desert Rat* (London: Pan, 1971).

Crisp, Robert, *Brazen Chariots* (New York: Ballantine Books, 1968).

*Daniell, Brigadier R.B.T., *Journal of a Horse Gunner* (Sevenoaks, Kent: Buckland Publications, 1998).

David, Saul, *Churchill's Sacrifice of the Highland Division, France 1940* (London: Brassey's, 1994).

Davies, W.J.K, *German Army Handbook, 1939-1945* (New York: Arco, 1984).

*Dawnay, Brigadier D. (et al), *The 10th Royal Hussars in the Second World War, 1939-1945*. (Aldershot, UK: Gale & Polden, 1948).

*de Guingand, Major General Sir Francis, *Operation Victory* (London: Hodder & Stoughton, 1947).

Delaney, John, *Fighting the Desert Fox* (London: Cassell, 1999).

*Denholm-Young, Colonel C.P.S., *Men of Alamein* (Stevenage, Hertfordshire: Tom Donovan, 1987).

Dimbleby, Jonathan, *Destiny in the Desert. The Road to El Alamein – the Battle that Turned the Tide of World War II* (New York: Pegasus Books, 2013).

Doherty, Richard, *Ubique. The Royal Artillery in the Second World War* (Stroud, Gloucestershire: The History Press, 2008).

*Douglas, Keith, *Alamein to Zem Zem* (New York: Chilmark Press, 1966).

Douglas-Home, Charles, *Rommel* (London: History Book Club, 1973).

Edwards, Roger, *Panzer. A Revolution in Warfare, 1939-1945* (London: Arms & Armour Press, 1989).

Fletcher, David, *Tanks in Camera, 1940-1943. Archive Photographs from the Tank Museum* (Stroud, Gloucestershire: Sutton Publishing – Budding Books, 2000).

Fonvielle-Alquier, François, *The French and the Phoney War, 1939-1940* (London: Tom Stacey, 1973).

Fort, Adrian, *Archibald Wavell. The Life and Times of an Imperial Servant* (London: Jonathan Cape, 2009).

Forty, George, *British Army Handbook, 1939-1945* (Stroud, Gloucestershire: Sutton Publishing, 1998).

Forty, George, *The Desert War* (Stroud, Gloucestershire, UK: Sutton, 2002).

Fraser, General Sir David, *Alanbrooke* (New York: Atheneum, 1982).

Fraser, General Sir David, *Knight's Cross. A Life of Field Marshal Erwin Rommel* (New York: Harper Collins, 1993).

French, David, *Military Identities. The Regimental System, the British Army, and the British People, c.1870-2000* (Oxford: Oxford University Press, 2005).

French, David, *Raising Churchill's Army. The British Army and the War Against Germany* (Oxford: Oxford University Press, 2000).

Freyberg, Colonel Lord, *Bernard Freyberg, V.C. Soldier of Two Nations* (London: Hodder & Stoughton, 1991).

Fuller, J.F.C., *The Second World War, 1939-1945* (New York: Duell, Sloan and Pearce, 1949).

*Gilbert, Adrian, *The Imperial War Museum Book of the Desert War* (London: Sidgwick & Jackson, 1992).

Gough, General Sir Hubert, *Soldiering On* (London: Arthur Barker, 1954).

Green, Michael, *American Tanks and AFVs of World War II.* (Oxford: Osprey, 2014).

Greenwood, Alexander, *Field Marshal Auchinleck* (Durham, UK: Pentland, n.d.).

Gregg, Victor and Stroud, Rick, *Rifleman, a Front-Line Life* (London: Bloomsbury, 2011).

Hamilton, Nigel, *Monty* (London: Hamish Hamilton). *Vol.1: The Making of the General, 1887-1942* (1981); *Vol. II: Master of the Battlefield. Monty's War Years, 1942-1944* (1983).

Hammond, Bryn, *El Alamein, the Battle that Turned the Tide of the Second World War* (Oxford: Osprey, 2012).

*Harding, Field Marshal Lord, *Mediterranean Strategy, 1939 – 1945, The Lees Knowles Lectures for 1959* (Cambridge: Cambridge University Press, 1960).

Harrison, Frank, *Tobruk. The Great Siege Reassessed* (London: Arms & Armour, 1996).

Hillson, Norman, *Alexander of Tunis, A Biographical Portrait* (London: W.H. Allen, 1952).

*Horrocks, Lieutenant General Sir Brian, *A Full Life* (London: Collins, 1960).

Imperial War Museum, *The British Army. The Definitive History of the Twentieth Century* (London: Cassell, 2007).

*Johnson, Brigadier R.F., *Regimental Fire! The Honourable Artillery Company in World War II* (London: HAC and Williams, Lea, 1958).

Jones, John Philip, *Battles of a Gunner Officer* (Barnsley, South Yorkshire: Pen & Sword, 2014).

Kaplan, Philip, *Chariots of Fire* (St. Paul's, MN: MBI, 2003).

Keegan, Sir John, *The Second World War* (Norwalk, CT: Easton Press, 1989).

*Kippenberger, Major General Sir Howard, *Infantry Brigadier* (London: Cumberlege – Oxford University Press, 1951).

Lamb, Richard, *Churchill as War Leader* (New York: Carroll & Graf, 1991).

Lande, D.A., *Rommel in North Africa* (Osceola, WI: 1999).

Latimer, Jon, *Alamein* (Cambridge, MA: Harvard University Press, 2002).

LeMay, Benoît, *Erich von Manstein, Hitler's Master Strategist* (Havertown, PA: Casemate, 2010).

Lewin, Ronald, *Montgomery as Military Commander* (London: Batsford, 1971).

Liddell Hart, Sir Basil, *History of the Second World War* (London: Collins, 1970).

Liddell Hart, Sir Basil, *Memoirs, Vol I (1895-1938), Vol II (The Later Years)* (New York: Putnam, 1965).

Liddell Hart, Sir Basil, *The Tanks. The History of the Royal Tank Regiment, Vols I & II* (New York: Praeger, 1959).

Lovegrove, Peter, *Not Least In the Crusade, A Short History of the Royal Army Medical Corps* (Aldershot: Gale & Polden, 1956).

Lucas, James, *Rommel's Year of Victory* (London: Greenhill Books, 1998).

Lucas, James, *War in the Desert. The 8th Army at El Alamein* (New York: Beaufort, 1982).

Lucas Phillips, Brigadier C.E., *Alamein* (London: Heinemann, 1962).

*MacGill, Dr. John Sylvanus, *Journal of Wartime Experiences in France (1940), North Africa (1941-1943), and the United States (1943).* (Unpublished).

Makepeace-Warne, Anthony, *Brassey's Companion to the British Army* (London: Brassey's, 1995).

Mead, Richard, *Churchill's Lions: A Biographical Guide to the Key British Generals of World War II* (Stroud, Gloucestershire: Spellmount, 2007).

Mead, Richard, *The Last Great Cavalryman: The Life of General Sir Richard McCreery, Commander, Eighth Army* (Barnsley, South Yorkshire, Pen & Sword, 2012)

Melvin, Major General Mungo, *Manstein, Hitler's Greatest General* (New York: Thomas Dunne, 2010).

*Merewood, Jack, *To War with the Bays. A Tank Gunner Remembers, 1939-1945* (Cardiff: 1st the Queen's Dragoon Guards, 1996).

Minney, R.J., *The Private Papers of Hore-Belisha* (London: Collins, 1960).

Money Barnes, Major R., *The British Army of 1914* (London: Seeley Service, 1968).

*Montgomery of Alamein, Field Marshal the Viscount, *Memoirs* (London: Collins, 1958).

Moorehead, Alan, *The Desert War. The North African Campaign, 1940-1943* (London: Hamish Hamilton, 1965).

Neave, Airey, *Flames of Calais, A Soldier's Battle, 1940* (Barnsley, South Yorkshire: Leo Cooper, 2013).

Nicolson, Nigel, *Alex. The Life of Field Marshal Earl Alexander of Tunis* (London: Weidenfeld & Nicolson, 1973).

Oatts, Lieutenant Colonel L.B., *Emperor's Chambermaids. The Story of the 14th/20th King's Hussars* (London: Ward Lock, 1973).

Parkinson, Roger, *Auchinleck, Victor at Alamein* (London: Granada, 1977).

*Pimlott, John (ed.), *Rommel in His Own Words* (London: Greenhill, 1994).

Pitt, Barrie, *The Crucible of War. Western Desert 1941* (New York: Paragon House, 1989).

Pitt, Barrie, *Year of Alamein 1942* (New York: Paragon House, 1990).

Place, Timothy Harrison, *Military Training in the British Army, 1940-1945* (London: Frank Cass, 2000).

*Pownall, Lieutenant General Sir Henry, *Chief of Staff, Diaries, Vol.I, 1933-1940* (London: Archon Books – Leo Cooper, 1973).

Reid, Brian Holden, *J.F.C. Fuller, Military Thinker* (New York: St. Martin's Press, 1987).

Richardson, General Sir Charles, *Send for Freddie* (London: William Kimber, 1987).

*Rommel, Field Marshal Erwin, with Sir Basil Liddell Hart (ed.), *The Rommel Papers* (Norwalk, CT: Easton Press, 1988).

Royle, Trevor, *Montgomery. Lessons in Leadership from the Soldier's General* (New York: Palgrave Macmillan, 2010).

*Sadler, John, *El Alamein, The Story of the Battle in the Words of the Soldiers* (Stroud, Gloucestershire: Amberley, 2010).

Salmond, J.B., *The History of the 51st Highland Division, 1939-1945* (Edinburgh and London: Blackwood, 1953).

Schofield, Victoria, *Wavell, Soldier and Statesman* (Barnsley, South Yorkshire: Pen & Sword, 2007).

Simpson, Emile, *War From the Ground Up: Twenty-First Century Combat as Politics* (London: Hurst Publishers, 2013).

Stewart, Adrian, *The Campaigns of Alexander of Tunis, 1940-1945* (Barnsley, South Yorkshire: Pen & Sword, 2008).

Taylor, A.J.P., *The Second World War. An Illustrated History* (London: Purnell, 1975).

Thompson, Major General Julian, *Desert Victory, Forgotten Voices* (London: Random House, 2011).

*von Manstein, Field Marshal Erich, *Lost Victories* (Chicago: Henry Regnery, 1958).

Walker, G. Goold, *The Honourable Artillery Company, 1537-1947* (Aldershot, Hampshire: Gale & Polden, 1954).

Warner, Philip, *Auchinleck, the Lonely Soldier* (London: Cassell, 1981).

Warner, Philip, *Horrocks: The General Who Led from the Front* (London: Hamish Hamilton, 1984).

*Wavell, Field Marshal Earl, *Generals and Generalship. The Lees Knowles Lectures Delivered at Trinity College, Cambridge in 1939* (Harmondsworth, Middlesex: Penguin Books, 1941).

Winton, Harold R., *To Change an Army. General Sir John Burnett-Stuart and British Armoured Doctrine, 1927-1938* (Lawrence, KS: University of Kansas Press, 1988).

JOHN PHILIP JONES

American academic, born and educated in Britain. Economics Tripos, Trinity Hall, Cambridge.

27-year career in international business, mainly with the J. Walter Thompson advertising agency, in Britain, the Netherlands and Scandinavia. This was followed by 27 years teaching and research at the Newhouse School of Public Communications, Syracuse University, New York. Full professor with academic tenure; Syracuse University's Chancellor's Citation for Exceptional Academic Achievement. Emeritus since 2007. Concurrently with my job at Syracuse, I was for many years a visiting professor at universities in Australia and Denmark.

2,000,000 words in print. Author of 17 books on marketing and economics (translated into 10 languages); plus more than 70 articles in professional and academic journals. Most of my books, in various language editions, can be found on amazon. I am a life-long student of warfare and have for 60 years been a member of the Honourable Artillery Company, London. I have walked over all the major battlefields of Europe, North America and South Africa. Since retiring I have begun writing works of military history. Three published titles are listed below.

John Philip Jones, *The Successes and Sacrifices of the British Army in 1914. Soldiers Marching, All to Die* (Lewiston, New York: The Edwin Mellen Press, 2009).

John Philip Jones, *Johnny. The Legend and Tragedy of General Sir Ian Hamilton* (Barnsley, South Yorkshire: Pen & Sword, 2012). One of six books short-listed by the Royal United Services Institute for the best military study published anywhere in the world in 2012/2013.

John Philip Jones, *Battles of a Gunner Officer. Tunisia, Sicily, Normandy, and the Long Road to Germany* (Barnsley, South Yorkshire: Pen & Sword, 2014)

I have founded a Military History Group for members of the Oxford & Cambridge Club, London. This is now flourishing.

Married for 57 years to Wendy Maudlayne, née Hoblyn. Two children, both married. We have travelled extensively, on pleasure and business. (I have been employed as a consultant in over 40 countries.)

INDEX

The Index covers the main text of the book, but not the Maps, Plates and Bibliography. Each of the Maps and Plates has a detailed caption. The Bibliography is organized alphabetically by author.

Individual soldiers' ranks are as they were during the events described or shortly afterwards, e.g. JSM was at first a captain and later a major. I use surnames and first names, but not titles granted, e.g. Sir Harold Alexander. Similarly, awards and decorations are not mentioned, with the single exception of the Victoria Cross.

Roger Smith Hotel, Washington DC, 216-217

Rommel, General Erwin, xxii-xxiii, 36, 39, 56, 92, 100, 103-107, 110-114, 126, 136-137, 139, 144-147, 165-166, 175, 181, 184, 189, 195, 199

Rommel's 'dash for the Wire'(during Operation *Battleaxe*), 112-113

Roosevelt, Franklin, 146-147, 178

Rotterdam, 34

Rouen, 45, 47, 51-53, 55

Royal Air Force, 11, 16, 23, 27, 29, 81, 91, 101, 110, 125, 141, 176, 183-184, 190, 201, 215

Royal Navy, 23, 43, 81, 110

Russia, xvii, 80, 109, 125, 194

Ruweisat Ridge, 165, 177, 179-180

Sacramento, CA, 216, 219

Sahara Desert, 200

Saint-Valery, 48, 56

Salisbury Plain, 81-83

San Francisco, 216, 219

Saunnu, 126-127

Scheldt, River, see Escaut, River

Schlieffen Plan, 32

Schwerpunkt, 10

Scout car, 56, 120-121, 131-132, 137, 142

Sedan, 26

Seine, River, xvi, 47, 55-56

Sfax, 212

Siam, 125

Sichelschnitt, Operation, 33-37, 47, 101

Sicily, 56, 207

Sidi Barrani, 95, 103, 118, 124

Sidi Omar, 110-111

Sidi Rezegh, 111-112

Sigint/Enigma/Ultra (Signals Intelligence from Bletchley Park), 108, 126, 175, 184

Sikorski, General Wladyslaw, 90

Simpson, Anthony, xxvi

Singapore, 125, 146

Singer, Captain Grant Washington, 185

Smales, Brigadier John, xv, xxv-xxvi

Sollum, 95, 107, 110-111, 124

Somme, River, xvi, xxii, 44, 48, 54-55, 185

Stalin, Joseph, 173

Stalingrad, 177, 188, 195

Stamford, 82

Stewart, Dr. William, xxvi, 21

Stilwell, Lieutenant General Joseph, 31

Stone family, Washington DC, 218-219, 222

Stuka dive bomber, 26, 106, 129, 146

Stumme, General Georg, 182

Suez, 95, 101-102, 123

Sun compass (Gnomon), see Desert navigation

Sussex, West, 81

Supercharge, Operation, 184

Switzerland, 178

Syria, 102

Tanks, Models of:

British:

Light (1940), 12-14, 17-18, 38, 45, 84

Cruiser (1940), 13-14, 17-18, 45, 84, 86

Cruiser (Crusader, 1941), 87-88, 113, 141, 147, 179

Cruiser (Valentine, 1941), 201

Infantry (Matilda), 13-14, 17-18, 38, 84, 104